EVIDENCE
OF
EXTRATERRESTRIALS

About the Author

Warren Agius is a longtime UFO researcher who is known for his unbiased approach to factual evidence. He has personally interviewed UFO contactee and bestselling author Whitley Strieber, as well as the late ufologist Stanton Friedman.

WARREN AGIUS

EVIDENCE

OF

EXTRATERRESTRIALS

OVER 40 CASES
Prove Aliens Have Visited Earth

Llewellyn Publications
Woodbury, Minnesota

First Edition
First Printing, 2021

Cover design by Kevin R. Brown

Llewellyn Publications is a registered trademark of Llewellyn Worldwide Ltd.

Library of Congress Cataloging-in-Publication Data (Pending)
ISBN: 978-0-7387-6713-0

Llewellyn Worldwide Ltd. does not participate in, endorse, or have any authority or responsibility concerning private business transactions between our authors and the public.

All mail addressed to the author is forwarded but the publisher cannot, unless specifically instructed by the author, give out an address or phone number.

Any internet references contained in this work are current at publication time, but the publisher cannot guarantee that a specific location will continue to be maintained. Please refer to the publisher's website for links to authors' websites and other sources.

Llewellyn Publications
A Division of Llewellyn Worldwide Ltd.
2143 Wooddale Drive
Woodbury, MN 55125-2989
www.llewellyn.com

Printed in the United States of America

*To my better half Laura, without whom this book
would not have been possible.*

Ad astra.

Contents

Part 2: Crashes and Landings

Part 3: Military Pursuits

Part 4: Government Projects

Introduction

I have always been drawn to the unknown. From a young age I have looked up at the sky and wondered if there's more life than just what we know of here on Earth. At fourteen years of age I picked up *Alien Agenda* by the late Jim Marrs and as I eagerly read each page, I became more captivated by the concept of extraterrestrials. From there on, I have read countless books on the phenomenon and started carrying out my own research on the topic. The hunger to know more and to learn about the possibility of advanced beings sharing the universe with us intensified. There have been many sleepless nights of pondering the possibilities of who we are sharing the universe with and what their intentions could possibly be. For over five years I have been collecting information on unidentified flying object (UFO) cases, acquiring declassified documents and carrying out interviews with experts in the field, most notably with the late Stanton Friedman.

The study of UFO phenomena is often overlooked and ridiculed, and although many people believe that there is life outside our planet, the idea of these beings visiting our planet is considered a "tin-foil-hat conspiracy theory." Whenever the term UFO is brought up, most people immediately picture little green men piloting a flying saucer, even though this is rarely the case. The reality is that the majority of UFO cases can easily be explained as a natural phenomenon or a misidentification. It is only in very few cases that the reported UFO is, in actual fact, an extraterrestrial aircraft. It is for this reason that we must keep in mind that just because an object is unidentified, it does not mean that it is extraterrestrial in origin; a bird, a military aircraft, or a satellite can be unidentified flying objects.

I have had countless conversations with people who have mocked the phenomenon and disregarded it as being unimportant. These experiences are what motivated me to write this book. What follows is a comprehensive account of every significant UFO sighting that has proved to me that extraterrestrials exist, they have been visiting our planet, and they are truly more advanced than us in every aspect. The cases covered in the following chapters are very thought-provoking and as we shall see, this phenomena is far greater than many people are aware of. It is also important to point out the fact that all of the details that are mentioned in this book are accurate and are not dramatized in any way. As a matter of fact, an important guideline that I followed throughout the making of this book is that each and every case has been approached in an unbiased and objective manner.

I truly hope that this book will expand your thinking and will evoke you to ask existential questions about life and the universe. Many people believe that there is life out there, but not many people consider that these extremely advanced beings visit our planet and could pose a threat to our security. I hope that this book will help you gain more knowledge and awareness on the phenomenon. The following cases are events that have happened in our history and I firmly believe that these cases prove what my younger self wanted to know: that extraterrestrial life does exist, it always has, and these beings have visited our planet much more frequently than one might think.

Classification of Sightings

Dr. J. Allen Hynek—an American astronomer who is well known for the extensive research he has done on unidentified flying objects, in addition to being the advisor for the United States Air Force's Project Blue Book, Project Sign, and Project Grudge—created a classification list for UFO reports. The classification has nine levels and every UFO report would fall under one of the nine categories. The cases that we shall cover in this book will mostly fall under one of the first four categories.

Level 1: Nocturnal Lights—This category includes reports of lights in the night sky.

Level 2: Daylight Discs—This level refers to reports that include unidentified flying objects in the daytime. These reports usually describe a disc-shaped or cigar-shaped object carrying out erratic maneuvers, appearing and disappearing out of nowhere, and traveling at great speeds.

Level 3: Radar-Visual—This category includes all of the reports in which the unidentified flying object has been tracked on radar. The radar sighting improves the credibility of the report.

Level 4: Close Encounters of the First Kind—This category includes reports that are made by individuals who have had a visual sighting of an unidentified flying object from a close distance (seemingly no more than 500 feet away). Since the individual is in close proximity to the UFO, these accounts usually contain great detail and description of the flying object.

Level 5: Close Encounters of the Second Kind—This level includes the reports in which physical contact with an entity has been made or a type of physical effect has been induced. The effects do not necessarily have to be anatomical, but may include malfunctioning of electrical equipment and vehicles, radioactive readings ,and trace markings on the ground.

Level 6: Close Encounters of the Third Kind—These reports include the presence of an extraterrestrial entity.

The following classifications are extensions added by others and not by Dr. J. Allen Hynek himself:

Level 7: Close Encounters of the Fourth Kind—Close encounters of the fourth kind include occurrences in which an individual has been abducted by an interplanetary flying object or the beings piloting the aircraft. This category also includes reports in which an individual experienced a distorted sense of reality. Such cases would include symptoms such as hallucinations or missing time, which is when the individual cannot recall what had happened in a certain time frame. Missing time is extremely common whenever an individual has had physical contact with an extraterrestrial.

Level 8: Close Encounters of the Fifth Kind—These reports include communication between a human being and an extraterrestrial. Communication can be both vocal and telepathic, although most abductees report that communication was solely made through telepathy.

Level 9: Close Encounters of the Sixth Kind—Close encounters of the sixth kind refer to cases in which a death of a human being or an animal is associated with a UFO sighting.

Part 1
Modern Sightings

Over the years, many individuals have claimed to have seen UFOs. Perhaps everyone has heard another person claiming they have seen strange lights in the sky or strange objects disappearing into thin air. More often than not, these UFOs are not extraterrestrial. I'm sorry to break it to you, but the majority of the UFOs turn out to be natural phenomena—simply satellites or other celestial bodies. With that being said, there are a few instances in which the reported UFOs turn out to be interplanetary and extraterrestrial in origin. In the following chapters, we will examine cases in which the evidence shows that the reported unidentified objects are interplanetary. What separates these cases from the rest is the presented evidence, which makes the extraterrestrial hypothesis the only plausible one.

Before going into the cases, I find it crucial to encourage you, the reader, to approach the following chapters with an open mind. So many people dismiss the phenomenon just because of their preconceived beliefs, and no matter how much evidence is presented, they will simply bury their heads in the sand. One of the key moments throughout the several years I have spent researching the phenomenon was when I realized the real threat to humanity is not conflict between nations, but these visitors whom we do not understand. If the visitors pose a threat to our safety, then we truly do not stand a chance. The one thing we do know is that, as we shall see, these beings are infinitely superior, and if they wanted to, they could wipe out humanity in a heartbeat. It is crucial for governments all over the world to take the phenomenon seriously. This is not a matter of trying to figure out if extraterrestrials exist or not (because they do), but rather to understand how their advanced technology works, and what this implies for the future of humanity and planet Earth.

Chapter 1
The Battle of Los Angeles

Date: February 25, 1942
Location: Los Angeles, California, United States

The following event has been dubbed "The Battle of Los Angeles" due to the military's full-scale response to the observed unidentified flying objects. This event is one of the few that has over a thousand firsthand eyewitnesses, making it one of the most remarkable cases to date, and it all happened just three months after the attack on Pearl Harbor.

It was February 25, 1942, when at around 02:25 the air raid sirens went off throughout Los Angeles, warning the people that an aerial attack was imminent. Since just three months earlier the Americans had experienced the worst military attack of their history so far, everyone was apprehensive. The United States Army prepared the citizens very well in the case that the Japanese were to make an attack on American soil. Numerous drills were carried out, preparing both the people as well as the army; however, the air raid siren that went off on the twenty-fifth was far from a drill.

On that day, naval intelligence had been tracking an unidentified object on radar in Southern California. Those collecting intelligence could not identify the object nor could they communicate with it. However, due to the recent events, they assumed that it was a Japanese aircraft about to attack one of the most densely populated cities in America. As the object started approaching the city of Los Angeles, the air raid sirens went off and the residents made their way out of their houses, completely unaware that they were about to witness one of the most compelling UFO cases to date.

The military had been tracking the unidentified object for well over half an hour on radar and orders were given to intercept the aircraft and respond accordingly. Although no American military jets were scrambled, Paul T. Collins, a witness of the sighting and an employee of the Douglas Aircraft Company, later reported that military jets were actually on the runway waiting for authorization to intercept. However, that permission was not granted, and many have questioned that decision, considering an unidentified aircraft had entered the American airspace without permission just months after an attack.

Shortly after the air raid sirens went off, thousands of individuals witnessed an enormous silvery object flying high in the sky, surrounded by smaller objects, flying in a V formation. At that point in time, it became very apparent both to the army and to the thousands of witnesses that these aircraft were unlike any aircraft anyone had seen in the sky. Assuming that the aircraft were about to drop bombs, the army followed orders and started shooting antiaircraft shells at the objects. The shells of such ammunition are designed specifically to shoot down any aircraft with great precision. In a span of one hour, a total of 1,430 antiaircraft shells were fired at the objects but to no avail. The unidentified objects were completely unaffected by the ambush. The army kept shooting at the objects, leaving thousands of witnesses perplexed by what they were witnessing. How were these aircraft shielded from the ammunition? The UFOs remained in the sky for over an hour, hovering motionlessly. Although every American was expecting another attack to occur, no bombs were dropped. The awaited attack never came, leaving many to wonder if these aircraft were truly Japanese.

After an hour in the sky and an hour of nonstop bombardment, at around 04:15, the large aircraft and the accompanying smaller ones disappeared from the sky. It is unknown how these objects were able to withstand the antiaircraft ammunition. Many have speculated that the objects must have had a shield of some sort protecting them. With the newly declassified videos showing fighter jets pursuing UFOs, one of the extraordinary characteristics of these unidentified aircraft is their antigravity propulsion system. Theoretically, if an aircraft has the capability to produce its own gravitational field, a force field is certainly in the realm of possibilities.

The following day, a full detailed report written by General George Marshall was sent to President Franklin D. Roosevelt, recounting the events of the previous night:

"The following is the information we have from GHQ at this moment regarding the air alarm over Los Angeles of yesterday morning. From details available at this hour:

1. Unidentified airplanes, other than American Army or Navy planes, were probably over Los Angeles and were fired on by elements of the 37th Coast Artillery Brigade (AA) between 3:12 and 4:15 am. These units expended the 1,430 rounds of ammunition.

2. As many as fifteen airplanes may have been involved, flying at various speeds from what is reported as being 'very slow' to as much as two hundred miles per hour and at elevations from nine thousand to eighteen thousand feet.

3. No bombs were dropped.

4. No casualties among our troops.

5. No planes were shot down.

6. No American Army or Navy planes were in action

Investigation continuing. It seems reasonable to conclude that if unidentified airplanes were involved, they may have been from commercial sources, operated by enemy agents for purposes of spreading alarm, disclosing locations of antiaircraft positions, and slowing production through blackout. Such conclusion is supported by varying speed of operation and the fact that no bombs were dropped."

The Eyewitnesses

As stated in the beginning of this chapter, this case is one of the very few cases that includes over a thousand eyewitnesses. As with any case, the more witnesses there are, the better the credibility of the case, especially if the accounts corroborate one another. The following statements are only a few of the hundreds that were made shortly after the events came to an end in the early hours of February 25. The witnesses include regular civilians as well as high-level officials and experts.

Peter Jenkins, an employee of the *Los Angeles Herald Examiner*, recalled seeing "a *V* formation of about twenty-five silvery planes overhead, moving slowly across the sky toward Long Beach."[1] A Long Beach police officer named J. H. McClelland was on duty when the air raid siren went off. In a statement he said, "An experienced naval observer was with me using powerful Carl Zeiss

1. Jim Marrs, *Alien Agenda: Investigating the Extraterrestrial Presence among Us* (New York: Harper Paperbacks, 1998), 63.

binoculars and said he counted nine planes in the cone of a searchlight. He said they were silver in color. This group passed along from one battery of searchlights to another and under fire from antiaircraft guns, flew from the direction of Redondo Beach and Inglewood on the land side of Fort MacArthur and continued toward Santa Ana and Huntington Beach. Antiaircraft fire was so heavy we could not hear the motors of the plane."[2]

Collins, the employee of Douglas Aircraft Company and an expert in aerospace engineering, stated that he had observed "several unidentified red objects appearing from nowhere and then zig-zagging from side to side five miles per second." He also confirmed that fighter jets were warming up on the runway, awaiting confirmation to pursue and intercept the UFOs. For whatever reason, however, that authorization was never granted.

"Planes of the Fourth Interceptor Command were, in fact, warming up on the runways, waiting for orders to go up and intervene the unknown intruders," Collins said. "Why, everybody was asking, were they not ordered to go into action during the twenty-one-minute period between the first air raid alert at 02:25 and the first artillery firing at 03:16."[3]

As we shall see in later chapters, when an unidentified object infiltrates a nation's airspace, military jets are immediately scrambled and are ordered to pursue and intercept the unidentified aircraft. When we take into consideration that the United States was still recuperating from the Japanese attacks on Pearl Harbor, it becomes even more illogical that the air force did not authorize the military jets to scramble. Could it be that the air force knew

---

2. Marrs, *Alien Agenda: Investigating the Extraterrestrial Presence among Us,* 63.

3. Paul Collins, "World War II UFO Scare," *FATE Magazine* 40, no. 7, issue 448, July 1987.

the UFOs were not Japanese, but were something far superior and advanced, and it would have been futile to scramble military jets?

The final witness statement comes from an American anthropologist named C. Scott Littleton, who believes that the objects in the sky were extraterrestrial and interplanetary in origin. Littleton states, "The most efficient explanation is that it is what we'd call today a UFO: something not of this world."[4] Such a hypothesis does make sense when we take into consideration the fact that these objects withstood antiaircraft ammunition for over an hour and then disappeared into thin air.

The Unidentified Flying Objects

It must be reiterated that the fact that hundreds of individuals were eyewitnesses to the event proves that these events did truly happen.

The classified memorandum written by General Marshall states that there were "as many as fifteen planes." The eyewitness reports describe one enormous main object that was surrounded by smaller ones flying beside it in a V formation. The movements of the smaller UFOs were erratic, zig-zagging from side to side. On the other hand, the main object remained stationary in the sky. It is interesting to note that the UFOs were described as being noiseless, although it could have been the case that the firing of the ammunition was overpowering the noise being emitted from the objects.

The most interesting aspect of this event is the fact that these UFOs were able to withstand the ammunition being fired at them for over an hour. So much ammunition was fired that several sur-

---

4. Kevin Burns, producer, "The Return," *Ancient Aliens*, May 25, 2010, A&E Television Networks.

rounding properties were damaged. Wesley Craven, a historian who wrote extensively on the Army Air Force in the Second World War, stated that due to the chaos of that night, one individual lost his life due to heart failure.[5]

After withstanding the ambush for over an hour, the UFOs were left completely unaffected and proceeded to disappear from the sky. The objects were no longer tracked on radar and no more visual contacts were reported. The UFOs had completely vanished, leaving everyone to wonder what they had just witnessed.

The Army's Explanation

"As far as I know, the whole raid was a false alarm and could be attributed to jittery nerves," said Frank Knox, the navy secretary.[6] Knox stated that the events did not occur the way hundreds of individuals had reported. In fact, he said the whole event was a delusion caused by the trauma the American people felt after the attack on Pearl Harbor. This statement implies that the hundreds of eyewitness reports made by civilians as well as high-level officials must have been inaccurate and mistaken, and that the army had spent an hour shooting at objects that were simply not there.

Such a statement is questionable for many reasons. When we take into consideration the facts, this statement simply does not hold true. Firstly, naval intelligence had tracked the unidentified objects on their radar. If, as Knox stated, the event was the result of jittery nerves, then the targets would not have showed up on radar. Following this contradiction, the Coast Artillery Association stated that they had released a weather balloon at 01:00, which was

---

5. Wesley Frank Craven and James Lea Cate, *The Army Air Forces in World War II*, vol. I (Chicago: University of Chicago Press), 284.

6. Marrs, *Alien Agenda: Investigating the Extraterrestrial Presence among Us,* 63.

what the thousands of individuals must have witnessed in the sky. This statement still does not match up with the events and witness statements. Even if it is true that a weather balloon was released in the sky, if the army had shot over a thousand antiaircraft shells at a weather balloon, it most certainly would have been shot down. Apart from that, the description given by the eyewitnesses does not match up with that of a weather balloon. The shape, color, and maneuvers of the reported UFOs contradict those of a weather balloon.

After these explanations were repudiated by the public, Knox provided a third explanation that remained the main explanation for the case. Knox stated that the UFOs were, in actual fact, Japanese commercial aircraft sent to cause psychological distress. During the Second World War, the Japanese did actually make use of hydrogen balloons (known as the Fu-Go balloons) to instill fear amongst their enemies. However, if what was in the sky was truly a commercial aircraft then how come it was not shot down? Once again, why weren't any American fighter jets scrambled? Even if an attack did not actually occur, why was the United States Army completely defenseless and unable to protect its civilians?

Conclusion

Three statements were provided by officials and none of the three statements hold true. It is evident that the military does not want to disclose to the public what was truly in the sky on the night of February 25, 1942. Is this because they believe the truth will cause panic, or is it because they themselves do not know?

When we compare the characteristics and capabilities of the UFOs to terrestrial aircraft, it is evident that the UFO technology is far superior to ours.

Chapter 2
Ghost Rocket UFOs

Date: 1946
Location: Sweden

One of the earliest reported UFO waves occurred throughout 1946, with the majority of the sightings taking place in Scandinavian countries, predominantly Sweden. Reports were also made in Greece, Italy, and India. The reports were similar in nature: individuals reported seeing strange rocket-shaped or missile-shaped objects in the sky, leaving no trail behind nor emitting any noise. In over two hundred instances, radar operators received radar returns, and between May and December there were over two thousand sightings reported. The question many researchers have asked and the main question we shall explore in this chapter is whether these rocket-shaped UFOs were interplanetary, V-type German missiles, or meteors.

The first report of a UFO was made on February 26, 1946, in Finland. The report stated that multiple individuals observed a number of meteors falling from the sky, even though no investigation was conducted nor any evidence provided. Throughout the year, over two thousand reports were made, mostly from Sweden, where individuals reported seeing rocket-shaped objects soaring through the sky. Some reports described multiple objects flying in formation horizontally without leaving any trace or emitting any noise.

As the reports increased, newspapers all over Sweden and neighboring countries started publishing articles on the phenomenon. The following is an article published on the Swedish newspaper *Dagens Nyheter* on May 24,1946:

"Two night watchmen in Landskrona-Posten sight wingless, cigar-shaped body of dimensions of a small airplane, which at regular intervals spurted BUNCHES of sparks from its tail. Estimated altitude at only 100 meters and moving at ordinary airplane speed to southwest."

As the article states, some reports described the UFOs as having a cigar shape. Throughout the year, debris was found and collected from these unidentified aircraft and analysis showed a significant number of unknown elements. It was even reported that one of these ghost rockets had crashed into Lake Kolmiarv in Sweden in July 1946. Given the rise in reports and the public mass panic as a result of these sightings, the United States Embassy in Sweden issued the following telegram, dated July 11, 1946, and it read:

"For some weeks there have been numerous reports of strange rocket-like missiles being seen in Swedish and Finnish skies. During the past few days reports of such objects being seen have greatly increased. Member of legation saw one Tuesday afternoon. One landed on beach near Stockholm same afternoon without causing any damage and according to press, fragments are now being studied by military authorities.

"Local scientists on first inspection stated it contained organic substance resembling carbide. Press this afternoon announces one such missile fell in Stockholm suburb 14:30.

Missiles observed made no sound and seemed to be falling rapidly to earth when observed. No sound of explosion followed, however.

"If missiles are of Soviet origin as generally believed, purpose might be political to intimidate the Swedes in connection with Soviet pressure on Sweden being built up in connection with current loan negotiations or to offset supposed increase in our military pressure on Sweden resulting from the naval visit and recent bikini Atoll tests or both."[7]

A Swedish Air Force pilot flying over central Sweden on August 14, 1946, encountered one of these unidentified missile-shaped flying objects. At around 16:00, the unnamed pilot reported seeing a dark cigar-shaped object just two hundred feet above his aircraft. The cigar-shaped object had a diameter of approximately three feet, and it was fifty feet long, flying at an estimated speed of four hundred miles per hour.

The unconventional characteristics of the aircraft included the absence of wings or exhaust plume. The object had also maintained a constant altitude over the ground throughout the entire encounter, which lasted a number of minutes before the cigar-shaped UFO disappeared from the skies.

The Investigations

Multiple investigations had been carried out by a number of countries to determine the origin of these ghost rockets. In 1946, the only two countries that had technology advanced enough to possibly create these ghost rockets were the Germans and the Soviets, and thus it was initially assumed that these ghost-rocket sightings

---

7. Timothy Good, *Beyond Top Secret: The Worldwide UFO Security Threat*, (London: Pan, 1997), 20.

were missiles created by the aforementioned countries. However, there was no evidence to prove this hypothesis, leaving the Swedish defense and nation vulnerable.

The Swedish authorities asked the United States and the United Kingdom for assistance. Intelligence expert in long-distance bombing techniques Lieutenant General James Doolittle, together with General David Sarnoff, an expert in aerial warfare, made their journey to Stockholm to start their investigation. Given the ever-growing mass panic surrounding the reports, it was established that the authorities should start covering-up the sightings by limiting media coverage. The director of intelligence for the British Air Staff, Reginald Victor Jones, was also involved in the investigation, examining reports that were made by radar experts.

The data the investigators found left them with even more unanswered questions. The officers now had enough evidence to conclude that the ghost rockets were not missiles, which for the authorities meant that they must have been bright meteorites or illusions witnesses created due to wartime nerves. Unsurprisingly, the extraterrestrial hypothesis was not considered even though the meteorite hypothesis was debunked by several researchers. Since these ghost-rocket sightings usually lasted for a number of minutes and included the UFOs making erratic maneuvers, the Swedish authorities were back at square one with no explanation as to what these sightings could have been.

After a number of months, reports of these ghost rockets started showing up all over Europe. In Greece, professor Paul Santorini was one of the leading scientists who was provided with a team of engineers to investigate the ghost rocket sightings. In the investigation, Santorini was able to rule out the possibility of the objects being missiles, however, his investigation was shortly halted by the Greek army. Santorini was told that after conferring with foreign officials, the Army thought it would be in the nation's and the world's best interest if the investigation was discontinued. Just days after, Santorini was visited by "foreign scientists" who informed him that these sightings involved foreign powers and technology that no nation on Earth could protect themselves from. Interestingly enough, it was later revealed that these officials were from the United States' Pentagon.

Back in Sweden, after several months of investigations, the military officials released a statement, disclosing that there had been no progress or leads in the investigation, and up to that point, these rocket-shaped UFOs were still unidentified.

"Swedish military authorities said today that they had been unable to discover after four months of investigation the origin or nature of the ghost rockets that have been flying over Sweden since May.

"A special communique declared that 80 percent of one thousand reports on the rockets could be attributed to celestial phenomena, but that radar had detected some two hundred objects that the phenomenon of nature or products of the imagination cannot be, nor can be referred to as Swedish airplanes.

"The report added, however, that the objects were not the V-type bombs used by the Germans in the closing days of the war."[8]

Conclusion

The sightings are still, to this day, unexplained. Over fifty years after the initial reports, in 1997, a document was declassified that stated that the extraterrestrial hypothesis was the most plausible explanation. The top secret United States Air Force document, dated November 4, 1948, reads as follows:

---

8. Good, *Beyond Top Secret*, 23.

"For some time, we have been concerned by the recurring reports on flying saucers. They periodically continue to pop up; during the last week, one was observed hovering over Neubiberg Air Base for about thirty minutes. They have been reported by so many sources and from such a variety of places that we are convinced that they cannot be disregarded and must be explained on some basis, which is perhaps slightly beyond the scope of our present intelligence thinking.

"When officers of this Directorate recently visited the Swedish Air Intelligence Service, this question was put to the Swedes. Their answer was that some reliable and fully technically qualified people have reached the conclusion that 'these phenomena are obviously the result of a high technical skill that cannot be credited to any presently known culture on earth.' They are therefore assuming that these objects originate from some previously unknown or unidentified technology, possibly outside the earth."[9]

---

9. Good, *Beyond Top Secret*, 238.

Chapter 3

Nine UFOs Encountered above Mount Rainier

Date: June 24, 1947
Location: Mount Rainier, Washington, United States

One of the earliest modern UFO sightings was made by pilot Kenneth Arnold. On June 24, 1947, a US Marine Corps C-46 aircraft had crashed at Mount Rainier, a mountain range close to Seattle and a $5,000 reward was offered to anyone who could locate the debris of the aircraft. On July 24, Arnold was flying a CallAir A-2 aircraft from Chehalis to Yakima, Washington. Having a few hours to spare, Arnold thought he would fly over Mount Rainier and attempt to locate the debris.

It was around 15:00 when Arnold was flying over the city of Mineral at an altitude of 9,200 feet. Noticing a bright light to his rear left, Arnold was able to locate just one other aircraft in the airspace, which was a DC-4 aircraft. Within a few seconds, a second bright light appeared, this time in front of him. It could not have possibly been the DC-4 aircraft he had observed as there was no way it could have traveled that fast, and Arnold had not seen any other aircraft in the vicinity. As he got a better look at the light, Arnold noticed that there were nine bright objects emitting the light. The lights were extremely close to the mountains and were flying at approximately the same altitude as Arnold.

At first, Arnold assumed that it must have been another aircraft that he had failed to previously locate. His assumption was quickly proven wrong as he noticed the long chain of nine separate objects flying in formation. They had no wings, nor did they leave any trails. Moreover, the objects were lustrous and had a semicircular convex shape, as well as a flat and shiny surface. One of the nine objects had a slightly different shape, that of a crescent. It was at this moment that Arnold knew this was no ordinary aircraft.

Just twenty-three miles away, the nine aircraft started flying toward Arnold's aircraft, their silhouette appearing dark against the bright surrounding. To confirm that the lights were not reflections, Arnold opened his side window and got an unobstructed view of the UFOs. Their shape and position remained unchanged. Knowing full well these aircraft were unconventional, he used his aircraft's instruments to calculate the incredible speed they were traveling. In just one minute and forty-two seconds the objects traveled fifty miles, meaning that they must have been traveling well over seventeen thousand miles per hour, three times the speed of any aircraft in 1947. The objects continued moving rapidly toward the south as they disappeared out of sight.

The Aftermath

Arnold landed in Yakima at approximately 16:00 and he immediately informed the airport manager of his encounter. To his surprise, a pilot on board another CallAir aircraft had made a similar report just minutes prior to Arnold's sighting. The only explanation authorities could provide Arnold was that the UFOs must have been guided missiles.

Knowing full well that the description of a missile did not match up with what he had seen in the sky, Arnold went to the *East Oregonian,* a newspaper published in Pendleton, Oregon. At the newspaper's offices, Arnold spoke with reporter Bill Bequette, who at first did not take Arnold's claims seriously. However, as Arnold began recounting his experience in detail, Bequette's doubts were erased. The following day, an article was published in the newspaper recounting Arnold's encounter with the unknown. The article, which was picked up by newspapers across the country, reads as follows:

"Nine bright saucer-like objects flying at 'incredible speed' at ten thousand feet altitude were reported here today by Kenneth Arnold, Boise, Idaho, pilot who said he could not hazard a guess as to what they were.

"Arnold, a United States Forest Service employee [sic] engaged in searching for a missing plane, said he sighted the mysterious objects yesterday at three pm. They were flying between Mount Rainier and Mount Adams, in Washington state, he said, and appeared to weave in and out of formation. Arnold said that he clocked and estimated their speed at twelve thousand miles an hour.

"Enquiries at Yakima last night brought only blank stares, he said, but he added he talked today with an unidentified man from Ukiah, south of here, who said he had seen similar objects over the mountains near Ukiah yesterday.

'It seems impossible,' Arnold said, 'but there it is.'"[10]

As Arnold's report started getting more coverage, several other individuals came forward and stated that they had seen similar objects in the sky on the same day. One witness was Fred Johnson, who at the time was at Mount Adams. Through his telescope Johnson stated that he had seen six round and bright objects flying

---

10. "Supersonic Flying Saucers Sighted by Idaho Pilot," *The Chicago Sun*, June 26, 1947, 2.

in formation. The objects came to a point in the head and had a general oval shape. As he took out his compass to determine their flight location, he noticed that his compass was spinning. Another unnamed witness was just twenty miles south of Yakima at a tower in Diamond Gap. The witness stated that he saw flashes in the sky moving in a straight line for a number of minutes before they disappeared.

The Investigation

An investigation into Arnold's report was initiated in early July 1947. Air Force personnel Lieutenant Frank Brown and Captain William Davidson interviewed Arnold on July 12 and found him to be a very reliable witness. In their report, Brown and Davidson stated that "Mr. Arnold actually saw what he stated he saw. It is difficult to believe that a man of his character and apparent integrity would state that he saw objects and write up a report to the extent that he did if he did not see them."[11]

A number of explanations have been provided for Arnold's case. The first explanation we shall examine was put forward by renowned UFO skeptic Philip J. Klass. In Klass's newsletter titled *The Skeptic UFO Newsletter* from July 1997, Klass stated that the nine objects Arnold had encountered in the sky were in actual fact meteorites.[12] This explanation does not hold true for several reasons; the first being that Arnold reported seeing the UFOs close to the mountain range. If the objects had been meteorites, then they would not have maneuvered and would have impacted on

---

11. Ted Bloecher, *Report on the UFO Wave of 1947* (Washington, D.C.: National Investigations Committee on Aerial Phenomena, 1967), 24.

12. Philip J. Klass, "New Research Suggests Kenneth Arnold's UFOs Were Meteor-Fireballs," *Skeptics UFO Newsletter* 46 (July 1997): 1–2, https://skepticalinquirer.org/the-skeptics-ufo-newsletter/.

the mountains. No explosions or impacts were reportedly seen by Arnold or any of the other witnesses. The second reason is that meteorites can travel up to 160,000 miles per hour. The UFOs were too slow to be meteorites and the objects' maneuverability disproves this hypothesis.

Astrophysicist and skeptic Donald Menzel provided a number of possibilities for the UFO sighting. The first explanation he provided was in 1953 and he stated that Arnold had seen a cloud of snow that was blown from the mountains and had reflected the sunlight. He also suggested that the objects could have been a thin layer of fog, haze or dust, caused to move by air circulation. These two hypotheses could not have been the case for a number of reasons. Firstly, no wind current is strong enough to carry snow clouds over fifty miles from Mount Rainier to Mount Adams, where witness Fred Johnson was when he spotted the UFOs. Even if it was the case that this could be possible, this does not explain the rapid speed, maneuverability and the intense brightness of the objects.

Ten years later in 1963, Menzel came out with three more explanations. Menzel stated that the UFOs could have been mountaintop mirages, orographic clouds (clouds commonly seen on mountains caused by a lift of air), or wave clouds in motion. Given that mountaintop mirages can only form under a stable atmosphere and above the mountain peaks, this immediately disproves Menzel's theory. Mount Rainier has an elevation of over fourteen thousand feet and Arnold stated that the nine UFOs were approximately at the same altitude as his aircraft (roughly at nine thousand feet). Moreover, orographic clouds appear motionless and are not bright clouds. This is another discrepancy in Menzel's theory since the objects were intensely bright and also traveled at a fast speed. The wave cloud explanation also does not match up with

Arnold's report as wave clouds are not semi-circular in shape nor do they carry out maneuvers or travel faster than any aircraft from that time period. Having provided five explanations and having all five explanations disproved, Menzel provided one final explanation in 1971. This time, Menzel stated that the UFOs could have been water drops on Arnold's window. However, if Menzel had paid attention to the details that Arnold provided in his witness statement, he would have noticed that Arnold had opened his window to get an unobstructed view of the objects, and when he did so the objects remained in the sky.

Although the multiple explanations Menzel provided were disproved, the United States Air Force stated that the most plausible explanation for the sighting was that what Arnold had seen was, in actual fact, a mirage.

Conclusion

Given that the mirage explanation does not truly explain what Arnold had seen in the sky on June 24, 1947, many have wondered if the objects were interplanetary. Kenneth Arnold's sighting was the first of many sightings reported in 1947, with one of the most infamous UFO crashes occurring just a month later in the New Mexico desert.

Chapter 4

The Green Fireballs

Date: December 5, 1948
Location: United States

The Green Fireballs is a term used to describe a series of UFO sightings in 1948. These mysterious objects were referred to as the green fireballs as they were exactly that; green balls of fire flashing across the sky. The majority of these sightings were observed over military and research bases, which sparked interest and concern from the government.

The first report was made on December 5, 1948, by a United States Air Force pilot, Captain Goede, who was on board a C-47 aircraft. Captain Goede recalls that at around 21:27 he observed "a green ball of fire flashing across the sky ahead of them."[13] Captain Goede and his copilot were approximately ten miles east of Albuquerque when they saw the fiery green object. At first, the two pilots just assumed that the object was a meteor or a weather phenomenon of some sort. The last thing they assumed the object to be was an extraterrestrial aircraft.

As the pilots continued watching, the green fireball, which was on the east side of their aircraft, then moved closer toward their

---

13. Edward J. Ruppelt, *The Report on Unidentified Flying Objects: The Original 1956 Edition* (New York: Cosimo Classics, 2011), 48.

aircraft. As it proceeded to level with the C-47, it was evident that this was not a natural phenomenon. Whatever that object in the sky was, it was aware of the C-47's position. As the fireball leveled with the aircraft, the two pilots were able to get a better look at the object and they were able to rule out some possibilities of what the object could have been. The UFO was described as being very large in size. It had a spherical shape and was also emitting a bright green glow. Shortly after the green fireball leveled with the air-craft, it accelerated at an alarming speed and disappeared. Captain Goede and his copilot were unable to locate the UFO again. After the sighting came to an end, they informed Kirtland Air Force Base, located just outside of Albuquerque, of their encounter. What the pilots did not know, however, was that other pilots had reported seeing the same phenomenon on the same night.

Just five minutes after the initial sighting, a second report was made by another pilot who reported seeing a similar object out-side the cockpit window. The unnamed pilot was on board Pio-neers Airlines Flight 63 when he suddenly noticed a green glowing object in the sky. Just like Goede and his copilot, the pilot on board the Pioneers flight at first assumed that this green object was either a shooting star or another natural phenomenon, however, this the-ory was disproved. The green fireball started approaching the air-craft as it changed its color from green to red. As it was increasing its speed, the object got larger in size, which forced the pilot to make a quick sharp turn to avert disaster and avoid collision with the object. The fireball then started descending toward the ground until it disappeared.

There are a lot of similarities between the two reports. The first similarity is the description the pilots provided of the object. The object in both reports was described as having a spherical shape and a glowing bright green color. The pilot on board Flight 63 also reported that the object was able to change its size and color. The most interesting characteristic of the reports is the spatial awareness the UFO seemed to possess. The fact that the objects were able to mirror the maneuvers carried out by the aircraft implies that whatever was piloting the green fireballs was aware of the aircraft's position in space and time.

The Investigation

Following the two separate reports, the Kirtland Air Force Base launched an investigation to determine the origin of these green fireball sightings. From the beginning of the investigation, the intelligence officers assumed that the object must have been a meteor, which is the reason why Dr. Lincoln LaPaz was included in the investigation. LaPaz was an American astronomer known for being a pioneer in the study of meteors and meteorites. Because of his expertise on meteors, his insight was essential in order for the investigation to be a valid and accurate one.

To find out if the green fireballs were truly meteors or not, LaPaz plotted the path of the green fireballs in accordance to the reports made on the night. This path would follow the course of the fireball, and if the object was in fact a meteor that made it to earth to become a meteorite, then debris would be located at the site of where it would have eventually hit the ground. If no debris were to be found, then the meteor/meteorite hypothesis would have been ruled out. On December 5, 1948, a total of eight separate reports were made and LaPaz took into consideration all of these reports when calculating the fireballs' path.

To the air force's surprise, no debris or remnants of a meteor/meteorite were found at the calculated locations. Moreover, apart from the fact that no debris was found, there were further factors that proved to LaPaz that the green fireballs could not have been meteors. First and foremost, the flat trajectory of the green fireball was unlike that of a meteor. Secondly the objects also changed in size and maneuvered in a way that was impossible for a meteor. As has been stated, it is evident that whatever was piloting the green fireballs was aware of the aircraft's location in space.

As the days went on, the number of green fireball reports increased, heightening the pressure on the air force to provide an explanation. Thus far, the investigation was inconclusive, and all the facts were pointing to one theory: that these objects were not natural. The air force wanted to have first-hand evidence of the fireballs, which is why on December 8, 1948, two intelligence officers got on board a private aircraft in an attempt to witness the green fireballs for themselves. It did not take the officers very long to witness the UFOs. Shortly after their take off at around 18:33, as the aircraft was flying at an altitude of 11,500 feet twenty miles east of Las Vegas, the officers noticed that just two thousand feet above their aircraft was a green fireball. Similar to the previous reports, the green fireball leveled with their aircraft and started approaching it at a rapid speed. Luckily, the pilot was able to swerve just in time to avoid the fireball. As for the two officers, it was now proven to them that these reports were truly authentic, and that these fireballs were not meteors but something else, something being controlled by an intelligent entity.

The description the two officers provided of the UFO was similar to the previous reports. The fireball was described as being significantly larger than a flare, which ruled out that possibility as well. They also described the object as being large and capable of mirroring every maneuver their aircraft had carried out.

Project Twinkle

The pressure on the air force continued to grow as the phenomenon lacked an explanation. In an attempt to resolve the numerous reports that were being made, the air force created Project Twinkle in 1949. The project, which was run by Land-Air Corporation, operated phototheodolites at White Sands, New Mexico. The aim was for the phototheodolites to photograph any unusual activity and any unidentified objects flying past the cameras. Apart from that, a twenty-four-hour manned watch was to be set-up in New Mexico to accompany the phototheodolites and to confirm any unusual sightings.

Another factor that indicated the green fireballs were piloted by intelligent beings is the fact that the green fireball sightings stopped shortly after the manned watch was set up. From October 1, 1950, to March 31, 1951 (the duration of the second contractual period), not a single green fireball sighting was made. Since no further sightings were reported, Project Twinkle was discontinued on the basis that no information was being gathered. However, many have questioned why the sightings had suddenly stopped. Could it be the case that perhaps whoever was piloting the green aircraft had become aware that instruments were set up to capture the sightings?

Project Twinkle was destined for failure from the get-go. It was poorly funded and was not given any importance. A final report was written just a year and a half later, even though insufficient data had been collected to come to a conclusive explanation. Apart from not being able to identify the origin of the green fireballs, the report suggested that no more funds were to be wasted on the project. Albeit the fact that there was no data to back up the claim, the report stated that the sightings were natural phenomena. Although the green fireballs were reported to be completely natural, the air force refused to declassify any material related to the sightings.

The Sightings Continue

After Project Twinkle failed to explain what the green fireballs were, Edward J. Ruppelt, the director of Project Blue Book, started an investigation of his own in early 1952. The sightings were once again on the rise and he wanted an explanation. In his book titled *The Report of Unidentified Flying Objects*, Ruppelt mentions a meeting he had with a group of scientists who worked at the Los Alamos Laboratory. When discussing the green fireball sightings, one of the scientists who had witnessed these UFOs for himself described the sighting as follows:

"Take a soft ball and paint it with some kind of fluorescent paint that will glow a bright green in the dark. Then have someone take the ball out, about 100 feet in front of you and about ten feet above you. Have him throw the ball right at your face, as hard as he can throw it. That's what a green fireball looks like."[14]

During the meeting with the scientists, it seemed evident to Ruppelt that these highly qualified individuals all seemed to have the same opinion: these fireballs were not a natural phenomenon, but were an aircraft of some sort, an extraterrestrial one, piloted by an intelligent entity. Many came to the conclusion that the green fireballs were "an unmanned test vehicle that was being projected into our atmosphere from a spaceship hovering several hundred miles above the Earth."[15]

This was not the only instance in which credible scientists had claimed that the UFOs were extraterrestrial. In a meeting two

---

14. Ruppelt, *The Report on Unidentified Flying Objects: The Original 1956*, 53.

15. Ruppelt, *The Report on Unidentified Flying Objects: The Original 1956*, 53.

years prior, a group of scientists had made a similar statement. Ruppelt stated that "two years ago I would have been amazed to hear a group of reputable scientists make such a startling statement. Now, however, I took it as a matter of course. I'd heard the same type of statement many times before from equally qualified groups."[16]

Meteors or Alien Aircraft?

On July 24, 1948, nine months after the initial sighting, the green fireballs were observed once again, this time near Socorro, New Mexico. LaPaz took dust samples, but this time the results showed that the dust contained large copper particles. This interested LaPaz because when copper is burned, it gives off a yellow green hue, which explains why the fireballs were green in color. However, copper is not usually found in meteors, which further proved that these green fireballs were not and could not have been meteors. What this finding proved was that the object was producing enough heat to burn the copper, producing the green color all the reports described.

With the meteor hypothesis ruled out, this left LaPaz and the authorities with one other viable explanation, the extraterrestrial hypothesis, the same explanation that several scientists had come to.

"I'm sure the yellow-green fireballs aren't ordinary meteorite falls. I have been observing the skies since 1914 and I have never seen any meteoritic fireballs like them."[17]

What is amazing about the air force's statement is that it completely contradicted the explanations the experts had provided.

---

16. Ruppelt, *The Report on Unidentified Flying Objects: The Original 1956*, 53.
17. National Investigations Committee on Aerial Phenomena, *The UFO Evidence*, ed. Richard Hall (Washington, DC: Quarto, 1964), 135.

LaPaz, as well as several scientists, who work at the most reputable government laboratory in the country, stated that the green fireballs could not have been meteors. It would only have been logical for the air force to trust the experts, alas, this was not to be the case.

In the final Project Twinkle report from 1951, it was stated that the sightings were completely natural. The green fireballs were simply "a flight of birds, planets, meteors and possibly cloudiness."

Chapter 5

Cigar-Shaped UFO Spotted in the Clear Night Sky

Date: May 29, 1950

Location: Mount Vernon, Virginia; United States

Captain Willis Sperry together with copilot William Gates and flight engineer Robert Arnholt were en route to San Francisco from New York on board a DC-6 aircraft with stops at Washington, DC, Nashville and Tulsa. The clear night sky, together with the full moon, was the perfect condition for a nighttime flight.

It was around 21:15 when the DC-6 aircraft was flying over Mount Vernon in Virginia at an altitude of 7,500 feet. Around that time, copilot Gates saw a bright fluorescent light straight ahead. What made the light stand out from the stars of the night sky was that the light was radiating and appeared to be much brighter than any of the stars in the sky. The light was dead ahead of the airplane and at that point the pilots assumed that it must have been an unregistered aircraft. As the lights continued to approach the DC-6 at a rapid speed, Gates grabbed onto the controls and quickly veered the aircraft to avoid collision. The object's silhouette was visible against the full moon, and its cigar shape, together with the dark metallic color and the lack of wings or exhaust plumes, convinced Gates, Sperry, and Arnholt that this was not an ordinary aircraft nor was it a terrestrial one. The imagery was somewhere between astonishing and terrifying.

Leveling the aircraft after the sharp turn, Sperry made a left turn, and to his surprise the object followed. The cigar-shaped UFO had halted its course and started moving in a parallel direction, imitating every turn and every maneuver Sperry made. It was crystal clear to these three witnesses that no terrestrial aircraft could possess the unconventional characteristics the disk-shaped UFO did. With that being said, the air traffic control operators at the Washington Air Traffic Control Center in Leesberg, Virginia, were unable to track any object other than the DC-6 aircraft on their radar. Within a few seconds the object made a sudden acceleration and disappeared to the east, not to be seen again.

The Investigation

This case was investigated by Project Blue Book and a formal interview with the three men was conducted on February 4, 1955. Although the investigation was initiated five years after the actual incident, the three men were able to recollect every single detail perfectly. Wolfgang Benjamin Kelmperer, the officer conducting the interview, acknowledged Sperry's credibility, as well as his sixteen years of experience and fifteen thousand flight hours. It was undeniable that Sperry was an experienced pilot and was a credible eyewitness, which was a vital aspect for the case's reliability.

Over the years, many other individuals came forward with stories that corroborated the sighting the three men had had. Colonel Henry "Hank" Myers, President Harry Truman's pilot, was flying from Nashville to Knoxville on the same night of Sperry's sighting. On his journey, Myers reported seeing a similar bright object that could have been the same UFO Sperry, Gates and Arnholt had encountered.

According to the interview with Kelmperer, "Much later, Sperry learned that 'Hank Myers, later pilot of President Truman's plane, was flying an AA airplane on the same evening and observed a brilliant bluish object between Nashville and Knoxville at such a time that it could well have been the same UFO.'

"The possibility that the UFO seen by Sperry and his copilot was a meteor was emphatically discounted by both. Capt. [sic] Sperry does not believe that the seemingly erratic apparent movement of the object could have been an illusion produced solely by the three veering maneuvers of their own aircraft. The observation of the bright light being at what they called the rear of the oblong or cigar shaped silhouette of the object as it passed for a fleeting fraction of a second in front of the disk of the full moon seems hard to reconcile with the brilliant visibility of this light during the earlier head-on approach phase, unless it is assumed that the luminous area was much larger than the cross section of the body."[18]

Conclusion

Sperry held out from involving the authorities of his sighting and perhaps this was the reason why a formal investigation by the air force never took place. With that being said, we must keep in mind that the high status of the second eyewitness, Colonel Myers, enhances the credibility of this UFO case. The characteristics of the UFO are without a doubt unconventional characteristics no terrestrial aircraft would possess. The lack of wings and exhaust plume are details that in and of themselves support the fact that the UFO was interplanetary and extraterrestrial in origin.

---

18. W.B. Klemperer, February 4, 1955 interview.

Chapter 6

UFO Caught on Tape

Date: August 15, 1950
Location: Montana, United States

The Mariana UFO sighting is considered to be one of the first UFO cases that included photographic evidence. It was August 15, 1950, when Nick Mariana, the manager of a minor-league basketball team, together with his secretary Virginia Raunig, was inspecting an empty baseball field in Montana prior to their fixture.

It was a beautiful sunny day, not a single cloud in sight. The time was around 11:25 when Mariana and Raunig were in the empty baseball field. Mariana's attention was caught by a bright light in the sky. As he looked up, he brought the sighting to Raunig's attention and the pair then noticed there were two objects in the sky. The objects were flying too close in proximity and too fast to be conventional aircraft. Apart from that, the objects were rotating on their axis. Mariana rushed to his car where he had his 16mm camera and was able to record part of the sighting before the two silvery UFOs disappeared.

The sixteen second footage shows the two objects traveling at a great speed before they disappear out of sight. This was the first time anyone had caught a flying saucer on camera, undeniable proof that these saucers, which were a topic of popular discussion at the time, truly existed. The following day the local newspaper wrote an article about the footage and the news spread like wild-fire, becoming the most famous UFO videotape to date.

The Footage

The Mariana UFO footage can easily be found online. The sixteen second video footage shows the two bright objects in the daylit sky. Mariana and Raunig estimated that the UFOs were traveling around two hundred to four hundred miles per hour. They also estimated the UFOs' diameters to be approximately fifty feet and the distance between the two objects to be approximately 150 feet apart.

When the footage was forwarded to the United States Air Force, the case was immediately shrugged off and an explanation was provided without any investigation. The air force stated that the two bright objects were reflections from two F-94 jets that were in the sky at the time. The explanation seemed legitimate and difficult for the ordinary person to disprove. With that being said, two years later in 1952, Edward J. Ruppelt, the head of Project Blue Book, believed that the case had been prematurely dismissed without a proper investigation. Ruppelt reopened the case and sent the footage to a laboratory for analysis.

The analysis indicated that the objects could not have been birds, weather balloons or meteorites. Firstly, if the two objects were weather balloons, they would have traveled along the wind's direction, not in the opposite direction, and at a much slower speed. Secondly, the speed of the objects was significantly faster than a bird, yet slower than a meteorite. The analysis also showed that the objects had different properties than a jet. The shape and color did not substantiate the air force's statement. Later in 1952, an intelligence officer in Great Falls, Montana, went through Malmstrom Air Force Base's entire records to check if any fighter-jets had been in the sky at the time of the sighting. It was the case that two F-94 jets were in the sky, however, in a completely different part of the city, clouding the official statement even more.

The investigation that Ruppelt was leading was indicating that the air force was either involved in a cover-up or else they had an explanation that they were not disclosing to the public. In regard to the official explanation provided by the air force, Ruppelt stated that "the two jets weren't anywhere close to where the two UFOs had been. We studied each individual light, and both appeared too steady to be reflections. We drew a blank on the Montana movie. It was an unknown."[19]

To confirm the findings from the analysis, Ruppelt sent the footage for a second independent analysis. This time the footage was analyzed by Robert Baker who worked for the Douglas Aircraft Company. Baker's findings were similar to the first analysis; the objects could not have been natural phenomena or reflections.

"Preliminary analysis excluded most natural phenomena. After about 18 months of rather detailed, albeit not continuous, study using various film-measuring equipment at Douglas and at UCLA, as well as an analysis of a photogrammetric experiment, it appeared that neither of these hypothesized natural phenomena explanations had merit."[20]

Conclusion

The two independent analyses came to the same conclusion, that the two objects caught on footage by Mariana could not have been reflections as the air force had stated. The contradiction led many to

19. Ruppelt, *The Report on Unidentified Flying Objects: The Original 1956*, 220.

20. Robert Baker, testimony at the Committee of Science and Astronautics Symposium on Unidentifed Flying Objects, July 29, 1968, http://files.ncas .org/ufosymposium/baker.html#oralstmt.

believe that a cover-up was involved, and the truth was being concealed from the public. Although the statement was debunked by many scientists, the air force did not comment further on the case.

If the two aircraft were not weather balloons, fighter jets, or birds, could it be that they were interplanetary objects? Could it be that the air force dismissed the case because they couldn't disclose to the public that an extraterrestrial aircraft had infiltrated American airspace and there was no way the air force could protect the nation?

Chapter 7

The McMinnville
UFO Photographs

Date: May 11, 1950
Location: McMinnville, Oregon, United States

The McMinnville photographs remain to this day one of the highest quality photographs that capture an extraterrestrial aircraft. The photographs, which show a flying disk, are still the most iconic photographs in the study of the UFO phenomenon. The authenticity of the photographs is what makes this case indisputable proof of the existence of extraterrestrial life.

Evelyn and Paul Trent lived in a rural area just nine miles southwest of McMinnville, Oregon. The Trents led a very simple and humble lifestyle, depending on their livestock and farm for their livelihood. At around 19:30, Evelyn was walking back to her house after feeding the animals. The sun was setting, and Evelyn would never have thought that she would be a witness to one of the most important sightings in the study of UFO phenomenon.

Evelyn had almost arrived at the house when she noticed a "metallic looking, disk-shaped object" in the sky.[21] The sight startled Evelyn and she ran into the house, calling for her husband Paul to immediately come out and witness the disk-shaped object

---

21. Condon Committee Report, Case 46, 1968.

for himself—the aircraft was a captivating and fascinating sight. Paul quickly ran back into the house to get his camera and captured two photographs of the disk-shaped object, which sped away into the distance shortly after.

As the object disappeared, Evelyn and Paul were left bewildered; had they just caught an extraterrestrial aircraft on their camera? The couple immediately reported the sighting to the local authorities, who forwarded the case to the Condon Committee, a group of scientists from the University of Colorado in charge of studying UFO cases. Paul and Evelyn were interviewed separately and the two described the object as having a disk-shape and made of a silver metallic material. The surface was extremely bright and reflective, similar to aluminum. The diameter of the object was estimated to be between twenty to thirty feet, and it lacked the usual features of an aircraft such as wings, exhaust plumes, and windows. Although the object accelerated at an incredible speed, it did not emit any noise, nor did it leave a trail behind.

The Investigation

Apart from the interviews, Evelyn and Paul were also instructed to take a psychological test to indicate whether they were mentally well or not. The results indicated that both Evelyn and Paul were of sound mental health and the event was certainly not a hallucination caused by an underlying psychiatric condition.

In early June of the same year, Paul took his photographs to *The Telephone Register Newspaper* to get answers, as the authorities certainly had not provided any. Prior to publishing the photographs, the newspaper agency analyzed the photographs to confirm that the story was not a hoax and to ensure that Paul had not tampered with the film. On June 8, the following article was published on the front page of the gazette:

"In view of the variety of opinion and reports attendant to the sources over the past two years, every effort has been made to check Trent's photos for authenticity. Expert photographers declared there has been no tampering with the negatives. The original photos were developed by a local firm. After careful consideration, there appears to be no possibility of a hoax or hallucination connected with the pictures. The *Telephone Register* believes them authentic."[22]

The photographs were analyzed for a second time in 1975 by Bruce Maccabee, a Navy optical physicist and avid researcher on the phenomenon of UFOs. To ensure reliability, Maccabee used densitometric measurements and the actual position of the objects in the frame. The investigation showed that there was no evidence that a string or a wire was suspended from the power lines to the flying saucer. This ruled out the hypothesis that the pictured flying disk was a model. Apart from that, Maccabee also highlighted the fact that the underexposed land and the properly exposed sky were consistent with the time Evelyn and Paul had reported seeing the object. At 19:30, the west would have been brighter than the east and this was the case in the photographs as well.

In the official Condon Report, William Hartmann, who was a well-noted planetary scientist and one of the scientists who made up the Condon Committee stated, "This is one of the few UFO reports in which all factors investigated—geometric, psychological and physical—appear to be consistent with the assertion that an extraordinary flying object, silvery, metallic, disk-shaped, tens of meters in diameter, and evidently artificial, flew within sight of two witnesses."[23]

22. Bill Powell, "At Long Last—Authentic Photographs of Flying Saucer," *Telephone Register Newspaper*, June 8, 1950.

23. Condon Committee Report, Case 46, 1968.

Conclusion

The McMinnville photographs are one of the few authentic photographs that captured an interplanetary flying object. Although the object is technically unidentified, it is not possible for a terrestrial aircraft to have the properties that the disk possessed. Apart from being some of the most iconic photographs in the study of the phenomenon, this case is a crucial one that supports the extraterrestrial hypothesis.

Chapter 8

The Lubbock Lights

Date: August 1951
Location: Lubbock, Texas, United States

In the summer of 1951, the authorities of Lubbock, Texas, and Albuquerque, New Mexico, were flooded with calls from residents who reported seeing a number of lights in the sky flying in a *V* formation. Apart from the visual sightings, the unidentified lights were captured on film and tracked on radar, becoming what is now known as the Lubbock Lights.

An Atomic Energy Commission's Sandia Corporation employee and his wife were enjoying the summer evening in their backyard in Albuquerque when a salient light caught the attention of the couple. As the light got closer to the house, the couple noticed that the light was a V-shaped aircraft flying at an altitude of eight hundred to one thousand feet. At the aircraft's end were six to eight bright bluish lights. The size of the aircraft was described as being larger than a B-36 aircraft, which has a wingspan of 230 feet. Without emitting any noise, the *V* shaped object hovered above their house as it continued flying toward the city.

The couple had seen B-36 bombers flying over their house multiple times and they were familiar with the shape and characteristics of the aircraft. Conversely, the *V* shaped aircraft was completely unfamiliar to them. As the unidentified aircraft disappeared over the horizon, the couple called the local authorities, who relayed the report over to air traffic control operators. The operators were able to confirm that there were no known aircraft flying over the designated location; the only two aircraft flying over Albuquerque were a Constellation aircraft, which was flying fifty miles west of the city, and an air force B-25, which was flying south.

The report was the beginning of a busy night for the authorities. Just twenty minutes later, the second and most credible report was made by a group of university professors in Lubbock, Texas. The group of professors consisted of Dr. W. Robinson, professor of Geology; Dr. A. Oberg, professor of chemical engineering; W. Ducker, head of the petroleum engineering department; and Dr. E. F. George, professor of physics; who were drinking tea and conversing about micrometeorites in Robinson's backyard. Their conversation ended abruptly as they noted a number of bluish-green lights flying in a semicircular formation. Naturally, the professors were knowledgeable enough to distinguish a meteor from an unnatural phenomenon and this was a clear-cut example of the latter. For a number of seconds, the professors counted a total of fifteen to thirty lights flying over the house before they disappeared into thin air.

For the next hour the professors talked amongst themselves of what the lights could have been, but the sighting was too short for them to discern any notable characteristics. Luckily enough, just an hour later, the lights reappeared. This time the lights were not flying in a particular formation but were maneuvering erratically before disappearing within a few seconds once again. Throughout the month of August, the four professors saw these bright lights on a total of twelve occasions.

Over the course of a month, several other reports were made by multiple individuals who reported seeing these mysterious *V* shaped lights in the sky. Another report was made by an elderly couple in Lubbock on August 25. As the wife was outside taking sheets off the clothesline, she was taken aback when she saw a large aircraft hovering noiselessly in the sky. The wife ran into the house, pale as a ghost, telling her husband of the sighting. Her husband was able to confirm the sight for himself. In an interview with Edward J. Ruppelt, the head of Project Blue Book, the elderly man described his wife as being "white as the sheet she was carrying" the second she walked in the house.[24]

One final witness report we shall look at was made by two women six days after the initial sighting. On August 31, a mother and her daughter were driving through Matador, Texas, which is 70 miles from Lubbock. At around 12:30 they noticed a strange pear-shaped object just 140 meters to the side of the road. The object was flying at a low altitude, approximately 110 meters above ground level. The ladies parked the car to the side of the road and exited to get a clearer view of the ominous object. As they got a clearer view, they noticed that it was "the size of a B-29 fuselage" and it was drifting slowly and noiselessly.[25] An interesting detail that the ladies included in their report is that the UFO did not have any exhaust plumes, but it did have a porthole on its side. After a couple of seconds, the object accelerated away and disappeared, leaving no traces behind. Although the report differed from the earlier ones, this was one of numerous UFO reports made throughout the month of August.

Apart from the visual reports, on August 26, an aircraft was recorded on radar traveling nine hundred miles per hour at an

24. Ruppelt, *The Report on Unidentified Flying Objects: The Original 1956 Edition*, 104.

25. Ruppelt, *The Report on Unidentified Flying Objects: The Original 1956 Edition*, 102.

altitude of thirteen thousand feet. In actual fact, two different radars were able to record the aircraft, which remained visible on radar for a total of six minutes. An F-86 military jet was also scrambled and ordered to intercept. However, once the jet climbed into the air, the target disappeared from the radar, forcing the pilot to return to base. The pilot on board the fighter jet explained how the object disappeared off the radar the second the F-86 was scrambled, as though it was aware of the jet's position and intent.

The Photograph

One important witness was Carl Hart, an amateur photographer who managed to capture the lights on film on August 31. On the night of the sighting, Hart was laying in his bed looking outside his window when a group of lights flying in a *V* formation started appearing out of nowhere. Hart had finally witnessed the lights everyone was talking about for himself. Using his Kodak 35mm camera, Hart was able to take a total of five photographs of the lights, which he developed the following day.

The high-quality photographs had captured what everyone in Lubbock was talking about; the *Lubbock Avalanche-Journal* even published the photographs in the newspaper. It did not take very long for Hart's photographs to gain attention. Soon after, *Life* magazine published an article and the photographs of the Lubbock lights. The report was being covered in countries all over the world, and Ruppelt wanted to authenticate the photographs for himself to ensure that this was not a hoax or a publicity stunt. Ruppelt managed to obtain four out of the five negatives and took them to Wright Patterson Air Force Base where they were analyzed by experts.

By the time Ruppelt had collected the negatives, many people had handled the film, and although they were not in an excellent shape for analysis, the experts at the air force base were able to confirm that the images did indeed show lights flying in an inverted V formation. The question that Ruppelt wanted to resolve now was whether the lights could have been stars, but in all of the four negatives, stars were visible in the background, implying that the V shaped lights were significantly brighter than the stars in the sky. In the official report, Ruppelt states that "the photos were never proven to be a hoax, but neither were they proven to be genuine."[26]

The Investigation

Incongruous with the analysis and the witness reports, the air force stated that the lights were plovers, a type of wading bird. This ludicrous explanation was immediately dismissed, firstly for the fact that plovers cannot mysteriously appear and disappear, and secondly, due to the fact that in a span of twenty minutes the lights were seen in Albuquerque and in Lubbock.

With the backlash that the air force received, a second statement was provided that was just as confounding as the first one. Ruppelt had stated that the air force did have an explanation for this sighting, however they were unable to disclose this information to the public. In his book *The Report on Unidentified Flying Objects*, Ruppelt said, "They weren't birds, they weren't refracted light, but they weren't spaceships. The lights that the professor's saw—the backbone of the Lubbock Light series—have been positively identified as a very commonplace and easily explainable natural phenomenon. It is very unfortunate that I can't divulge

---

26. Ruppelt, *The Report on Unidentified Flying Objects: The Original 1956 Edition*, 107.

exactly the way the answer was found because it is an interesting story of how a scientist set up complete instrumentation to track down the light and how he spent several months testing theory after theory until he finally hit upon the answer. Telling the story would lead to his identity and, in exchange for his story, I promised the man complete anonymity."[27]

Conclusion

The Lubbock Lights were witnessed by hundreds of individuals and numerous reports were made, one of which was by a credible group of university professors. Although protecting the scientist's identity is a valid thing to do, Ruppelt could have easily provided the explanation but used a pseudonym or withheld his name from the statement. Many have wondered whether the lights were the B-2 stealth bomber, which is why the air force did not disclose the explanation.

The first operational flight of the stealth bomber took place in 1989, thirty-eight years after the Lubbock sightings, which in and of itself disproves the hypothesis. Apart from that, one common factor was that the lights hovered silently and at a low altitude. Even if it was the case that the B-2 bomber was in the sky prior to the official operational flight, if it had flown overhead it would have left a thundering noise. All military aircraft that break the sound barrier produce a sonic boom, and yet, the mysterious V-shaped aircraft was completely noiseless. Although Ruppelt stated that the lights can easily be explained by a natural phenomenon, he did not state what this phenomenon was. Over the years,

---

27. Ruppelt, *The Report on Unidentified Flying Objects: The Original 1956 Edition*, 110.

several meteorological officers have stated that they cannot explain the sightings using natural phenomena.

To this day we do not know what the Lubbock lights truly were. Were they natural phenomena as Ruppelt had stated, or were they extraterrestrial aircraft? I myself believe that the latter explanation makes the most sense considering the salient characteristics, the ability for the aircraft to appear and disappear, and most of all, for the fact that even when analyzed at an air force base, no one was able to provide any explanation.

Chapter 9

The Washington, DC UFO Wave

Date: July 1952
Location: Washington, DC, United States

In the summer of 1952, one of the most publicized UFO sightings took place in the capital of the United States, Washington, DC. For two weeks, reports of strange lights in the sky were made by numerous individuals, including high-level officials. The sightings were given so much attention by the media that President Harry S. Truman himself had contacted Edward Ruppelt, the head of Project Blue Book, to inquire into what the mysterious lights were.

The first wave of sightings started on July 19, 1952. At 23:40, Edward Nugent, an air traffic control operator who worked at the Washington National Airport, noticed seven unidentified objects on radar. The objects were fifteen miles south of the city and there were no aircraft in the vicinity at the time. The unidentified objects were also not following a preestablished flightpath, which is necessary for every aircraft when it enters a country's airspace. Nugent immediately informed his superior, Harry Barnes, who was the senior air-traffic control operator on duty. Barnes observed the objects and noticed bizarre characteristics that were dissimilar to conventional aircraft. From the get-go, Barnes knew that whatever these seven objects were, they certainly were not a conventional or military aircraft.

"We knew immediately that a very strange situation existed," Barnes said. "Their movements were completely radical compared to those of an ordinary aircraft."[28]

Before contacting the air force, Barnes checked whether it could have been the case that Nugent's radar had in some way malfunctioned. When contacting the Washington National Airport's radar-equipped tower, Howard Cocklin and Joe Zacko, two of the radio operators working there, confirmed that this was not a glitch. They, too, had been tracking the seven objects on their radar, and they had also made visual contact with the objects. Outside the tower's windows, Cocklin and Zacko had seen a bright white light in the sky that proceeded to accelerate at a rapid speed and disappear.

The mysterious light was also observed by S. C. Pierman, a Capital Airlines pilot, who was awaiting approval to take off from Dulles International Airport. Pierman had been waiting for take-off approval for several minutes, but it was delayed as the radio control operators ha informed him that there was an unidentified aircraft flying above the runway. Outside the cockpit windows, Pierman noticed "white, tailless, fast moving lights" that were flying above the runway.[29] The shape, color and speed of the aircraft seemed to be something out of a science fiction movie. Throughout Pierman's sighting, he was in contact with Barnes who was tracking the objects on the radar. The second that the objects disappeared from the sky, Barnes noted that they had disappeared off the radar scope too.

---

28. Jerome Clark, *The UFO Book: Encyclopedia of the Extraterrestrial* (Detroit: Visible Ink Press, 1998), 653.

29. Peter Carlson, "50 Year Ago, Unidentified Flying Objects from Way Beyond the Beltway Seized the Capital's Imagination," *The Washington Post*, June 21, 2002.

It was now time for Barnes to forward the report to the air force. He contacted Andrews Air Force Base in Maryland, informing them of the situation. Barnes notified them that two separate radars had been tracking several unidentified objects and that visual contact had been made by three individuals. William Brady, the radio control officer at the Air Force Base, had also seen the lights in the sky. For the next two hours the unidentified lights remained visible in the Washington sky. Brady described the phenomenon as an "object that appeared to be like an orange ball of fire."[30]

Throughout the two hours, more high-level officials had seen the lights, one of them being Sergeant Charles Davenport. At around 02:00, Davenport reported seeing a bright light traveling at a very high speed, carrying out erratic maneuvers, such as moving from side-to-side. At one point in the encounter, Davenport noted that next to the main bright light was a secondary silver-colored object, which was carrying out similar erratic maneuvers before it accelerated at an incredible speed. The main bright light followed shortly thereafter and the two lights had disappeared out of the sky.

It was around 03:00, over three hours after the initial sighting, when an F-94 military jet was scrambled from New Castle Air Force Base. The pilot was instructed to patrol the sky and pursue the lights if they had reappeared. Just like the previous UFO cases, the second the fighter-jet took off from the base, the targets disappeared off the radar.

The UFOs returned to the Washington sky the following weekend, making it even more eventful than the previous one. On July 26, 1952, an unnamed pilot, flying a *National Airlines* aircraft, was flying over the capital, when at around 20:15 he observed a number of

---

30. Carlson, "50 Years Ago."

bright lights outside the cockpit window, flying at a higher altitude than the aircraft. The objects also showed up on the airborne radar as well as the radar at Andrews Air Force Base. At the base, Sergeant Charles Cummings made visual contact with the UFOs that were moving significantly faster than a shooting star, however, they left no trails behind. On radar, the objects were travelling at roughly seven thousand miles per hour, and at approximately 23:30, two F-94 fighter-jets were scrambled from New Castle Air Force Base.

Captain John McHugo and Lieutnenant William Patterson were instructed to pursue the objects as they were flying toward the capital city. Patterson was able to make visual contact with four glowing white objects outside his cockpit window, and although he was tracking them on his radar, he was unable to lock-down with them. Interestingly enough, as Patterson was closing down the distance, the objects responded and surrounded his fighter-jet, two on each side. Speaking to the air traffic control operators, Patterson stated: "...they're all around me. What should I do?"[31]

His question was left unanswered; no one provided him with instructions. Each time the objects retreated from the fighter-jet and Patterson attempted to close down on them once again, they would surround his aircraft each time. Even though the objects were at an extremely close proximity, Patterson could not describe them in any other way except for bright glowing spheres. The cat-and-mouse chase was terminated after numerous minutes as it was evident that Patterson was clearly unable to identify them or pursue them. It was clear that the unidentified flying objects were the ones in control of the airspace.

---

31. Dan Gilgoff, "Saucers Full of Secrets," *Washington City Paper*, December 14, 2001, https://www.washingtoncitypaper.com/news/article/13023374/saucers-full-of-secrets.

The Air Force's Explanation

National and international newspapers were covering the stories, each coming to their own conclusions, some claiming they were meteorites, others claiming they were alien aircraft. Everyone was waiting for an explanation, even President Truman himself, who had contacted Captain Edward Ruppelt.

The air force stated that the blips on the radar were caused by a temperature inversion, a phenomenon that occurs when a layer of warm air and a layer of moist air cover a layer of cool and dry air, causing blips to appear on radar. A press conference was also held on July 29 by Major General John Samford, the Director of Intelligence. During the press conference, Samford took questions and also gave a second possibility of what the lights could have been. Samford stated that the lights and the objects on radar could also have been a flock of birds, which radio control operators mistook for aircraft: "The radar screen has been picking up things for many years that, well, birds, a flock of ducks. I know there's been one instance in which a flock of ducks was picked up and was intercepted and flown through as being an unidentified phenomenon."[32]

What is interesting about this press conference and the explanations given, is that on the same day, Gilbert Levy, the chief of the counterintelligence divisions of the Air Force Office of Special Investigations, wrote a report about the wave of the UFO sightings. His report, which was released in 1975, stated that the air force did not know what the lights were and that the temperature inversion explanation was provided just to keep the public off the air force's back. His report stated "The Director of Intelligence

---

32. Press conference held by Major General John Samford, July 29, 1952.

advises that no theory exists at the present time as to the origin of the objects and they are considered to be unexplained."[33]

On the same day, even the FBI asked the Air Force Intelligence for a debriefing session. N. W. Philcox, who was the FBI liaison officer, wrote in his report "[Commander Boyd] advised that it is not entirely impossible that the objects sighted may possibly be ships from another planet such as Mars. He advised that at the present time there is nothing to substantiate this theory, but the possibility is not being overlooked. He stated that Air Intelligence is fairly certain that these objects are not ships or missiles from another nation in this world. Commander Boyd advised that intense research is being carried on presently by Air Intelligence, and at the present time when credible reporting's of sightings are received, the Air force is attempting in each instance to send up jet interceptor planes in order to obtain a better view of these objects. However, recent attempts in this regard have indicated that when the pilot in the jet approaches the object it invariably fades from view."[34]

Conclusion

In this case, the air force provided two explanations: one for the public and another for the security and intelligence wings of the United States government. The two explanations are vastly different. The one given to the public stated that the lights and radar targets were a result of a temperature inversion, whereas the one given to the security departments stated that the air force did not have an explanation as to what the phenomenon was, and it could have been the case that the UFOs were extraterrestrial in origin.

---

33. Loren Gross, *UFO's: A History 1952: July 21st - July 31st* (Fremont, CA: Privately published, 1986), 56.

34. N. W. Philcox, FBI Memorandum, 1952.

Many high-level officials, such as Barnes, did not accept the temperature inversion explanation. Those who had seen the objects with their own eyes knew that these objects were piloted by an intelligent being. The characteristics and maneuvers were unnatural and could not have been a natural phenomenon. Barnes said, "The UFOs were monitoring radio traffic and [behaved] accordingly since the objects disappeared as soon as the jets were scrambled."[35]

---

35. Clark, *The UFO Book*, 656.

Chapter 10
"We Flew Above Flying Saucers"

Date: July 14, 1952
Location: Norfolk, Virginia, United States

Just one week prior to the UFO wave in Washington, DC, another significant UFO report was made. While en route to Miami from New York, Captain Fred Koepke, First Officer William Nash, and Second Officer William Fortenberry were on board a Pan American World Airways DC-4 aircraft. With clear skies, it seemed that this would be a routine flight for the three individuals. The weather conditions were perfect for a night-time flight. With no clouds in the sky, the city lights stood out as they were flying eight thousand feet over Norfolk, Virginia. However, just a few minutes into the flight, they came face to face with the unknown.

As Nash was looking down at the city lights, he noticed a red light had suddenly appeared in the sky, flying just below the aircraft's starboard position. As he got a better look at it, what he thought was one light turned out to be six unidentified flying objects flying in an echelon formation at a tremendous speed toward the aircraft. Nash immediately called out for the others to look out the window to see what was unfolding. Koepke, Nash, and Fortenberry just stared in awe as the lights flew in formation directly below the aircraft. In an article later written by Nash and

Fortenberry, the two recounted, "They had the fiery aspect of hot coals, but of much greater glow—perhaps twenty times more brilliant than any of the scattered ground lights over which they passed or the city lights to the right."[36]

The six aircraft were flying in formation approximately two thousand feet above the ground. They had a perfectly circular shape with well-defined edges and a wingspan of over 100 feet. What proved to the three men that these objects were extraterrestrial was that after a few seconds, the six objects flipped on their edge and started flying in a vertical position. Koepke compared the UFOs to a coin standing vertically, and estimated the aircraft were about fifteen feet wide. The objects then returned to their original horizontal position, still in formation, and made a sharp angular turn before they sped off into the distance.

Their encounter did not end there though. Within a few seconds, two other UFOs flew directly below their aircraft, heading toward the same direction the other six UFOs were. Although they were similar in shape, they were considerably less bright and as they caught up with the other six aircraft, the eight red lights started flickering sporadically as they began a vertical climb, blinking out and disappearing one by one. The entire encounter lasted around twelve seconds and the pilots estimated that the objects had covered fifty miles in just twelve seconds, which means that they must have been traveling at twelve thousand miles per hour. Although the objects were traveling at a speed that would have broken the sound barrier, no sonic boom was heard.

---

36. William B. Nash and William H. Fortenberry, "We Flew Above Flying Saucers," *TRUE Report on Flying Saucers*, 1967, http://www.seektress.com /above.htm.

The Investigation

The DC-4 aircraft landed in Miami shortly after midnight. The following day, the three men were interviewed separately by Air Force Intelligence officer Major John Sharpe, together with four other officials. Although they did not get an inclination as to what the lights were, the men were told that seven other individuals had made similar reports within thirty minutes of their sighting.

The investigation carried out by Project Blue Book acknowledged the authenticity of the report and the credibility of the witnesses. With that being said, this case was listed as an unknown, which meant that the reported UFOs were not a natural phenomenon, a celestial body, nor a misidentification or a delusion. This did not stop astrophysicist and skeptic Donald Menzel from discounting the encounter. Although the official investigation itself could not find an explanation, Menzel stated that firstly, the pilots were not credible sources and secondly, the red lights were reflections from the cockpit and "immaterial images made of light."[37]

Conclusion

Menzel's scrutiny of the encounter is not only illogical but also unfounded. In the witness reports, the witnesses stated that the objects could not have been reflections due to their maneuverability. Although the case is officially listed as unknown, it does seem as though these objects were interplanetary; the ability to appear and disappear out of nowhere, breaking the sound barrier without producing a sonic boom, and their unconventional characteristics are all factors that support an extraterrestrial hypothesis.

---

37. Donald H. Menzel and Lyle G. Boyd, *The World of Flying Saucers: A Scientific Examination of a Major Myth of the Space Age* (Garden City, NY: Doubleday, 1963), 263.

In Nash and Fortenberry's article, they write, "Though we don't know what they were, what they were doing, or where they came from, we are certain in our minds that they were intelligently operated craft from somewhere other than this planet. We are sure that no pilot, able to view them as we did, could conceive of any earthly aircraft capable of the speed, abrupt change of direction, and acceleration that we witnessed, or imagine any airplane metal that could withstand the heat that ought to have been created by friction in their passage through the dense atmosphere at two thousand feet. Whether they were controlled from within or remotely, we can't say, but it is impossible to think of human flesh and bone surviving the jolt of their course reversal." [38]

---

38. Nash and Fortenberry, "We Flew Above Flying Saucers."

Chapter 11
President Carter's UFO Sighting

Date: January 6, 1969
Location: Georgia, United States

Apart from being the thirty-ninth president of the United States, Jimmy Carter is also an avid believer in extraterrestrial life. During the electoral campaign of 1976, Carter claimed that if he were to be elected, he would release every piece of information the government had on alien life. Unsurprisingly, even though he was elected, he wasn't granted permission to release any classified information. What many people do not know about Carter is that he himself had seen a UFO in 1969 when he was giving a speech in Georgia.

"One thing is for sure. I will never make fun of people who say they have seen unidentified objects in the sky. If I become president, I will make every piece of information this country has about UFO sightings available to the public and the scientists."[39]

On January 6, 1969, at 19:15, as Carter was delivering a speech at the Lions Club in Georgia, one of the attendees noticed a bright object in the sky and pointed it out to Carter. The object was located to Carter's left side, flying at a low altitude, and was significantly

---

39. Timothy Good, *Above Top Secret: The Worldwide UFO Cover-up* (London: Sidgwick & Jackson, 1987), 368.

brighter than the moon and stars. Hovering silently over the tree-tops, the object started changing its color in a sequential order, from a bright white to blue, red, green, and then back to white. The spherical object remained in the sky for a total of twelve minutes before it disappeared from the sky.

"There were about twenty of us standing outside of a little restaurant, I believe, a high school lunchroom, and a kind of green light appeared in the western sky," Carter later recalled. "This was right after sundown. It got brighter and brighter. And then it eventually disappeared. It did not have any solid substance to it, it was just a very peculiar-looking light. None of us could understand what it was."[40]

In several interviews throughout the years, Carter has frequently been asked about what he thought the unidentified light was. In one interview in 2005, Carter said, "All of a sudden, one of the men looked up and said, 'Look over in the west!' and there was a bright light in the sky. We all saw it. And then the light, it got closer and closer to us. And then it stopped, I don't know how far away, but it stopped beyond the pine trees. And all of a sudden, it changed its color to blue, and then it changed to red, then back to white. And we were trying to figure out what in the world it could be, and then it receded into the distance."[41]

The Investigation

Nearly seven years after the sighting, a number of theorists looked into the event. Naturally, so much time had passed that many of

40. Robert Sheaffer, *UFO Sightings: The Evidence* (Amherst, NY: Prometheus Books, 1998), 20–21.

41. Will Hylton, "The Gospel According to Jimmy," GQ Magazine, December 6, 2005, https://www.gq.com/story/jimmy-carter-ted-kennedy-ufo-republicans.

the witnesses had forgotten details about the sighting. Out of the twenty witnesses, only one of them remembered the details vividly; the other witnesses simply stated that they recalled seeing a strange object in the sky.

Not having a lot of details to work with, a conclusion was drawn shortly after the initiation. The report stated that the unidentified light was a bright Venus. Robert Sheaffer, a UFO skeptic, stated that the position of Venus matched the position of the UFO in the sky.

Sheaffer later wrote, "Mr. Carter reports that his UFO was in the western sky at about thirty degrees elevation. This almost perfectly matches the known position of Venus, which was in the west-southwest at an altitude of twenty-five degrees."[42]

However, over the years, many have criticized this conclusion. It's been argued that if the light was a bright Venus, it would have been noticed much earlier in the night. Moreover, Carter said that the object changed its color from blue to red, green, and to white, and hovered over the treetops before it disappeared, not to be seen again. These characteristics have proved to many that what Carter and the other witnesses saw was not a bright Venus but an interplanetary aircraft.

Conclusion

Although the characteristics described by Carter do not resemble features of Venus, we must keep in mind that there is not enough evidence to come to a definite conclusion. We cannot prove that the object was extraterrestrial, nor can we confirm that it was a bright Venus.

---

42. Robert Sheaffer, "President Carter's 'UFO' Is Identified as the Planet Venus," *The Humanist*, July/August 1977, 46.

Chapter 12
UFOs Patrol the
New Zealand Sky

Date: December 21 and 30, 1978
Location: Kaikoura, New Zealand

A series of unidentified lights were seen over New Zealand on December 21 and 30, 1978. The following case has a substantial amount of evidence that proves that the UFOs could not have been a natural phenomenon. In *The Journal of Scientific Exploration* parapsychologist John Beloff wrote the following about the Kaikoura sightings: "The New Zealand UFO sightings of the twenty-first of December 1978 are unique among civilian UFO reports because there is a large amount of documentary evidence, which includes the recollections of seven witnesses, two tape recordings made during the sightings, the detection of some unusual ground and airplane targets, and a 16mm color movie."[43]

On December 21, 1978, numerous reports were made by locals who described seeing strange lights in the sky. The lights were seen from the South Island, also known as Te Waipounamu. One of the reports was made by employees of Safe Air airline. The individuals

---

43. John Beloff, "Parapsychology: The Continuing Impasse," *The Journal of Scientific Exploration* 1, no.2, (1978): 191–196.

were on board an Armstrong Argosy aircraft when, out of nowhere, five white flickering lights surrounded their plane.

The lights were described as being as large as a house and they were also being tracked on the aircraft's radar. When contacting the Wellington air traffic control, the operators were also able to track the objects on their radar. The objects were making an odd rectangular pattern. The five unidentified targets were not following a predetermined flight route that raised alarm; coincidentally or not, however, the objects disappeared off the radar and out of the sky before the military were informed.

Just nine days later, on December 30, a similar encounter was reported, this time by a television crew who were on a flight en route to Christchurch. Luckily enough, crew members on board the flight were equipped with cameras and thus were able to capture the lights on film. Just like the previous report, several enormous bright white lights surrounded the aircraft and disappeared within a few seconds, only to reappear once again shortly thereafter. On the second time, the pilots were more prepared and captured the lights on their 16mm camera. After a couple of minutes, the lights disappeared, but the substantial amount of evidence, most particularly the photographic evidence, was enough for experts to come to a definite conclusion.

The Investigation

Dr. Bruce Maccabee, the same Navy optical physicist who analyzed the McMinnville photographs, had the following to say regarding the Kaikoura lights: "The main reason for the uniqueness of these sightings is the amount of information that is available for analysis. The information that is available for most other sightings is only that which is extracted from the memories of the witness(es). A relatively small fraction of all other sightings involve photographs or "landing traces" and a few have radar contacts associated with visual sightings ("radar-visual" sightings). However, there is no sighting (by civilians, at least), other than the N.Z. sightings, which has (a) two independent tape recordings made at the time of the events, (b) reports of unusual ground-based (search) and airborne (weather) radar targets that were coincident with visual sightings, (c) a color movie (16 mm professional camera and film), as well as (d) the memories of a sizeable number of credible witnesses (five)."[44]

The first explanation provided by the Royal New Zealand Air Force stated that the lights were a bright Venus, yet they did not take into account that Venus would not have been visible in the sky at the time of the sighting. With that being said, a second hypothesis was put forward: the lights were meteorites. Once again, the good old meteorite explanation, which is responsible for every UFO sighting.

Sir Bernard Lovell, a physicist and astronomer at the Jodrell Bank Radio observatory, stated that the lights could have been unburned meteorites, even though the lights were reported to shine for a number of minutes and unburned meteorites only last a few seconds before disappearing. Moreover, Lovell did not take into account the objects' maneuverability or the analysis of the photographic evidence, which ruled out the meteorite hypothesis.

The third and final explanation provided by the Royal New Zealand Air Force was that the lights were a reflection off a squid hunting fleet. In a report titled "Investigations of Unidentified & Radar Sightings East Coast South Island," the New Zealand Defense Force stated the following: "Not only would the squid

44. Bruce Maccabee, "Analysis and Discussion of the Images of a Cluster of Periodically Flashing Lights Filmed Off the Coast of New Zealand," *Journal of Scientific Exploration* 1, no.2 (1987): 152, https://www.scientificexploration.org/journal/volume-1-number-2-1987.

boats give a good source of radar return whilst in transit to the squid fishing ground, but they generate a very large amount of light when fishing at night. Each boat generates about 200 kilowatts of light to attract squid to its lures, and this light source cannot be discounted as a cause of some of the visual sightings."[45]

There are a number of reasons why many experts, including Maccabee, discounted this explanation. First and foremost, the pilots were aware of the squid boats in the sea; they had seen them prior to the UFO sighting and were well aware of their position. The boats themselves were roughly one hundred meters away from where the individuals reported seeing the bright lights in the sky. As a matter of fact, the pilot at first thought that the lights were reflections off the boats, and it was only after he noticed that the lights were moving northward (the opposite direction the squid boats were traveling) that he knew the object was unnatural.

Another reason that disproves this hypothesis is that no records were found showing that there were any squid boats in Pegasus Bay, where the sightings had taken place. William Ireland, an independent researcher, was unable to find any records. It is important to note that by law, every squid boat has to provide its exact fishing location to the authorities. One final crucial point is that the pilot was making a climb through the clouds to find out whether the lights were reflections off the squid boats, or truly interplanetary aircraft. When the aircraft was flying through the clouds, the pilot noted how the lights climbed to the same altitude, lighting up all surrounding clouds. On multiple occasions, the pilot made turns toward the objects to get a better look at them, however, with each turn, the unidentified flying objects made a parallel opposite turn,

---

45. New Zealand Defense Force, Investigations of Unidentified and Radar Sightings East Coast South Island, 1987, http://files.afu.se/Downloads /Documents/New%20Zealand/AIR-1080-6-897-Volume-1-1978-1981.pdf.

proving that an intelligent being was piloting the UFOs and was maneuvering relative to the aircraft's position. If the lights had truly been reflections, then they would have remained in a stationary position.

Conclusion

This is one of those cases where all of the evidence points to one direction. It has been proven that these lights could not have been squid boats nor any other natural phenomenon. The characteristics of the object, as well as the maneuvers and capabilities, show that an intelligent being was piloting this aircraft. As with the previous cases and as we shall continue to see later on in the book, some certain events cannot be attributed to natural phenomena and the only plausible hypothesis is the extraterrestrial one.

Chapter 13

UFO Observed by
JAL 1628's Flight Crew

Date: November 17, 1986
Location: Alaska, United States

Japan Airlines Flight 1628 was a cargo aircraft carrying French wine, en route to Tokyo from Paris, with stops in Keflavik in Iceland and Anchorage in Alaska. On board the Boeing 747 aircraft was Captain Kenju Terauchi, copilot Takanori Tamefuji, and flight engineer Yoshio Tsukuba.

It was around 17:10 when the Boeing was flying over northeastern Alaska at an altitude of thirty-five thousand feet. It was just after sunset; the sky was clear, and it was a smooth flight under an almost full moon. Although the conditions were optimal for a flight, things did not go as the crew members were expecting. Just two thousand feet below the aircraft, Terauchi noticed a set of lights that he could not identify nor track on his radar. Given that they were flying close to Elmendorf Air Force Base, the captain assumed that it was a military aircraft patrolling the sky, so he did not think much of it.

Several minutes later, the lights were still in the sky, traveling the same route as the Boeing. The lights had remained on the left side and had not changed direction or altitude. At the Anchorage

Air Traffic Control Center, the radio operator could not locate anything on the radar except for the Boeing. The operator also confirmed with the Air Force Base that there were no military aircraft in the vicinity. Although nothing was showing up on the radar at Anchorage, the radio operator at Elmendorf's Regional Operational Control Center started getting a strong primary return on radar, confirming Terauchi's sighting.

The only clouds in the sky were thin spotty ones below the aircraft; above the aircraft the sky was clear, and the lights were distinctly visible. Tamefuji and Tsukuba had also noted that the lights were now straight ahead, and it was at that moment that they noticed that there were two sets of distinct lights joined together. Rectangular in shape, the lights were maneuvering erratically, moving from a horizontal to a vertical position. To confirm that the sighting was not a result of a reflection, the cockpit lights were turned to dark, but the lights remained visible, lighting up the entire sky. The witness reports provided by the crew members described the lights as having no definite shape; they were simply lights arranged in a rectangular shape, similar to lights on a passenger plane. The numerous lights were flashing in front of the aircraft, just one thousand feet ahead. In an attempt to capture the objects on camera, Terauchi grabbed the camera he had with him, but it failed to focus on the lights. Even when trying to focus the camera in manual mode, the camera would not focus on the UFOs.

After approximately eight minutes, the two lights became extremely bright, as though they were shooting off bright flares. In his witness report, Terauchi stated that "the inside of the cockpit shined brightly, and I felt warm in the face."[46] The light emitted from

46. Kenju Terauchi, "Meeting the Future," translated by Sakoyo Mimoto, FAA Alaskan Region Airway Facilities Division, January 2, 1987, https://documents .theblackvault.com/documents/ufos/jal1628/733667-001-007.pdf.

the objects was so intense that the captain could feel the warmth on his face, which came to an end after a few seconds. The two rectangular lights then transitioned into small circular orbs and proceeded to move toward the aircraft's side, mirroring every move and turn. On several occasions Terauchi tried to communicate with Anchorage Air Traffic Control, but the communication was being interrupted, presumably due to the objects' close proximity.

The bright spherical lights started moving toward the rear side of the aircraft, slightly below the horizon. Well behind the aircraft, the pilots started losing sight of the lights and after a short moment, a third object appeared above the horizon. The third object was significantly brighter than the city lights and much more intense. Terauchi described the object as being the "mothership" as the two other lights proceeded to fly toward it. It was not until this point in the encounter that Terauchi and his colleagues started fearing for their safety. They were now sharing the sky with three unidentified and, most definitely, extraterrestrial aircraft. For this reason, Terauchi contacted Anchorage and requested a change in course and also requested immediate permission for landing. Although this was approved, the lights remained visible in the same location, even though the Boeing had made an angular turn, meaning that the lights were paralleling the same maneuvers relative to the aircraft's position in space.

Running low on fuel, Terauchi did not have the time for excess flying and was able to make a safe landing at Talkeetna. The three objects maintained their distance and the air force base even offered for a military aircraft to be scrambled and escort the cargo, however, Terauchi declined the offer after hearing about Thomas Mantell's death as he was chasing a UFO (see chapter 31). After fifty minutes, the three objects disappeared from the sky and out of view.

"The thing was flying as if there was no such thing as gravity. It sped up, then stopped, then flew at our speed, in our direction, so that to us it looked like it was standing still. The next instant it changed course. There's no way a jumbo could fly like that. If we tried, it'd break apart in mid-air. In other words, the flying object had overcome gravity."[47]

The Investigation

Within a few hours after the aircraft landed, the Federal Aviation Administration launched an investigation and interviewed the crew members separately. It was not until March 5, 1987, four months after the sighting, that a report was issued stating that the radar readings were a split radar, caused by the primary signal from the Boeing reflecting off the aircraft's surface, resulting into two separate radar targets. The report, however, failed to acknowledge the visual sighting that all three crew members had mentioned in their witness reports.

"FAA's Regional Public Affairs Officer Paul Steucke pointed out that FAA normally does not investigate UFO sightings but pursued the JAL incident in its role as the operator of the air traffic control system. He said the agency's objective was to determine if there was an unreported aircraft in the vicinity of the JAL flight that could present a safety hazard.

"As part of the inquiry, Steucke said, radar data of the JAL flight track was reviewed by FAA experts at the agency's Technical Center in Atlantic City, N.J., using identical equipment. They determined that a second radar target near the JAL flight at the time

47. Shukan Shincho, "JAL Pilot's UFO Story Surfaces After 20 Years," *Japan Today*, December 8, 2006.

of the reported sighting was not another aircraft but rather a split radar return from the JAL Boeing 747.

"Technically, this is known as an 'uncorrelated primary and beacon target return.' It means that the primary radar signal reflected off the aircraft's surface did not correlate exactly with the pulse emitted by the aircraft's radar beacon transponder. This phenomenon is not unusual and gives the impression of two separate radar targets."[48]

Interplanetary Aircrafts or Planets?

Although the report issued by the FAA did not acknowledge the visual sightings, it did not dispute or invalidate their encounter, either. Having said this, UFO skeptic Philip Klass provided an explanation himself before the transcripts of the witness interviews were made available. Klass stated that the lights were simply a bright Jupiter or Mars.

Foolishly enough, since Klass did not wait for the witness recordings to be released, he did not take into account the position of the UFOs in space. He also did not take into consideration the pictorial information provided, or the maneuverability described by Terauchi and Tamefuji. At the time of the sighting, Jupiter and Mars were on the opposite side of the sky. Even if they were in the same location, the UFOs maneuvered in ways that neither Jupiter nor Mars can.

---

48. Federal Aviation Administration, "FAA Releases Documents on Reported UFO Sighting Last November," U.S. Department of Transportation press release, February 4, 1987, http://www.nicap.org/docs/861117_flight1628 .pdf.

Conclusion

Was the sighting a genuine encounter with extraterrestrial aircraft or was it simply a hoax? Although the three witnesses were independently interviewed, their statements and descriptions corroborated with one another's. Moreover, Terauchi had well over ten thousand flight hours; would a highly experienced pilot report something he did not deem to be unnatural, possibly tarnishing his credibility?

Chapter 14

The Black Triangle UFO Wave over Belgium

Date: November 1989
Location: Belgium

The black triangle UFO, often depicted in science fiction movies, is based on reports made by several Belgians in November of 1989. The Belgian wave included some of the first reports in which individuals reported seeing a black triangle hovering in the sky.

The First Sightings

The first reported sighting was made on November 29, 1989. It was around 17:20 when two sergeant majors of the Belgian Gendarmerie were patrolling the road between Eupen and Kittenis. As the gentlemen were driving down the road, they noticed bright white lights hovering slightly above the side of the road, approximately two hundred meters away from their car. The object was moving slowly, and the officers immediately noticed its dark triangular silhouette.

On each of its corners, the triangular-shaped aircraft had a bright white light and a pulsating red glow in its center. To their amazement, the dark triangle started approaching their vehicle, leaving them in complete shock. As it approached their vehicle, they noticed that although the object was enormous and hovering at a low altitude, it was completely noiseless. Even when the dark triangle was directly overhead, the two patrolmen could not hear any noise. The dark triangle continued flying toward Eupen's city center, coming to a halt over Gileppe Dam. Its pulsating red glow increased in intensity just before it disappeared into thin air.

Following this extraordinary and strange sighting, the two gentlemen knew that they had to forward this case to the air force. When they contacted the air force base at Liège Bierset, the radio control operators confirmed that there was no air traffic at that time and location. However, they also stated that they had been tracking an unidentified target on their radars, which was also being picked up by two other air force bases, one at Aachen in Germany and the other at Maastricht in the Netherlands. On that day over fifteen reports of a similar nature were made.

The reports kept coming in throughout the month of December. One particular report was made by Belgian Army Lieutenant Colonel Andre Amond. He and his wife were driving toward Gembloux to pick up their son from the railway station. It was at around 18:15 when the couple spotted three bright white lights and a pulsating red light in the center. At the time of the sighting, Amond and his wife were driving through a small wooded area that was completely dark, and thus, they had a clear and unpolluted view of the lights. The lights were moving horizontally, gliding through the sky very slowly and were completely silent. Being a lieutenant in the army, Amond knew full well that there was no military aircraft that slightly resembled what he was seeing before his very eyes.

Amond continued following the lights as they hovered above a farm in Sart Ernage. For a brief moment, the couple lost sight of the object. However, determined to keep on pursuing the lights, he rapidly drove to the other side of the farm. As he did so, he noticed that the lights were still in the sky, and given that he was at the highest point of the street, he had an unobstructed and panoramic view of the phenomenon that was unfolding right before his very eyes. It was at this moment that the encounter took a turn. The three bright lights transformed into one intense light in the center, and the triangular aircraft started descending vertically, directing the bright spotlight toward Amond's position.

His wife frantically started screaming for Amond to get back in the car and for them to drive away. As he got in the car and started driving away, he looked back at the object, which was now in a horizontal position and the original characteristics of the dark triangle had reemerged; one pulsating red light in the center and three bright white lights at the corners. Shortly after Amond started driving away, the triangle shot up toward the sky and disappeared.

In his witness report, Amond described the object to be twice the size of the moon and was "larger than the head-light of a big transport aircraft." He also stated that he had felt threatened and unsafe by the object's presence: "The object with this enormous, anomalous, luminous mass showed itself somewhat aggressive. We heard no engine noise…This object was silent!"[49]

Characteristics of the Black Triangle

After Amond witnessed the UFO, he wrote to the Belgian Ministry of Defense, pointing out three characteristics in particular he believed proved that the aircraft he had seen was extraterrestrial in origin.

The first notable characteristic was the speed the triangular UFO was traveling. Amond made a distinction between two

---

49. A. Amond, W. De Brouwer, P. Ferryn and S. Meesen, "ERNAGE 1989: The Facts and Their Analysis," Comité belge d'étude des phénomenes, 2008, http://www.cobeps.org/pdf/ernage_report.pdf.

points of his sighting. When he first saw the object, it was hovering very slowly, gliding through the sky. As a matter of fact, he had to slow his car down in order to wait for the object to catch up. On the other hand, when he had a panoramic view of the object, he noticed how the object was moving erratically in the sky at a fast speed. The triangular aircraft had also shot up toward the sky, faster than any aircraft he had seen throughout his career in the army.

The second characteristic is that the UFO was completely noiseless. Even when Amond parked his car at a secluded country road, neither he nor his wife could hear any noise being emitted from the UFO, not even when it sped off and disappeared. An interesting point that Amond made to the Ministry of Defense is that although at one point in the encounter the UFO was positioned exactly in front of the bright full moon, it did not reflect the moonlight and was covering it almost entirely. If it were a commercial aircraft, the moonlight would have reflected off of its surface; this characteristic proved that the object had a solid mass, and was not just simply lights.

The third and final point that Amond made was that he could not find an explanation as to what the dark triangle could have been. We must keep in mind that Amond was an experienced Lieutenant Colonel; he was familiar with all the military aircraft. In his letter, he stated that the object could not have been military, a helicopter or a hologram. He was adamant that "some kind of intelligence was involved" (Amond, 1989) and that the aircraft was most definitely extraterrestrial.

The Peak of the Sightings

Although reports were made from December 1989 through April 1990, March 30, 1990, in particular saw an increase in reports. At around 23:00, Belgian gendarme A. Renkin observed three unusual lights moving toward Thorembais-Gembloux from his home at Ramillies. Noticing that these lights were significantly brighter than any star in the sky, positioned in a perfect triangular shape, Renkin contacted the supervisor at the Glons Control Reporting Center. Renkin informed the supervisor that the three lights were changing from red to green to yellow, and he was certain that this was not a commercial or a military aircraft.

The supervisor at Glons Control Reporting Center immediately ordered for a number of gendarmeries to patrol the area where Renkin had seen the lights. Just ten minutes later, Renkin made a second call to the supervisor, as he now started to observe another set of lights moving toward the first triangle. The second lights were also in the shape of a triangle and had the same exact characteristics. Renkin's sighting was confirmed by the supervisor, who started tracking an unidentified target on radar at the same location where Renkin had reported seeing the lights. Thirty minutes after Renkin's call, the patrol arrived at the location and immediately noticed the two triangular lights in the sky. They, too, noted that the lights were brighter than the stars and were changing color sequentially. The objects remained in the sky for at least forty-five minutes. It was around 23:45 when one of the triangular objects began carrying out erratic maneuvers and started to approach the second aircraft. The erratic maneuvers were also recorded on the radar back at the air traffic control center.

A second air traffic control center, the Semmerkaze Traffic Center Control / Reporting Post, confirmed the radar sightings, and ordered for the first F-16 fighter jet to be scrambled from Beauvechain Air Force Base. An hour after the first report was made, the lights were still visible and at a stationary position in the sky. The numerous reports, made by multiple individuals, noted that from time to time, the objects would change the intensity of their lights.

The second F-16 fighter jet was scrambled shortly after midnight, and a total of nine interceptions were made by the pilots. From the nine attempts, the pilots were only able to lock down with the object on radar three times. However, later investigations showed that the lock-downs were made with the other F-16 in the sky, and not with the actual UFO they were pursuing. Although the pilots were able to locate the object on radar, no visual contacts were ever made. At one point, the Glons operators informed the pilots that they were above the target, however, not even at this point were the fighter pilots able to visually locate the aircraft.

During the encounter, the pilots noted that the unidentified aircraft would change its speed from 172 miles per hour, to 1,116 miles per hour. They also noted that it would drop from an altitude of nine thousand feet to five thousand feet in just a matter of seconds. At the time of the pursuit, the individuals on the ground were still able to locate the triangular lights, even though the pilots were unable to see them. At around 00:30, many reported seeing the two F-16 fighter jets turning in circles above the triangular UFO. They also noted that one of the triangular aircraft started emitting a bright red light that illuminated the sky, just as it sped into the distance and disappeared.

After several failed attempts to locate the triangular UFOs, the two F-16 fighter jets returned to base. Just minutes later, Captain Pinson who was part of the patrolling team, observed four white lights in the shape of a square. The lights made quick erratic movements before the intensity of the lights dissipated as they disappeared.

The Investigations

At the time of the sightings, Major General Wilfried De Brouwer was the chief of operations of the Belgian Air Staff. De Brouwer stated the following, which excluded all natural explanations: "The National Civil Aviation Authorities replied that no flight plans had been introduced to operate in that area. Normally, flight plans are mandatory for flights between sunset and sunrise, but in cases of military exercises and emergencies (ambulance or police), exceptions can be made for helicopters.

"If an ambulance helicopter had been operating, the pilot should have contacted the relevant air space surveillance authority and communicate the point of departure, point of arrive, intentions, etc.

"Furthermore, that evening, no military exercises had taken place over Belgium."[50]

De Brouwer also provided a number of reasons that further proved that the aircraft was interplanetary. The first was that the shape of the aircraft was unlike any other commercial or military aircraft. The aircraft also was the size of a jumbo jet and was able to hover without emitting any noise. Third, the aircraft was travelling well over five hundred miles per second and it was capable of accelerating from seventy-seven miles per second to over 250 miles per second almost instantly. Finally, the aircraft dropped from an altitude of ten thousand feet to five hundred feet in just five seconds.

In his investigation, De Brouwer also ruled out the possibility that the triangular aircraft could have been a military aircraft from the United Kingdom or the United States. He contacted the militaries of the two countries and inquired if there were any aircraft over

---

50. Wilfried De Brouwer in Amond, "ERNAGE 1989: The Facts and Their Analysis."

Belgium at the time of the sightings. Officials from both countries assured De Brouwer that no aircraft belonging to their air force were in the airspace. It is important to note that before any aircraft enters another country's airspace, authorization must first be granted.

A report was also made by Captain Pinson, one of the patrolmen who was on site at Thorembais-Gembloux, to investigate the triangle UFO report. Pinson's report stated that when he looked at the aircraft from a telescope, he was able to make out the dark silhouette of the triangular aircraft and the three bright lights at each of its corners. Pinson also stated that the sky was completely clear and that he and the rest of the gendarmes were able to see the stars very clearly.

Conclusion

The majority of the witness reports were made by high-level officials whose credibility cannot be questioned. The Belgian UFO wave is undoubtedly one of the most convincing cases that proves the existence of extraterrestrial life and the advanced technology that these beings are in possession of. It is for this reason that governments all over the world have the responsibility to take the phenomenon seriously and thoroughly investigate each UFO report.

Chapter 15

The Phoenix Lights

Date: March 13, 1997.
Location: Phoenix, Arizona, United States

A series of unidentified lights were observed over Phoenix, Arizona, Nevada, and Sonora, California on March 13, 1997. Thousands of individuals reported seeing the *V*-shaped lights in the sky over the aforementioned locations, and several individuals managed to capture these lights on their cameras.

The first report was made at 18:55 when a young man witnessed a group of six lights in the sky over Nevada. In his report to the National UFO Reporting Center, the unnamed man described the lights as having a *V* shape and being as large as a Boeing 747. The man reported that as the UFO flew overhead, it made the noise of a gust of wind and disappeared over the horizon. In the following two to three hours, multiple similar reports were made. The multiple reports described the *V*-shaped object to be as large as 900 feet and two miles wide. Although the object was enormous, many reported that the UFO glided through the sky without emitting any noise, even though some reported it to be flying at an altitude of one thousand feet. At different times, the altitude varied from one thousand feet to ten thousand feet.

The next report was made at around 20:15 from an unnamed former police officer in Arizona. As the man was driving, he noticed five red lights; four of which were flying in a *V* formation, with the fifth light trailing behind. Having just left his house, the former police officer returned back to his house and grabbed his binoculars to get a better look at the object. For two whole minutes, the man was able to observe the bright red lights as they hovered silently before they disappeared over the horizon.

Tim Ley was one of the witnesses who came forward and shared his experience in detail. Prior to his sighting, Ley was not a believer in extraterrestrials, nor was he interested in the UFO phenomenon. His opinion changed on March 13, 1997, when he, together with his wife Bobbi, his son Hal, and his grandson Damien, was at his house in Phoenix. Ley was just exiting his car when his son pointed to the sky as they saw five lights in the shape of an arc, hovering silently toward the house. As the lights approached the house, the size and shape of the UFOs changed too. In a report, Ley said "We could see the lights were also getting slightly larger and the spaces in between them increasing in distance...It now appeared that the middle light on top of the arc had elongated up, so that now the lights looked like the letter A without the bar across." [51]

Maintaining the formation perfectly, the lights flew overhead. As they did so, Tim noted that the lights were, in fact, one enormous aircraft and not five separate ones. The lights were maintaining their positions so perfectly that they must have been "locked together." [52] He then noted that the aircraft had a very dark structure; its perfect geometric shape and size was something out of a science fiction movie. It was so large that it spread over a couple

51. Tim Ley, "Tim Ley Family—Eyewitnesses of 3/13/97 Arizona UFO Flyover Event Called 'Phoenix Lights,'" *Tim Ley* (blog), 1998, http://www.artgomperz .com/a1999/aug/b7.htm.

52. Ley, "Tim Ley Family - Eyewitnesses."

of blocks and each arm of the V-shaped UFO was around 700 feet long. The aircraft was gliding through the sky at around thirty-five meters per hour.

Another witness, a truck driver named Bill Greiner, recounted his experience when he spoke to USA Today. Prior to the sighting, Greiner was a skeptic; he had never believed in UFOs or extraterrestrials. From his car window, as Greiner was driving on a mountain north of Phoenix, he saw the massive V-shaped aircraft in the sky: "Now I've got a whole new view. I may be just a dumb truck driver, but I've seen something that don't belong here."[53]

One last witness report to examine is the report made by Fife Symington, the former Arizona governor. On March 13, Symington saw a "massive delta-shaped craft silently navigate over Squaw Peak, a mountain range in Phoenix, Arizona."[54] Apart from being the governor of Arizona, Symington was also a pilot and a former air force officer. The former Arizona governor stated the following when asked about the Phoenix Lights: "I'm a pilot and I know just about every machine that flies. It was bigger than anything that I have ever seen. It remains a great mystery. Other people saw it, responsible people. I don't know why people would ridicule it. It was enormous and inexplicable. Who knows where it came from?"[55]

In later interviews, Symington also confirmed that this object was most definitely not man-made, and he also ruled out the explanation that the Air Force had provided for the sightings:

---

53. Richard Price, USA Today, June 18, 1997.

54. Fife Symington, CNN, November 9, 2007.

55. Symington, CNN, November 9, 2007.

"I can definitively say that this craft did not resemble any man-made object I'd ever seen. And it was certainly not high-altitude flares because flares don't fly in formation."[56]

The Military's Response

Although hundreds of reports were made describing the UFO in detail, the United States Air Force stated that what was in the sky was actually slow-falling, long-burning LUU-2B/B illumination flares that were dropped by four A-19 Warthog aircraft as part of a training exercise at the Barry Goldwater Range. As I shall point out, there are many discrepancies in this explanation.

The first inconsistency is the shape of the aircraft. Hundreds of reports were made on the day, and all of them described the UFO in the same way. Even if we have a look at the detailed witness reports mentioned previously in the chapter, it is clear that the aircraft in the sky was enormous, V-shaped, and had bright lights along its body. The witnesses also mentioned that the aircraft hovered slowly overhead, and even when it was at a low altitude, none of the individuals were able to hear any noise emitted from the UFO. This does not correspond to the general appearance of flares or of A-19 Warthog aircraft.

One important aspect of this explanation, which I find troubling, is the fact that the former governor of Arizona was not informed that long-standing flares were going to be dropped over the state. Would it not have prevented panic and anxiety amongst civilians if they had known that flares were about to be dropped as part of a military exercise? Moreover, even if this information was not made public, wouldn't the governor at least have been

56. Symington, CNN, November 9, 2007.

informed? When Symington heard of this explanation, he contacted the air force himself and started asking questions. Unsurprisingly, the air force refused to answer any questions and he was not given further explanations. Moreover, as with every other case, interviewing firsthand witnesses is usually the first thing done after an event like this. Although the Phoenix lights were observed by thousands, not one individual was interviewed or asked to provide a description of the object they had seen.

As mentioned in the beginning of this chapter, multiple individuals were able to capture these lights on film. Jim Dilettoso, the founder of the Arizona State University Computer Institute and the former NASA Industrial Application Center Technology Director, analyzed a number of these photographs and film footages using a number of computerized techniques. When analyzing one film in particular, Dilettoso came to the conclusion that these lights were artificial and could not have been flares, as the air force had proposed.

The analysis also showed that the spectrum of the lights did not match up with any known light in the sky. This ruled out the possibility of the lights being anything natural. Moreover, the lights also had a substantial amount of red, green and blue—colors that do not match-up with the description of a flare. Dilettoso also reported that the lights were pulsating in a repeated manner.

Conclusion

If we have a look at the eyewitness reports and the details that the individuals provided, the explanation the Air Force gave seems nonsensical. Many high-level individuals, such as the former Arizona governor, did not accept this explanation, and for good reason. With the explanation being ruled out, what was truly in the sky? Many explanations have been disproved, but the one hypothesis that was not even considered was the extraterrestrial hypothesis. Was this theory not even acknowledged due to the general taboo concerning the subject? Did the air force not even consider the theory a possibility to prevent mass hysteria and panic?

Chapter 16
UFO over Chicago's Airport

Date: November 7, 2006
Location: Chicago, Illinois, United States

With over a thousand flights a day, Chicago's O'Hare Airport is amongst the busiest airports in the world. What happens when a UFO is spotted hovering above one of the departure gates? How do the authorities respond to such an event? Although this is not a situation airport officials have to face often, the unexpected happened on November 7, 2006, at Chicago's airport.

The first sighting was made at around 16:30 by an unnamed United Airlines taxi mechanic, who was pushing back a B-737-500 from gate C17 that was scheduled to depart shortly thereafter. In his report, the individual stated that he "was compelled to look straight up, for some reason, and was startled to see the aircraft hovering silently."[57]

The individual described the UFO as being disc-shaped and silver in color. Its metallic surface had an angular size of roughly

---

57. Richard Haines et al., "Report of an Unidentified Aerial Phenomenon and Its Safety Implications of O'Hare International Airport on November 7, 2006," National Aviation Reporting Center on Anomalous Phenomenta, May 14, 2007, 9. https://static1.squarespace.com/static /5cf80ff422b5a90001351e31/t/5d02ec731230e20001528e2c/1560472703346 /NARCAP_TR-10.pdf.

twenty-six inches, and it was rotating silently at an altitude of five hundred to one thousand feet. This individual was not the only one who saw the object. Ten to fifteen of his colleagues were astonished at the sighting too. They even radioed the cockpit crew in the airplane they were pushing back to have a look at the unidentified object. Around two minutes after first seeing the object, the witness described how the UFO "shot off into the clouds" and disappeared.[58] The sighting lasted for approximately five minutes.

Aviation mechanics from different gates saw the object in the sky, too. A taxi mechanic, who was pushing an empty *United Airlines* aircraft back to the hanger, reported hearing a conversation over the radio between two pilots who had mentioned the disc-shaped object in the sky. The witness stated that he heard the pilots describing an unidentified aircraft that was seven hundred feet above ground level. The disc-shaped object hovered silently before it shot off through the clouds and disappeared.

In the report to the National Aviation Reporting Center on Anomalous Phenomena (NARCAP), one of the witnesses commented on how he and his colleagues were sure that this was not a conventional or a terrestrial aircraft. He stated that it "had means of propulsion that we don't know of. There were no downward facing engines for thrust that I could see on the bottom. There was no place for exhaust to be coming from and no visible air column that would keep something hovering."[59]

58. Haines, "Report of an Unidentifed Aerial Phenomenon," 9.

59. Haines, "Report of an Unidentified Aerial Phenomena," 101.

The Aftermath

Although the witnesses were all credible individuals, an official investigation was not carried out. Before we go into the aftermath and the explanation provided by the Federal Aviation Administration, I must state that the witnesses were knowledgeable individuals who certainly could differentiate a weather balloon or a natural phenomenon from an aircraft. These individuals spend their day working with aircraft. We must also acknowledge the severity of this report. Although this object is unidentified, it could have posed a threat to national security and the fact that an official investigation was not carried out is truly worrying.

"Anytime an airborne object can hover for several minutes over a busy airport but not be registered on radar or seen visually from the control tower, constitutes a potential threat to flight safety."[60]

As we have seen from the previous chapters in this book, it seems that the easiest explanation officials provide for a UFO sighting is that the sighting was a natural weather phenomenon. Elizabeth Cory, a spokesperson for the Federal Aviation Administration, stated that the silver disc-shaped object was simply a natural phenomenon caused by the atmospheric conditions. In her statement, Cory said "Our theory on this is that it was a weather phenomenon. That night was a perfect atmospheric condition in terms of low cloud ceiling and a lot of airport lights. When the lights shine up into the clouds sometimes you can see funny things. That's our take on it."[61]

---

60. Billy Cox, "O'Hare Incident Worth Revisiting," *Herald-Tribune*, August 21, 2007, https://www.heraldtribune.com/news/20070821/ohare-incident-worth-revisiting.

61. Haines, "Report of an Unidentified Aerial Phenomena," 16.

Although the FAA attributed the sighting to a weather phenomenon, they failed to explain what weather phenomenon this was and how it could have been mistaken for a disc-shaped aircraft hovering silently in the sky. Apart from this preposterous explanation, it is also difficult to understand why the employees, who reported seeing the unidentified object in the sky, were forced to stay silent.

Reporting for the *Chicago Tribune,* Jon Hilkevitch interviewed an airline employee who was one of the witnesses on the day. An unnamed individual told Hilkevitch that all United Airlines employees who were witnesses were immediately interviewed by management and they were instructed to "write reports and draw pictures of what they observed." The United employee went on to tell him that they were told that they could not talk to anyone about what they had seen.

Conclusion

Although this case is still unexplained, the FAA certainly wants to keep it that way. Numerous attempts have been made by investigators calling for the FAA to launch a formal investigation into the sighting. The administration refused to do so, even though the phenomenon was witnessed by over twelve credible individuals.

It is also important to highlight the fact that United Airlines and the FAA initially denied that such a sighting happened. Prior to *Chicago Tribune* filing a Freedom of Information Act (FOIA) request, the two entities denied that a UFO was seen hovering above the airport. Naturally, when the report was then made public, the FAA was forced to provide a response, albeit it was a nonsensical one.

One baggage handler who was interviewed by Hilkevitch summed up the situation perfectly. The individual stated "Some

of us are getting angry with this being hushed up with all the ter-
rorism and TSA idiots hanging around. If we see a funny looking
bag all damn hell breaks loose but park a funny silver thing a few
hundred feet above a busy airport and everyone tries to hush it up.
It just doesn't make sense."[62]

62. Haines, "Report of an Unidentified Aerial Phenomenon," 18.

Chapter 17
Pilot's Encounter with a UFO at Alderney

Date: April 23, 2007
Location: Alderney, British Crown Dependency

Ray Bowyer, an experienced pilot with over eighteen years of experience and over seven thousand flight hours, used to fly a Trislander aircraft from Southampton to Alderney on a daily basis. For over eight years, Bowyer had been flying the forty-five-minute flight without any problems; however, on April 23, 2007, Bowyer witnessed an aircraft in the sky that most definitely was not terrestrial.

"On April 23, 2007, my passengers and I witnessed multiple, as yet unidentified, objects over these islands while crossing the English Channel. They were very, very large. They were picked up on radar in two locations and one was witnessed by another pilot from a totally different vantage point."[63]

The flight took off from Southampton, England, at 14:00; the visibility was clear, and the weather conditions were ideal for a flight. Once the aircraft reached an altitude of four thousand feet, Bowyer put it on autopilot so that he could carry out the necessary paperwork and also keep a look out for any other nearby aircraft.

---

63. Leslie Kean, *UFOs: Generals, Pilots, and Government Officials Go On the Record.* (New York: Three Rivers Press, 210), 74.

As Bowyer and his passengers were flying ten miles south of the Isle of Wight, his attention was caught by a bright yellow light. At first Bowyer did not think too much into the sighting; he had assumed that it must have been an airplane or a reflection from the ground. A minute or so had passed and the bright light remained in the sky. Bowyer figured that if the light had been a reflection, as he had originally thought, then it would have disappeared by then.

Trying to identify what this source of light was, Bowyer grabbed his binoculars and noticed that this was not an airplane nor a reflection in the sky. The thin and elongated cigar-shaped object remains a vivid memory for Bowyer. The unidentified aircraft came to a point at both of its ends. It was then that he realized he was sharing the sky with an extraordinary object. Bowyer wasted no time; he immediately contacted the Jersey Air Traffic Control Centre to get any information available on the object. Paul Kelly, the operator who responded to Bowyer's call, confirmed that there were no identifiable aircraft close to his airspace. However, Kelly also informed Bowyer that he had located the target on his radar, and had also picked up a primary return signal.

Now that Bowyer had confirmed that the cigar shaped object was truly present in the sky, he could only hope that it would not interfere with the flight. Shortly thereafter, one of the passengers on board the aircraft noticed a second object in the sky, completely identical to the first one. The passenger informed Bowyer that a second cigar-shaped object was just beyond the first one. It had the same shape, color, and size.

As the second object came into view, Kelly contacted Bowyer, informing him that another pilot had seen the cigar shaped object in the sky from his cockpit windows. Patrick Patterson, a pilot flying a Blue Island airways plane, was forty kilometers from Bowyer's aircraft, and he too had seen the two anomalous aircraft in the sky. Patterson had described the objects to Kelly as being extremely bright, elongated, and thin.

Bowyer tried to get as close as possible to the two cigar-shaped objects. As a matter of fact, he had exceeded the point at which he was supposed to start his descent for landing, and at the closest range possible, the two UFOs were lined up one above the other. Unable to delay the descent any longer, Bowyer started the descent for landing. It was at this point that he and his passengers had seen the two UFOs for the last time. Commenting on what he thought the aircraft were, Bowyer stated the following: "If it was designed by an engineer, that man has to be shaken by the hand because it was a fantastic piece of equipment, if that is what it was. I can't really say much further than to say what I've said all along, that this thing is not from around here."[64]

Communication with Air Traffic Control

The following is the full conversation between Bowyer (R.B.) Kelly (P.K.) and Patrick Patterson (P.P.):[65]

14:09, R.B.: Do you have any traffic, ah, can't really say how far, but at my 12 o'clock level?

14:09, P.K.: No traffic at all in your 12 o'clock

14:09, R.B.: I've got a very bright object, well, I couldn't say how far. Extremely bright, yellow, orange object straight ahead. Very flat platform. Looking at it through my binoculars as we speak. Any more information on that aircraft please?

---

64. *Britain's Closest Encounters*, episode 4, "Aldernay Lights," directed by Nigel Levy, aired July 30, 2008, on Channel 5 in the UK.

65. Jean-Francois Baure, David Clark, Paul Puller, Martin Shough, "Unusual Atmospheric Phenomena Observed Near Channel Islands, UK, 23 April 2007," *Journal of Scientific Exploration* 22, no.3 (2008): 293–294.

14:10, P.K.: Five-four-four. Negative. Nothing at all in your 12 o'clock for the next 40 miles or so.

14:12, P.K.: Airline five-four-four, Roger. I do have, uh, primary contact now. A very faint primary contact just to the left across your 11 o'clock at this time at a range of about four track miles.

14:13, R.B.: Roger. I've got a definite contact at my 12 o'clock. A very bright yellow object, looking, well like a cigar.

14:14, R.B.: Looking through my binoculars as I am now. There is a second one just appeared behind the first one from where I am. Roger five-four-four. Just confirming that all the passengers can see this…aircraft. ah, I've got the island visual. It's dead ahead, can't say how far, probably five miles but it's staying the same size. Looks to be off the North, North-West coast of Alderney

14:14, P.K.: Roger, I do have a primary contact. Just one blob if you like, uh 8 miles or so to the west of Alderney

14:14, P.P.: Jersey eight-three-two. Zone asked us to look if we could see an object, which is being seen by A-line at the moment. We have got something at 8 o'clock resembling the description

14:15, R.B.: The second one appears to be beyond the first from where I am. It is exactly the same, it's got a gap. It is a cylindrical object, very bright yellow and there is a gap in the light about two-thirds the way along it.

14:15, P.K.: Airline five-four-four, Roger. Would you like to descend?

14:16, R.B.: Please. I better go down

14:16, R.B.: 2 thousand feet, 1021. It's very plain to see from where I am now without any binoculars.

Conclusion

On November 12, 2007, Bowyer addressed the US National Press Club about his sighting. In his speech, Bowyer expressed his disappointment at how the Chicago airport sightings, which took place the previous year, were handled. He urged the authorities to take UFO sightings more seriously, and appealed for any crew members to make reports if they were to see a UFO.

"I heard about the multiple witness sightings at Chicago O'Hare Airport, about a year ago now, on November 7, 2006. I was surprised to hear how it was handled. Despite many pilots and airport personnel witnessing the object hovering over the terminal, there was no investigation at all by the FAA. It appears as if pressure may have been applied to crew members by their company not to discuss this incident. I would have been shocked if I was told that the CAA in the UK would obstruct an investigation, or if the CAA told me that what I had seen was something entirely different. But it seems as if pilots in America are used to this sort of thing here.

"I would urge all fellow aircrew to report whatever they see as soon as possible and to stand up and be counted. It is only when crucial and critical witnesses such as air crew make reports that the authorities will be kick-started into a broader investigation of [these] phenomena. Thank you very much."[66]

---

66. Ray Bowyer's speech at the National Press Club, November 12, 2007.

Chapter 18

UFOs Interfere
with Nuclear Missiles

The following chapter will examine cases in which UFOs have directly interfered with nuclear missile weapons. Although this may seem like a bizarre claim, this is not all that uncommon. There have been numerous instances in which unidentified aircraft have been spotted flying over bases where nuclear missiles were being operated, causing the missiles to malfunction without a cause.

The Disclosure Conference

Such sightings have occurred so often that, on September 27, 2010, seven high-level United States Air Force personnel held a press conference in which they talked about their experiences with UFOs during their time in the air force. The press conference, which was held in Washington, D.C., was live-streamed on CNN, giving it international coverage. The seven officials who took part in the press conference included Lieutenant Robert Salas, a ballistic missile launch officer and a missile propulsion engineer; Lieutenant Colonel Dwynne Arneson, a strategic air command (SAC) officer; Lieutenant Robert Jamison, a combat targeting team commander and intercontinental ballistic missile (ICBM) targeting officer;

Colonel Charles Halt, deputy base commander (his story is covered in Chapter 26: The Rendlesham Forest Incident); Lieutenant Jerome Nelson, deputy missile combat crew commander; Patrick McDonough, nuclear missile site geodetic surveyor; and Captain Bruce Fenstermacher, combat crew commander.

Lieutenant Robert Salas

On the evening of March 24, 1967, while Salas was stationed at Malmstrom Air Force Base in Montana, strange lights were seen in the sky, hovering above a nuclear weapon storage site. The red glowing lights were seen by several air force personnel, including Salas, who was the ballistic missile launch officer. Whenever an unidentified object is spotted anywhere, it constitutes a threat to national security because it can never truly be known what the intention of the object is. When UFOs are spotted above a nuclear missile site, the threat becomes even greater.

Salas reported that the red glowing light was pulsating and had a diameter of roughly thirty feet. Just minutes after the sighting, all the missiles inside the storage unit went into a "No-Go" condition, which means that somehow all of the missiles had been disabled and could not be launched. At the time of the incident, Salas did not correlate the UFO sighting to the nuclear missiles. However, once he looked into the case, he noticed that there had not been any system failures and no other individual had disabled the missiles. The malfunction had occurred without cause. Moreover, the investigation showed that there had been a total guidance and control system failure. It must be accentuated no one individual can possibly disable any nuclear missile without authorization or the necessary equipment.

After the missiles went into their "No-Go" state, the red object was still hovering above the nuclear storage site, pulsating and lighting the night sky. More eyewitnesses saw the object and shortly after, while Salas went to investigate the nuclear storage site, the security stationed at the front of the gate informed him that the red light had accelerated at a very high speed and disappeared, without emitting any noise or leaving any trail.

During the 2010 press conference, Salas emphasized that the disabling could not have been carried out by any air force personnel. No individual could have disabled the nuclear missiles and to do so, one would need the necessary equipment and above all, authorization from their superiors.

"The security people had no equipment up there, no ability to affect any kind of system shutdown on our missiles," Salas said.[67]

The air force base had even confirmed that there were no military exercises at the time, and they did not have an explanation as to what the red light was. However, what Salas mentioned at the press conference definitely implied that the UFO had something to do with the missile incident, and that the air force did not want to disclose this information to the public.

"There was also a member of the Air Force Office of Special Investigations in the room. He ordered us not ever to talk about this. I even signed a non-disclosure statement to that effect," Salas said.[68]

Lieutenant Colonel Dwynne Arneson

Apart from being a strategic air command officer, Arneson also had a top secret clearance, something that not many individuals in the military possess. This clearance means that Arneson had access

---

67. National Press Club press conference, aired September 27, 2010 on CNN, https://www.youtube.com/watch?v=zT0EP4mP1lI.
68. Ibid.

to information that not only was highly classified, but could harm national security if it were to be disclosed to the public without the proper declassification and authorization.

Arneson was on duty at Malmstrom Air Force Base at the time of Salas' sighting. Arneson reported that he had received a message that multiple individuals had seen an unidentified red object hovering above the nuclear missile storage site, and that the missiles had malfunctioned shortly thereafter.

"I happened to see a message that came through my communications center," Arneson said. "It said…that 'A UFO was seen near missile silos'…and it was hovering. It said that the crew going on duty and the crew coming off duty all saw the UFO just hovering in mid-air. It was a metallic circular object and from what I understand, the missiles were all shut down. What I mean by 'missiles going down' is that they went dead. And something turned those missiles off, so they couldn't be put back in a mode for launching."[69]

Several years after the incident and his retirement, Arneson started working with Boeing. During his time there, he met with Robert Kaminski, one of the engineers at *Boeing*. Since *Boeing* is the main missile system contractor for the Air Force, it was carrying out an investigation into what had caused the system failure in 1967. Kaminski told Arneson that they could not find any technical explanation as to what had caused the malfunction. He also confirmed that several more UFO reports were made on the day, all stating that an unidentified bright light was seen in the sky, close to the Air Force Base. What makes this case even more bizarre, is that the Air Force had instructed Kaminski and the engineers to

69. National Press Club press conference, aired September 27, 2010 on CNN, https://www.youtube.com/watch?v=zT0EP4mP1lI.

discontinue the investigation immediately and to not follow-up on the report.

"I am convinced that somebody out there is trying to send us a message," Arneson said. "If I knew who they were, I probably would not be here."[70]

Lieutenant Robert Jamison

On March 24, 1967, when the nuclear missiles shut down at Malmstrom Air Force Base, Jamison, who was a missile targeting officer, was at home relaxing when he received a call instructing him to return to the base in order to bring the missiles back online.

Once Jamison arrived at the base, he was debriefed on the situation. Although he had not seen the UFO himself, he was told that an unidentified red light was seen hovering above the nuclear storage site. He was also informed that the missiles went offline at the exact moment the UFO was seen hovering above the site.

It was not unusual for a missile to go offline because of a malfunction; however, it had never happened before that more than two missiles went offline at the same time without cause. Speaking about his experience, Jamison said, "Very rarely does a missile malfunction. And I don't think any—much rarer would be two at the same time. But never ten....I know that the U.S. government does not obviously appreciate people, such as myself and these gentlemen, speaking out about this. What we're describing, on an ongoing basis, decade after decade at multiple Air Force bases is just disruption of our nuclear missiles."[71]

---

70. National Press Club press conference, aired September 27, 2010 on CNN, https://www.youtube.com/watch?v=zT0EP4mP1lI.

71. Ibid.

Lieutenant Jerome Nelson

Nelson was a deputy missile combat crew commander of the missile squadron in Roswell from 1962 to 1965. Nelson explained how on one occasion, while he was in the launch control center at the Roswell, New Mexico, base, the security guards contacted him and informed him that a "fully illuminated round object was hovering silently over the missile silo and shining a light down onto it."[72]

Nelson could feel the fear in the security guard's voice. The unidentified aircraft was shining a bright light directly onto the nuclear storage site and he was concerned that it would somehow affect the missiles. Nelson immediately reported the sighting to the base commander on duty.

After just five minutes, the UFO disappeared from the sky, however, this was not the only time that an event like this had happened while he was on duty. Nelson stated that similar events had occurred more frequently throughout the month. On more than three occasions, unidentified objects were seen hovering above the nuclear storage site at Roswell. Each time Nelson would inform the base commander of the sighting, the commander would simply dismiss it altogether. Surprisingly, Nelson was never debriefed on any of the sightings.

Patrick McDonough

In September of 1966, McDonough, who was a nuclear missile site geodetic surveyor, together with two other airmen, was instructed to carry out the initial geodetic surveys for the fifty missile sites in the United States.

---

72. National Press Club press conference, aired September 27, 2010 on CNN, https://www.youtube.com/watch?v=zT0EP4mP1lI.

On one particular evening, as the three men were setting up their instruments and carrying out their tasks, an unidentified object appeared in the sky, coming from the north and stopped directly above the three men and the Malmstrom missile storage site. McDonough described the UFO as having a round shape with a diameter of around fifty feet. He compared its size to that of a B-52's wingspan. It also had pulsating lights around its circumference and one bright light shining down onto the missile silo site. At an altitude of just 300 feet, the three men were able to get a detailed view of the object, however, just moments later, it shot off to the east side and disappeared. After the UFO disappeared, the three men gathered their equipment, jumped back into their trucks, and made their way back. The night, however, was not over just yet for McDonough and his colleagues.

As McDonough was driving over a hill, he somehow lost control of the truck and it completely flipped over. Luckily, none of the three men were injured, and after two hours of walking, they found a farmhouse where they were able to contact the highway patrolmen.

Surprisingly, as the three men were talking with the patrolman about their incident, he informed them that they had received over twenty reports from people saying that they had seen a strange light in the sky, in the vicinity where they had had the accident. The three men all wrote an official report, however, there was never a follow up. It was never mentioned by anyone in the air force.

"But I must say now, in my four years that I had with this geodetic survey squadron, I had worked on the latest missiles and aircraft in the United States Air Force inventory. And I worked everywhere on these guidance systems. And we, or I, never saw anything in the air force inventory that could perform like this UFO did. It's…I don't know what it was, but we sure didn't have any...I never saw anything like it. And I'd like to thank all of you for being here today and thank the National Press Club. Hopefully, someday, the...we'll know in the near future that...the government will perhaps release any information they have on UFOs."[73]

Captain Bruce Fenstermacher

In the fall of 1967, Fenstermacher, together with his deputy, were listening to a conversation between the flight security controller and the security alert team at Warren Air Force Base in Cheyenne, Wyoming. What was interesting about this conversation, is that the security alert team had reported seeing a "white pulsating light in the sky that's maybe seven or eight miles away."[74]

The witnesses informed the security controllers and Fenstermacher that the unidentified bright light was close to where the nuclear control facility was. To confirm the report, Fenstermacher called the operators who confirmed that a cigar-shaped object was truly hovering in the sky, pulsating a white light over the nuclear storage site. The operator went on to explain how the object was completely silent and, for several minutes, it remained in the sky, hovering directly above the control center.

Fenstermacher ordered the security alert team to go to the launch facility and as they did so, the cigar-shaped object started flying toward another launch facility site. After an hour and a half, the flight security control said that the UFO just suddenly and silently "went away up to a start size and then disappeared."[75]

The next couple of days during the meetings with the squadron commander, Fenstermacher stated that an officer, who he had

---

73. National Press Club press conference, aired September 27, 2010 on CNN, https://www.youtube.com/watch?v=zT0EP4mP1lI.

74. Ibid.

75. Ibid.

not previously seen at the base, had instructed everyone to keep silent and to not disclose any information to the public. The officer went on to explain how the sighting involved top secret material that could cause harm to national security if it was to be revealed to the public.

Another Interference

On October 26, 2010, Marc Ambinder, a former contributing editor at *The Atlantic*, reported that President Barack Obama had been informed that on October 23, fifty nuclear intercontinental ballistic missiles (ICBMs) had gone offline. The fifty ICBMs accounted for one-ninth of the entire missiles owned by the United States. For over an hour, all fifty missiles had gone into a 'LF Down' status, meaning that though the missiles were offline, they still could have been launched. However; they could only have been controlled from airborne command.

The commanders at the base informed the two other nuclear missile command centers, as well as the National Military Command Center in Washington of the situation, although at the time they were unaware of what had caused the missiles to go offline. Speaking about the incident, an unnamed military officer stated:"We've never had something as big as this happen. We can deal with maybe five, six or seven at a time, but we've never lost complete command and control and functionality of fifty ICBMs."[76]

What makes this incident even more bizarre is that Robert Hastings, a notable UFO researcher who has interviewed hundreds of former air force personnel and the same individual who had hosted the September 2010 press conference the previous

76. Marc Ambinder, "Failure Shuts Down Squadron of Nuclear Missiles," *The Atlantic*, October 26, 2010, https://www.theatlantic.com/politics/archive/2010/10/failure-shuts-down-squadron-of-nuclear-missiles/65207/.

month, received an abundance of reports in which individuals had seen a UFO in Wyoming on the same day the nuclear missiles had gone offline. Civilians, as well as military personnel, made similar reports, all of which described a cigar-shaped object hovering silently in the sky.

One of the witnesses who Hastings interviewed was a retired missile maintenance technician. On the morning of October 23, this witnesses had seen the Wyoming UFO as he was driving through western Cheyenne at around 08:30: "I've seen Goodyear blimps in person, overhead, and they are 'blimp' shaped. What I saw was very long and I don't remember seeing any structures under it. It didn't appear shiny, but dull and gray…I would guess it was 7:1, or seven [units] long to one [unit] wide, or so it looked. It was tapered on both ends and very big. It was not short and squat like normal blimps. It appeared to be moving northerly and was over the buttes east of town."[77]

Conclusion

It seems evident after all these witness reports that these visitors seem to have a particular interest in our nuclear missiles. Many have questioned the reason why, and although we may never find the answer, it could be the case they are interfering with our weapons to prevent further wars and global catastrophes. Could it be that these visitors are interfering in order to preserve life on Earth?

---

77. Robert Hastings, "Huge UFO Sighted Near Nuclear Missiles During October 2010 Launch System Disruption," The UFO Chronicles, June 21, 2011, https://www.theufochronicles.com/2011/06/huge-ufo-sighted-near-nuclear-missiles_19.html.

Chapter 19

UFO Shuts Down
Chinese Airport

Date: July 7, 2010
Location: Hangzhou, China

In the summer of 2010, an unidentified object was seen hovering above Xiaoshan Airport in Hangzhou, China. Unlike American authorities, who did not take the O'Hare airport UFO sighting seriously, the Chinese aviation authorities shut down the entire airport.

On July 7, 2010, at around 20:40, air traffic control operators at the Xiaoshan Airport were informed by the flight crew of a plane about to make its landing that an unidentified object was in the sky, hovering above the airport. After the sighting was confirmed by air traffic control operators, the authorities instructed all flights to be grounded, and those flights that were about to take off were delayed. They also diverted all incoming flights to Ningbo and Wuxi. For an hour, the airport was entirely shut down and a total of eighteen flights were disrupted.

Interestingly, local residents had been seeing strange lights in the sky prior to the airport sighting. One resident, Ma Shijun, reported that he saw a strange object emitting red and white rays of light. The time of his sighting was around 20:26: roughly fifteen minutes prior to the airport sighting. As Shijun and his wife were walking down the road, they felt a beam of light over their heads and once they looked up, they saw the strange object in the sky.

The Investigation

Naturally, after the unidentified aircraft shut down the airport for an entire hour, a proper investigation was launched by the Civil Aviation Administration of China. The day after the sighting, it was reported that the UFO might have been a military aircraft. However, this theory has not been confirmed.

Although we cannot come to any conclusions since the evidence is scarce, I must clarify that in every circumstance and country, every aircraft needs the proper authorization to be in the sky. If the UFO was a military aircraft, which it could very well have been, it is strange that the air traffic control operators were not informed. Even if it was the case that it was a classified aircraft, it is not logical for an airport to shut down for an entire hour unless absolutely necessary.

The Sightings Continue

Just one week after the Xioashan Airport sightings, on July 15, 2010, "four lantern-like objects forming a diamond shape" were seen hovering over Chongqing in Eastern China.[78] One witness reported that the four UFOs remained in the sky for over an hour before they started ascending farther into the atmosphere, until they disappeared.

The UFO sightings over China did not end in the summer of 2010. The following year, on August 20, 2011, *Shanghai Daily*

---

78. Stephan Kurczy, "China UFO Spotted Again. Why Skepticism is Warranted," *The Christian Science Monitor,* July 16, 2010, https://www.csmonitor.com /World/Global-News/2010/0716/China-UFO-spotted-again.-Why -skepticism-is-warranted.

reported that several pilots had seen UFOs in the sky. A pilot for Flight 6554 described the object as being a huge, bright white ball climbing out of the thick clouds. The object had a diameter of approximately ninety kilometers and remained in the sky for over twenty minutes. The object started losing its brightness until it gradually disappeared. At first, the pilot on board thought that this must have been an illusion of some sort or a weather phenomenon. However, he later learned that at least ten pilots had made the same report to the air traffic control operators.

On the same day, similar reports were made in Beijing at the same time the UFO was seen in Shanghai. Once again, although the two locations are at least one thousand kilometers apart, the reports made were very similar. Yu Jun, a former editor of a scientific magazine, stated that a large white ball of light appeared in the sky and it increased in its size. After five minutes, the object disappeared.

Conclusion

It is unclear whether these UFOs were military aircraft, natural phenomena or interplanetary objects. Although we will not have the answer to this question, it is clear that mysterious objects were in the Chinese skies in the summer of 2010 and 2011.

Chapter 20
Pilots Encounter UFOs off the Irish Coast

Date: November 9, 2018
Location: Ireland

A more recent sighting took place on November 9, 2018, off the Irish coast. The first sighting was made by a British Airways pilot at 06:47, who reported seeing a very bright light traveling at an incredible speed.

The pilot contacted the Shannon Airport air traffic control and inquired whether there were any military exercises happening over the south of Ireland at that time. Once the air traffic control operator confirmed that there were no military exercises happening, it became apparent that the pilot was sharing the sky with something extraordinary. Moments later, the UFO approached the aircraft, flying closely to its left side, right before it accelerated to the north and disappeared.

A second pilot, who was piloting a Virgin Atlantic Airways plane, also encountered the unidentified object in the sky. The pilot informed the air traffic control operators that numerous unidentifiable bright lights were in the sky. At first the pilot assumed that the lights were simply meteorites entering the atmosphere. However, shortly thereafter, the two bright objects approached the aircraft and accelerated at a very high speed, disproving his hypothesis. The pilot estimated the object to be traveling at Mach 1, which means that the UFOs had broken the sound barrier. However, no sonic boom was heard, which means that they must have been traveling through a vacuum, proving that this was an extraterrestrial object that did not abide by the laws of physics.

Communication with Air Traffic Control

The following is the transcript between the pilot on board the British Airways flight (B.A.), the pilot on board the Virgin Atlantic Airways flight (V.A.A.) and the air traffic control operator (A.T.C.). This part of the transcript is at the moment in which the pilots encountered the unidentified object in the sky.[79]

B.A.: Are there any uh, military exercises taking place right now?

A.T.C.: There is nothing showing on either primary or secondary [radar].

B.A.: Okay, it was moving very fast.

A.T.C.: Was it alongside you?

B.A.: It came up on our left-hand side and then rapidly veered to the north. It was a very bright light and then disappeared at a very high speed and was wondering, it did not seem to be on a collision course and was wondering what that could be.

V.A.A.: A meteorite or another object making some re-entry. There appears to be multiple objects following the same sort of trajectory. They were very bright from where we were

A.T.C.: Do you know the direction they were going in or anything?

79.VASAviation, "[Real ATC] Several Aircraft Witness a UFO Right Over Ireland!," YouTube, November 13, 2018, 7:17, https://www.youtube.com /watch?v=pv7x4dRye3U.

V.A.A.: It was in our 11 o'clock position uh, two bright lights over to the right and then climbed away at speed.

A.T.C.: Okay, we're passing it on now.

An Explanation

After the two sightings, the Irish Aviation Authority released a statement reporting that an official investigation would be underway. Since the sightings occurred only a few years ago, all information remains classified and no official explanation has yet been given.

"Following reports from a small number of aircraft on Friday 9 November of unusual air activity, the IAA has filed a report. This report will be investigated under the normal confidential occurrence investigation process."[80]

Conclusion

Although no official explanation has been provided, it is evident that what was in the sky on November 9 was extraterrestrial. The description, the maneuverability and the fact that the UFOs defied the laws of physics are all indications that they were interplanetary flying objects.

---

80. Lucia Binding, "UFO Investigated in Ireland After Multiple Aircraft Sightings," *Sky News*, November 12, 2018, https://news.sky.com/story/ufo-investigated-in-ireland-after-multiple-aircraft-sightings-11552908.

Part 2
Crashes and Landings

The Roswell case is one of the most renowned UFO crashes. This case is usually the first that comes to mind when people think of extraterrestrials. However, what many people are unaware of is that numerous other incidents exist in which extraterrestrial aircraft have crashed. In other instances, such aircraft have made a perfect and deliberate landing. One common factor amongst the following crashes and landings is the substantial amount of evidence that each case possesses. As we shall see, each and every case in this section has considerable evidence proving that extraterrestrials do exist, and, in some instances, interplanetary objects have even crashed here on Earth.

One pivotal question I often ask is what will happen if any military on Earth comes in possession of the technology that these beings possess? In the following cases it will be evident that the crashed object was extraterrestrial in nature, and with that we must ask, how will the militaries use this technology if they do acquire it? Once they get this technology in their possession, will they try and duplicate it and use it in future wars? Or is the extraterrestrial technology simply too advanced and complex for mankind to even comprehend?

As we have seen in the previous section of the book, the reported UFOs display maneuvers that physically cannot be carried out by terrestrial aircraft. This will also become evident in the subsequent chapters. What will happen to mankind if any countries ever acquire technology that essentially makes them the most superior and threatening nation in the world?

Chapter 21
The Aurora Crash

Date: April 17, 1897
Location: Aurora, Texas, United States

The first reported UFO crash of modern times occurred in 1897 in Aurora, Texas. It was in the early hours of April 17 when local judge J.S. Proctor was awoken by a loud, explosive sound coming from outside his house. When Proctor walked out of his house, he noticed debris scattered all over his property, and saw that an object had hit the windmill next to his house. Proctor described the debris found on his property as being metallic, similar to aluminum. Many people from all over Aurora began gathering around his house, as they too had heard the explosion.

With several witnesses reporting seeing the debris, some even seeing an extraterrestrial body, word of the crash spread quickly. By the time authorities arrived at the scene, a portion of the debris had already been dumped in the well, which was situated below the windmill. The remaining debris was buried with the alien body, which had allegedly been found at the crash site. Although many have questioned whether an alien body was truly recovered from the site, a number of witnesses reported seeing the humanoid body. Investigations at the local cemetery also revealed a grave marker locating where the alien body had been buried.

The people of Aurora placed a large stone with a flying saucer engraved on it at the grave where the humanoid body was allegedly buried. A proper funeral and burial also took place. S.E. Haydon, writer for *The Dallas Morning News* wrote the following on the front page of the newspaper on April 19, 1897: "About 6 o'clock this morning the early risers of Aurora were astonished at the sudden appearance of the airship that has been sailing through the country.

"It was traveling due north, and much closer to the ground than ever before. Evidently some of the machinery was out of order, for it was making a speed of only ten or twelve miles an hour and gradually settling toward the earth. It sailed directly over the public square, and when it reached the north part of the town collided with the tower of Judge Proctor's windmill and went to pieces with a terrific explosion, scattering debris over several acres of ground, wrecking the windmill and water tank and destroying the judge's flower garden.

"The pilot of the ship is supposed to have been the only one on board, and while his remains are badly disfigured, enough of the original has been picked up to show that he was not an inhabitant of this world.

"Mr. T. J. Weems, the United States signal service officer at this place and an authority on astronomy, gives it as his opinion that he was an inhabitant of the planet Mars. Papers found on his person—evidently the record of his travels—are written in some unknown hieroglyphics and cannot be deciphered.

"The ship was too badly wrecked to form any conclusion as to its construction or motive power. It was built of an unknown metal, resembling somewhat a mixture of aluminum and silver, and it must have weighed several tons.

"The town is full of people to-day who are viewing the wreck and gathering specimens of the strange metal from the debris. The pilot's funeral will take place at noon tomorrow."[81]

Eyewitness Reports

Since this incident occurred over a century ago, authorities did not carry out an investigation, or if they had done so, there are no records indicating it. With that being said, witnesses were tracked down and interviewed by the Mutual UFO Network (MUFON) in 1973. The two witnesses interviewed were Charlie Stephens and Mary Evans, who were both young at the time and recalled their parents visiting the crash site.

Jim Stephens, father of the then ten-year-old Charlie, was one of the individuals who went to the crash site after he had seen a bright light, followed by a fire on Proctor's property. Charlie recalled that in the early hours of the morning, his father noticed a large fire emerging from more than three miles away. Once his father arrived at the scene, he reported seeing metallic-like fragments scattered all over the ground. When interviewed by the MUFON investigative team, Charlie did not recall his father mentioning having seen any alien bodies. On the other hand, Mary Evans, who was fifteen years old at the time, recalled her parents telling her that they had seen a torn alien body beside the metallic debris, which was scattered all over Proctor's property. Evans explained how the metallic fragments were compared to aluminum, and also that a funeral was going to be held for the alien body, which was found at the site.

---

81. S.E. Haydon, " A Windmill Demolishes It," *The Dallas Morning News,* April 19, 1897, 5.

Although Charlie's father did not recall seeing an alien body at the crash site, this was confirmed not only by the article Haydon wrote just a couple of days later, but also by Aurora Town Marshal H.R. Idell. Perhaps the most credible witness of this case is Idell, who confirmed that a stone with a flying saucer was indeed placed upon the humanoid's grave as a marker. He also confirmed to the MUFON team that, before it was stolen, the marker had been there for over fifty years and that this was not a fabrication of any kind.

The Debris

In 1973, Bill Case, the director for MUFON and an author for the *Dallas Times*, initiated an investigation to determine whether this story was simply part of Aurora's folklore, or something otherworldly. The investigation did, indeed, prove that an explosion had occurred and that the recovered debris displayed unusual characteristics.

Before discussing the findings of the analysis, it is important to note that the goal behind this investigation was not to prove whether the metallic debris was extraterrestrial or not, but rather to find out if the crash had truly happened. Using highly sophisticated metal detectors, the MUFON team was able to locate metal fragments just 100 meters from the crash site. John F. Schuessler, an aerospace engineer and a director for MUFON wrote the following: "From all indications there was definitely an explosion. The pattern established by metals recovered indicates the craft exploded on the lower right side, first blowing bits and pieces over a two- or three-acre area east and northeast of the well site on top of a rocky limestone hill. Immediately, the rest of the craft exploded, throwing other samples to the north and west."[82]

---

82. John Schuessler, "Metal From a Crashed UFO?"

The metal sample was analyzed using x-ray fluorescence, soft x-ray spectroscopy, and optical metallography. These three methods showed that the metal had unusual properties when compared to regular aluminum. The analysis showed that the metal contained large grains, indicating that the metal had melted, and then proceeded to cool back down. This detail proved the material was exposed to temperatures that were high enough to cause metal to melt. Moreover, the analysis also showed that the metal had an unusually high purity level of aluminum and only a slight presence of iron. The reason why this finding is unusual is due to the fact that the commercial aluminum that we are all familiar with, which contains iron, is also composed of copper and zinc. The absence of these elements indicate that the metal was unconventional.

A more recent investigation, carried out by the television series *UFO Hunters* in 2008, came to even more interesting and remarkable findings. During the investigation, Tim Oates, the grandson of Brawley Oates (who was the current owner of the property previously owned by Proctor) was interviewed and gave the investigative team permission to unseal the well to take a water sample. The sample taken from the well, where the debris had been deposited just after the crash, was analyzed and the findings showed that it had an abnormally high level of aluminum and that the water was immensely contaminated. This revelation also indicated, or rather provided a reason, for why Brawley Oates developed cysts, goiters, and severe arthritis when he first moved to the property.

The Grave

As part of the investigation, the MUFON team also searched the local cemetery where the humanoid remains were allegedly buried. When the team's metal detectors were placed over the grave where the marker was located, the detectors immediately picked up a signal. So far in the investigation, it was apparent that the crash truly did happen. However, in order to prove or disprove whether an alien body was truly buried or not, the investigators needed to exhume the grave.

Since the MUFON team had been granted permission from the cemetery association to investigate the grave, they assumed that they would also be granted permission to exhume the grave. Upon requesting access, not only did the association deny them permission, but they also denied them further access to the cemetery altogether. Making the situation even more suspicious was the fact that in their last visit to the cemetery, the MUFON team was unable to locate the grave marker and they also noted that there was a three-inch wide pipe going into the grave. Furthermore, when the metal detector was placed over the grave, no signals were picked up, indicating that the metal that was buried in the grave had been transported elsewhere.

Conclusion

Did the cemetery association remove the debris and perhaps the body from the grave site because the investigative team was too close to reaching the truth? More importantly, what had been buried in the grave that was so secretive that the investigators were denied permission to exhume it? Having no other option, the MUFON team had to terminate the investigation.

Although the investigators did not have sufficient evidence to prove that an alien body was buried in the grave, they were able to prove that a crash did indeed happen, and the analysis of the debris showed that the metal had unconventional characteristics.

With that being said, we must keep in mind that this incident occurred over a century ago and thus, the evidence is scarce. Although we cannot come to any definite conclusions, the following factors support the story that local residents have recounted for over a century; the story of how an interplanetary aircraft crashed and, together with the debris, an alien body was recovered:

1. Metal fragments were retrieved from the crash site, just 100 meters away from the windmill where the unidentified object had allegedly crashed.

2. The metal sample showed that it was exposed to high temperatures, proving that it was involved in an explosion.

3. The analysis of the metal and water samples showed that the debris had an unusually high aluminum purity level. The high aluminum levels were also the reason why Brawley Oates had developed severe arthritis, goiters and cysts.

4. The presence of a grave marker was confirmed by the town marshal, the eyewitnesses and the MUFON investigative team. The marker was a large stone with a flying saucer engraved on it.

5. The metal detectors proved that metal was buried in the grave.

6. After MUFON were denied access from exhuming the grave, the metal detectors were no longer able to detect any signals when placed over the grave, indicating that whatever was buried in the grave had been placed elsewhere.

Chapter 22
The Roswell Crash

Date: July 1947
Location: Roswell, New Mexico, United States

The Roswell crash is a common reference in the discussion of UFOs and perhaps the most famous UFO-related case to date. This incident put Roswell on the map, driving thousands of tourists every year to visit the crash site. However, what was it that crashed in the New Mexico desert? Was it a flying saucer as the air force had originally stated, or was it a weather balloon, a later explanation provided by the air force? The following case is not just about an extraterrestrial aircraft crashing in the desert, but it is also about a nationwide cover-up.

The Crash

On June 14, 1947, William Brazel and his eight-year-old son, Vernon, were walking from the ranch where Brazel worked at, located in Corona, just eighty-five miles northwest of Roswell.

In an article in the *Roswell Daily Record* on July 9, Brazel stated he and his son had encountered a large amount of debris scattered all over the ground. Brazel described the wreckage as being composed of "rubber strips, tinfoil and a rather tough paper and sticks."[83] It was not unusual for Brazel to discover remnants of weather balloons on his ranch, and thus he did not pay too much attention to the debris, assuming that it was just another crashed weather balloon. With that being said, over the next couple of days, several individuals in Roswell reported seeing strange flying objects in the sky. Two of the initial witnesses were Dan Wilmot and his wife who, in early July, reported seeing a saucer-shaped object in the sky.

It was July 2 when Dan Wilmot and his wife were enjoying the summer night outside their house in Roswell. The time was around 21:50 when Wilmot saw a bright, oval shaped light in the sky. The UFO was described as being "like two inverted saucers faced mouth to mouth" and had a diameter of at least twenty feet.[84] The object, which was at an altitude of approximately 1,500 feet, was travelling at an incredible speed, estimated to be well over 500 miles per hour. After remaining in the sky for a few seconds, it accelerated out of sight. At first, Wilmot did not share his sighting with anyone, in hopes that another witness would come forward and share their experience. However, no one did, and thus, on July 9, Wilmot contacted the *Roswell Daily Record* and told them about his sighting. Coincidentally enough, his report was made just a few hours before the military announced that they were in possession of a flying disk.

Going back to July 4, given that it was Independence Day, Brazel took his wife and two children out to the ranch with him. He had been hearing stories of people seeing flying saucers in the sky and that one of them had crashed somewhere in the desert. That

83. "Harassed Rancher Who Located 'Saucer' Sorry He Told About It," *Roswell Daily Record*, July 9, 1947.

84. "RAAF Captures Flying Saucer on Ranch in Roswell Region," *Roswell Daily Record*, July 8, 1947.

was when he thought; could it be that the debris that he had seen the previous month could be the saucer everyone had been talking about? As he got a closer to the debris, he started noticing how this was unlike any other weather balloon he had recovered previously, and, upon further inspection, he confirmed that the material was different to that of a weather balloon.

Brazel said, "I am sure that what I found was not any weather observation balloon. But if I find anything besides a bomb, they are going to have a hard time getting me to say anything about it."[85]

The following day, Brazel contacted the local town sheriff, George Wilcox, and informed him that he had recovered the crashed flying saucer everyone was talking about. Wilcox immediately forwarded the report to Roswell Army Airfield and Major Jesse Marcel, who, together with Lieutenant Colonel Sheridan Cavitt and Master Sergeant Bill Racket, accompanied Brazel back to the ranch and his house where they collected all the debris. Back at Brazel's house, the three men attempted to reconstruct the material and carried out several experiments to explore the material's properties. The debris was similar to aluminum foil; it was extremely lightweight and had the same silver color. The debris was laid out all over the kitchen floor, covering at least 180 meters, and it also had strange symbols and hieroglyphs engraved on its surface.

This was the last time Brazel saw the wreckage. Marcel piled all of the wreckage onto his truck and returned back to Roswell Air Force Base. July 8 was the start of a cover-up that is still going on to this day. On that day, Colonel William Blanchard instructed Lieutenant Walter Hault to issue a press release, stating that the air force was in possession of a flying disk. The statement was the first

85. "Harassed Rancher Who Located 'Saucer' Sorry He Told About It," *Roswell Daily Record*, July 9, 1947.

of its kind—no other air force on Earth had ever publicly stated that it was in possession of an extraterrestrial aircraft and technology. The same day, several newspapers broke the story, using headlines such as "RAAF Captures Flying Saucer on Ranch in Roswell Region," found in the Roswell Daily Record.

It is important to point out the fact that although there are many theories that alien bodies were recovered from the crash site, the military never declared such a thing, and Brazel did not report seeing any bodies either. Over the years, many theories have been postulated, claiming that four gray aliens were recovered. We shall examine some of these theories later on in the chapter.

At the time, the air force was not aware of the chaos such a statement would create. Shortly after the statement was issued, the debris was sent to the Fort Worth Air Force Base in Texas. At the air force base, the wreckage was placed in General Roger Ramey's office and just a few hours later, a second statement was released by the air force. Ramey stated that the wreckage was not of a flying disk but was a weather balloon. The statement was published in newspapers, along with a photograph of Ramey posing with the wreckage. Irving Newton, the warrant officer and forecaster at the base, also confirmed that the wreckage was of a weather balloon that had been released in the sky in order to obtain meteorological information they could not get from the ground.

Witness Reports

Although that was the last statement the air force had released, as the years passed, more witnesses came forward and shared their story. Perhaps the two most important and fascinating witness accounts were that of Bill Brazel, the son of William Brazel, and of Jesse Marcel Jr., the son of Major Jesse Marcel.

Jesse recalled that on one night, his father was sent out to investigate the ranch where the debris had been located. When Major Marcel returned home, his truck was full of the debris from the wreckage site. Jesse described the material as being similar to aluminum foil, and although the material was not made of metal, it was very tough and it could not be burned or torn. Whenever the material was bent, it would return back to its original shape. He also explained how it had hieroglyphics carved into its surface. Lastly, although Jesse was just eleven years old at the time, he remembered his father saying that the material was not from Earth. He explained how his father had said that no aircraft on Earth could reach the speed the object had reached before its crash.

Bill Brazel, the son of William Brazel, described how after his father discovered the debris, he was somewhat of a different man. After first reporting this discovery of the debris, Brazel was kept away from his family for a week and was interrogated relentlessly. Upon his return, he would not explain what had happened in that week, not even to his wife. Bill does not know the full extent of the story and has explained how his father took everything to the grave with him. In an interview with Charles Berlitz and William Moore, Bill stated the following: "He said they had told him to shut up because it was important to our country and was the patriotic thing to do, and so that's what he intended to do. He did say that they had shut him up in a room and wouldn't let him out. He was very discouraged and upset about the way they had treated him. They even had given him a complete 'head-to-foot army physical' before they would let him come home."[86]

---

86. Charles Berlitz and William Moore, *The Roswell Incident*. (New York: Fine Communication, 1997), 26.

A year or so after the crash, Bill kept finding pieces of the wreckage at the ranch. Although it did not amount to much, he was able to determine that the material was unconventional. Similar to Jesse's description, Bill stated that the material was very lightweight. Although it was very similar to tinfoil, whenever it was bent it would return to its original shape. It also could not be torn or scratched. Apart from the tinfoil-like material, Bill also recovered pieces of wood that were quite heavy, as well as a material that looked similar to wire or thread, although it was very strong and rigid. Even when using both hands, he could not snap it. The material that his father had brought home on July 4 had figures carved on its surface that looked similar to hieroglyphics.

However, the material did not stay in Bill's possession for long. Not long after Bill had found the materials, approximately two years after the crash, three military officials went to the house and wanted to speak with him. Since his father was away at the time, he had let them in, but what he did not know was that the three men were air force personnel sent to collect the wreckage he had been talking about. Bill recalled that one of the men had told him that it was very important for him to hand over the material to help the country's safety. Before they left, Bill was also asked to take the three men to the wreckage site to ensure that there was not any debris left.

In his statement, Bill also affirmed that the wreckage was not a balloon. He stated that he and his dad had picked up balloons on numerous occasions at the ranch, however, this material was vastly different from those weather balloons. Usually, with weather balloons there would be instruments attached to the material, but none were found with this wreckage. Bill stated that when his father went to turn the material in, he first went to the weather bureau. Even though the material was vastly different to a weather balloon's, his father had thought that it must have been an observational instrument of some sort. When he told the bureau office of his finding, they confirmed that the material was not of a weather balloon and they instructed him to take it to the sheriff's office instead.

The Alien Bodies

Since the crash in 1947, the Roswell story has been altered and revisited countless times by authors and conspiracy theorists. As we have seen in the witness statement reports, there was no mention of any alien bodies being retrieved from the crash site; if anybody would have found bodies, it would have been William Brazel, the rancher who had found the wreckage. It is fundamental to separate the truth from fiction, and the theory that alien bodies were found at the crash site is simply that, a conspiracy theory. Although this theory has not been proved, I think it is important to examine the details since this aspect has become a fundamental part of the Roswell crash story.

In 1991, the late Stanton Friedman, one of the most highly respected UFO researchers and nuclear physicists, interviewed Glenn Dennis, a mortician who worked at Ballard Funeral Home. The funeral home had a contract with the Roswell Army Airfield to provide mortuary services. Apart from being a funeral parlor, the company also operated an ambulance for the airfield, and it was not unusual for Dennis to drive down to the base after an incident was reported. In the interview with Friedman, Dennis stated that on one summer day in 1947, the parlor received several calls from the mortuary officer at the airfield asking what size the smallest coffin he could provide was. Apart from that, the officer also asked how a body would be prepared if it had been exposed to toxic elements and the sun for several days. Dennis went on to say that on the same day, he had to drive down to the airfield after an injury was reported. As he entered the building, Dennis allegedly saw a lot of material that resembled aluminum spread all over the floor, which was heavily guarded by air force personnel.

As Dennis walked down the hall, a nurse who was his friend frantically asked him why he was there and told him to leave the building immediately. She told him that if anyone had known he was there they would kill him. As she said that, two military officials noticed his presence and escorted him out. After two hours had passed, he received a call from, presumably the army, who told him that if he opened his mouth about what he had seen, they would shoot him dead.

His story did not finish there. The following day, his nurse friend called him and asked to meet up with him urgently. The nurse told him that that day he was at the airfield, the air force had brought in three little alien bodies from a crash site. Two of them were completely mangled, but the other one was in good condition. She described them as being child-like, very fragile, with no hair. They had deep eyes and very small indentations for ears. When it came to their arms, they did not have any fingers, but had suction cups that looked like tentacles instead. When Dennis asked her if they were found with the wreckage, the nurse told him that they were found about a mile or two away from the crash site. That was the last time Dennis had heard from his friend. After several days of not answering his calls, Dennis was told that she was transferred to a different air force base in England. A couple of months later, Dennis sent a letter to her, which was returned and stamped "deceased."

There are a number of reasons why I believe that no alien bodies were found at the crash site and why this aspect of this case is a hoax. Many investigators tried to trace down this nurse, but to no avail. At first, Dennis refused to provide a name, but after a while, he stated that the nurse was named Naomi Self. Investigators were able to find the military records that named all the nurses who worked at the Roswell base in the summer of 1947. There were only five female nurses, none of whom were called Naomi or had been transferred to England. After this was revealed, Dennis stated that the surname he provided was a fake one, but he refused to provide the real one.

Although the theory that alien bodies were recovered at the crash site was a fabrication, this does not mean that the government is not involved in a cover-up or that the recovered material was not extraterrestrial. The witness statement reports are all proof that the wreckage Brazel discovered was not a weather balloon. As we shall see in the following section, the typical weather balloon is vastly different compared to the recovered wreckage.

Weather Balloon
or Extraterrestrial Craft?

The air force stated that the weather balloon that had crashed in Roswell in 1947 was a Project Mogul weather balloon. Project Mogul was a top secret project by the air force that consisted of high-altitude balloons, as well as a number of sophisticated components attached to them being released in the sky. The goal was to detect long-distance sound waves generated by Soviet Union missiles. The Project Mogul balloon was made of rubber, which was quickly replaced by polyethylene plastic. The components attached to the balloon include acoustical sensors and radar reflecting targets. By the year 1942, it also became a requirement for test dummies to be on board all military aircraft tests, including weather balloons, which were deemed too dangerous for humans to be on. The test dummies were dressed in regular army uniforms and were equipped with parachutes.

Although the air force stated that the recovered material was that of a weather balloon, the facts show otherwise. When Brazel discovered the material, he did not report finding any test dummies or any of the components that the balloons are usually equipped with. Moreover, the material Brazel discovered and polyethylene plastic have completely different characteristics.

The witnesses who had handled the material all described it in the same way. Although it resembled aluminum foil, it would return to its original shape when bent and it also was heat and tear resistant. If we look at polyethylene plastic, the material that a Project Mogul weather balloon is made of, just like any other material, it has a melting point. When exposed to high temperatures for a long period of time, it would naturally melt. Apart from that, once plastic is bent, it cannot return to its original shape because stress cracks would start forming. Lastly, Brazel, his son, and Marcel all stated that on the surface of the material were strange symbols that were described as being similar to Egyptian hieroglyphics.

The most important factor that proves that the material was not a weather balloon is the fact that Brazel was aware of what a typical weather balloon looked like. He stated that on at least two occasions he had found wreckages from weather balloons that had crashed on the ranch. However, as he stated in the interview that was published in the *Roswell Daily Record,* Brazel was confident that what he had found was not a weather balloon. We must also keep in mind that Brazel did not gain anything from this. The only thing that he got was harassment and interrogations from the air force.

Why would he keep persisting that the material was extraterrestrial? It certainly would have been easier for him to just agree with the air force's statement and let the story die down.

Interview with Stanton Friedman

The late Stanton Friedman was a nuclear physicist and was also the first researcher to investigate the Roswell crash. Before his passing, I had the privilege to interview him in 2017 via email and ask him questions regarding the Roswell crash. Here is some of our discussion:

Q: *You were the first researcher to investigate the Roswell case. What do you think genuinely happened? Did an interplanetary flying object crash or was it a weather balloon?*

A: I personally think that the 509th Composite Bomb Group (stationed at Roswell Army Airfield) recovered the wreckage of a crashed alien spacecraft, as well as several alien bodies.

Q: *Do you think the government is in possession of any extraterrestrials or ET technology?*

A: I think they have had a living alien for a while and most certainly had wreckage from alien spacecrafts. I do not know whether they have learned how to duplicate the technology they were in possession of, but the Wright Brothers could not have duplicated a 747 or a V-2 rocket.

Q: *One of the most common questions skeptics ask is if extraterrestrials visit our planet then why don't they land on the White House lawn? What would your answer be?*

A: I think that is an incorrect question to ask. They are here for their own purpose, not ours. They do not need to justify their existence to us. Our rule is shoot first and ask questions later. Moreover, the president [of the United States] does not speak for planet Earth.

Q: *Why do you think aliens are so interested in humans? What is the reason behind all of the abduction cases?*

A: We may be the least interesting planet. Certainly, we have demonstrated many evil qualities such as killing 50 million people in World War II, as well as destroying over 1,700 cities. One of my books has twenty reasons why aliens visit; for example, Earth is the densest planet in the solar system, so it has much more heavy metals than any other planet.

Q: *Why do you think the government does not disclose any information on extraterrestrial life?*

A: There are a lot of answers to this question. No government wants its people to owe their allegiance to the planet instead of the sovereign. Nationalism is the only game in town.

Conclusion

The facts outlined in this chapter prove that what crashed near Roswell in the summer of 1947 was an interplanetary flying object. The material of the wreckage and the witness reports are sufficient evidence to prove that the material was extraterrestrial in origin.

The Roswell crash is undoubtedly one of the most credible and convincing cases that prove that extraterrestrials exist and have been visiting our planet. This incident can be seen as the case that sparked an interest in researchers to investigate the UFO phenomenon.

Although we do not have all the answers, and most of our questions will remain unanswered, there is enough evidence for us to understand that we are not alone in the universe, nor are we the superior species. The proof this case offers is enough for mankind to understand that the biggest threat is not other nations here on Earth, but outside visitors who have complete power and control.

Chapter 23

Rocket-Shaped UFOs
Land in Levelland

Date: November 2, 1957
Location: Levelland, Texas, United States

The Levelland sightings have compelling evidence that strongly suggests that the observed UFOs were interplanetary aircraft. Apart from the unusual features of the aircraft, the objects in this case were able to affect the operation of nearby vehicles. As we have seen in Chapter 19, it is not uncommon for UFOs to interfere with electrical systems, most notably, military systems. This capability and occurrence will become even more prominent in part 3, which will examine cases where military jets have pursued UFOs.

Joe Salaz and Pedro Saucedo were two farmers who on November 2, 1957, came face-to-face with an otherworldly object. It was around 23:00 when Salaz and Saucedo were driving back to their homes after a day's work. When they were four miles west of Levelland, their attention was caught by a bright blue light, flashing in the sky. The bright light proceeded to hover above their truck and, as it did so, the engine died, leaving Salaz and Saucedo stranded in the middle of the road.

At first, they thought that the bright light was lightning, which was a plausible assumption considering that thunderstorms had just passed. As Saucedo exited the vehicle to inspect the truck's engine, he was taken aback when, just three hundred feet away, he saw a rocket-shaped object in the middle of the road. It was approximately two hundred feet long and six feet wide. Each passing second felt like an hour, however, after only a few seconds, the object shot up into the sky, emitting bright yellow flames at its end. The object shot up with such velocity that a heat wave hit Saucedo, causing him to fall to the ground. For the next three minutes, the rocket-shaped object illuminated the entire sky. Once the object disappeared out of sight, the truck's engine revived. Saucedo recounted the event as follows:

> "I was traveling north and west on route 116, driving my truck. At about four miles out of Levelland, I saw a big flame, to my right front...I thought it was lightning. But when this object had reach to my position it was different, because it put my truck motor out and lights. Then I stop, got out, and took a look, but it was so rapid and quite some heat that I had to hit the ground. It also had colors - yellow, white - and it looked like a torpedo, about two hundred feet long, moving at about 600 to 800 miles an hour."[87]

Saucedo ran back to his truck and drove as fast as his vehicle would allow him to until they arrived at Whiteface, ten miles from Levelland. There, Saucedo found a phone booth and called A.J. Fowler, the officer on duty at Levelland. Thinking Saucedo was a drunk, the officer did not take this report seriously. Within a few minutes, several other reports started coming in from individuals all over Levelland.

---

87. J. Allen Hynek, *The UFO Experience: A Scientific Inquiry*, (Chicago: Henry Regnery Company. 1972), 260,

Just fifty minutes later, a second encounter was reported. Jim Wheeler was driving four miles east of Levelland when he had to bring his car to a stop after he had noticed a peculiar object in the middle of the road. In front of him was a two hundred-foot, egg-shaped object. At the same moment, his car engine died and the headlights went off, leaving him in the dark road with an unidentifiable and bizarre object straight ahead. Just like the previous report, after a few seconds, the egg-shaped object shot up toward the sky and disappeared out of sight. It was only until the object disappeared that the car's engine came back to life. In his official report, Wheeler described the object as a "brightly lit egg-shaped object, about 200 feet long."[88]

Approximately an hour after the first sighting was reported, Newell Wright, a nineteen-year-old Texas Tech student, was driving back home when "his car engine began to sputter, the ammeter on the dash jumped to discharge then back to normal, and the motor started cutting out like it was out of gas."[89] His car engine eventually died, and the headlights went off, too. As he exited the vehicle, Wright noticed that not too far away in the distance was a pear-shaped object, 125 feet long, in the middle of the road. Wright described the object to be made of a material similar to aluminum. Frightened at the odd sighting, Wright ran back to his vehicle where he proceeded to lock the doors and just stare straight ahead at the object, helplessly trying to restart the engine, although to no avail. After several minutes, the pear-shaped object shot up to the sky and disappeared in a split second, and it was only then that he was able to restart his car's engine and drive away.

---

88. Hynek, *The UFO Experience: A Scientific Inquiry,* 160.

89. Hynek, *The UFO Experience: A Scientific Inquiry,* 161.

Another sighting, which was not reported to officials, was witnessed by a couple who were driving along State Farm Road 1073, just a few miles away from where Saucedo and Salaz had had their encounter. Although the couple did not see any egg-shaped objects in the sky or on the ground, their vehicle was affected after a bright flash of light lit up the night sky. Throughout their drive, they noticed that their car radio had gone static a few times, but they did not think too much of it. At one point, a bolt of bright light lit up the entire sky and the car engine died, together with the headlights and car radio. The couple did comment on how strong the lightning must have been in order for the car's engine to die. After a couple of seconds, they were able to restart the car and continue on their journey.

The following day the husband heard of the multiple reports that were made by individuals stating their cars had malfunctioned following a brightly-lit object appearing in the sky and in the middle of the road. Although he and his wife did not see any objects, he assumed that this must have been the same phenomenon.

Officer Fowler had received multiple phone calls the night of November 2 from different people, all reporting the same incident. After receiving all those calls, Sheriff Weir Clem and Deputy Pat McCulloch were sent out to patrol the streets of Levelland, attempting to find the egg-shaped object that multiple people had reported seeing. At around 01:30, as they were driving along Oklahoma Flat Road, five miles from Levelland, the two officials noticed an oval-shaped light. The object was so bright that the two compared it to a red sunset. Just 300 yards from their position, the object lit up the entire highway, flying at an alarmingly low altitude. The object only remained in view for a few seconds before it disappeared out of sight.

By the end of the night, a total of fifteen reports were made, all of which were made by individuals in the Levelland area. The reports all described an oval-shaped object landing on the ground or hovering in the sky, which caused their car's engines and electrical systems to fail. The systems and the car would only start functioning again after the object disappeared out of sight.

The Investigation

The Levelland sightings were investigated by the United States Air Force's Project Blue Book, led by Dr. J. Allen Hynek at the time. Early on in the investigation, Hynek made it clear that the sightings and the vehicles malfunctioning could not have been a coincidence. A total of fifteen reports were made by independent individuals, all reporting the same incident.

"In terms of probabilities, that all seven cases of separate car disablement and subsequent rapid, automatic recovery after the passage of the strange illuminated craft, occurring within about two hours, could be attributed to coincidence is out of the statistical universe—if the reports are truly independent (and they are, according to the tests we've used throughout)." Hynek wrote.[90]

Surprisingly, even though these reports are evidently not a result of a weather phenomenon, the air force concluded that the sightings were ball lightning or St. Elmo's fire, which is luminous plasma created by a strong electrical field in the atmosphere. Before analyzing these two hypotheses, one important factor that must be mentioned is the fact that the air force investigator only spent a couple of hours at Levelland. How could fifteen independent reports be investigated in just a matter of hours? How could

---

90. Hynek, *The UFO Experience: A Scientific Inquiry,* 164.

the air force come to a definite conclusion if a proper investigation had not been carried out?

The first hypothesis proposed by the air force was that the sightings were ball lightning. Donald Menzel, an astronomer, astrophysicist and perhaps the biggest UFO skeptic, describes ball lightning as a "luminous ball whose diameter ranges from a few inches to several feet; the color may be red to orange or blue to white. These lightning balls appear most frequently toward the end of an electrical storm. They can hang motionless or drift in the air, gliding down chimneys and across the floor to radio or TV sets, float, a few inches above the ground or high in the sky."[91]

Apart from the bright lightning and the bright color, this explanation does not describe the reports made by the fifteen witnesses. Although Menzel provides an explanation as to what ball lightning is, he fails to explain how this correlates to an egg-shaped object landing on the ground, malfunctioning vehicles, and then shooting back up toward the sky and disappearing. It seems as though this explanation was used solely because thunderstorms were reported in the area on the day of the sightings.

The second hypothesis is that the sightings were St. Elmo's fires. This weather phenomenon appears as a bright light in the sky, very similar to ball lightning. Once again, this explanation does not corroborate with the witness reports. How can a brightly lit, egg-shaped object that causes a vehicle's engine to die and then shoots up in the sky before disappearing, be confused with bright plasma in the sky? The two are vastly different and difficult to misidentify.

---

91. Donald H. Menzel and Lyle G. Boyd, *The World of Flying Saucers: A Scientific Examination of a Major Myth of the Space Age* (Garden City, NY: Doubleday, 1963), 176.

This investigation was met with a lot of backlash. Dr. James McDonald, a senior physicist, spoke at the United States House of Representatives in 1968 and argued how it could not have been possible that these sightings were natural phenomena caused by an electrical field in the sky. McDonald stated that there was no lightning or thunderstorms; there was only a slight trace of rain. Moreover, at least ten vehicles were stopped and had malfunctioned due to the UFO's presence, and this was most certainly not a coincidence. Hynek, too, stated that the conclusion the air force came to was hasty and inaccurate. In his book titled *The UFO Experience* Hynek stated: "Observers reported overcast and mist but no lightning. Besides, had I given it any thought whatever, I would soon have recognized the absence of any evidence that ball lightning can stop cars and put out headlights."[92]

Conclusion

The facts speak for themselves. It is evident that the egg-shaped object was not a natural weather phenomenon. The air force's reaction and investigation foreshadowed how future UFO cases were to be handled; by completely dismissing them. As Hynek and McDonald stated, the explanations were insufficient and evidently not supported by any evidence.

---

92. Hynek, *The UFO Experience: A Scientific Inquiry*, 165.

Chapter 24
Encounter of the Third Kind

Date: April 24, 1964
Location: Socorro, New Mexico, United States

The following case is indubitably one of the most convincing and compelling encounters of the third kind. Not only did the witness report seeing an extraterrestrial aircraft land on the ground, but also reported seeing two humanoid figures alongside the aircraft. What follows is the account of Lonnie Zamora who, on April 24, 1964, had an otherworldly encounter.

Zamora was a sergeant police officer stationed in Socorro, New Mexico. It was around 17:45 when Zamora was on duty, chasing a speeding car in Socorro. At some point during the chase, Zamora heard a loud roar that lasted for at least ten seconds, followed by a large bluish orange flame just above where a dynamite shack was located. Naturally, Zamora assumed there had been an incident and the dynamite shack had exploded, and thus, he abandoned the car chase and began driving toward the location.

As he reached the top of the hill beyond where the shack was located, approximately two hundred yards away from his position, he noticed a shiny object and two figures standing beside it. From afar, the object appeared to be an upside down car, and Zamora initially thought that the two people needed assistance. As he started driving toward them, he noticed they were dressed in all white overalls. As the car approached the shiny object, one of the beings spotted Zamora and seemed startled by his presence. Zamora noted how they did not seem to have any unfamiliar characteristics, but, given that he only got a glimpse at the beings, he was unable to provide a detailed description of their appearance.

Zamora contacted the sheriff's office and informed them that he was assisting in a car accident and requested assistance. As he got closer to the object, he noticed that the shiny object was not a flipped car, as he had initially thought. Straight ahead was an aluminum, white-colored, oval-shaped object, which had an unusually smooth surface. In its center was a red insignia, which he assumed to be a lettering of some sort. Things continued to get even more bizarre. Once Zamora exited his vehicle, he heard a second loud roar, which rose in frequency. He also noted that as the frequency got louder, the oval-shaped object started ascending from the ground and a large, bluish orange flame radiated from beneath it. Zamora assumed that the object was about to explode so he turned and started running as fast as he could toward his vehicle, tripping and falling to the ground in the process. He covered his face expecting an explosion to happen at any second, but the roar simply dissipated.

As he lifted his head, he saw the object move away from him toward the dynamite shack, just fifteen feet off the ground. The object was moving at an incredible speed. It flew beyond the Mile Canyon mountains and disappeared in a matter of seconds. Once Zamora reached his vehicle, he radioed the sheriff's office once again and informed them of what he had just experienced.

Before going into the investigation, Zamora's sighting was confirmed by a second witness who was driving north of Highway 85 (now Old Highway 85) at the time. The witness stated that he had seen a strange object in the sky and also reported that he had seen a police car going up the hill toward the object's location.

The Investigation

Shortly after the object disappeared, State Patrol Sergeant Samuel Chavez and United States Army Captain Richard Holder arrived at the scene. The two officers noted how distraught Zamora seemed; he was unusually pale and was sweating profusely. Prior to their arrival, Zamora sketched the shape of the object on a piece of paper and the insignia that was on its surface. Once the area was secure, Zamora took Chavez and Holder to the location where he had first seen the strange aircraft.

At the landing site, they noted depressions on the ground and some brush that was on fire. Holder obtained soil samples and sent them to Dr. J. Allen Hynek for analysis. Once Zamora gained his composure, he was able to describe the encounter in a more detailed manner. He explained how when he had first seen the object, he noticed that it did not have any doors or windows. However, when he fell to the ground, he heard what he thought to be a door shutting closed, which would have explained the humanoids' disappearance. The oval-shaped object also had two legs that emerged from its center to the ground, acting as landing gear.

After a couple of hours, word of the sighting started to spread, and news stations and organizations started arriving at the scene. As the case started getting media coverage, Captain Hector Quintanilla, the head of Project Blue Book at the time, instructed Sergeant David Moody to go to the scene and carry out an investigation on the air force's behalf. Early on in the investigation, Moody was able to confirm that the object could not have been a military aircraft. He had contacted Kirtland Air Force Base and was told that all military helicopters were inside the hangars at the time. Moreover, meteorological stations confirmed that the encounter could not have been caused by atmospheric conditions.

The encounter was also independently investigated by the FBI, which noted that there were four smoldering areas and four depressed areas at the landing site. These depressed areas were sixteen by six inches arranged in a rectangular pattern, approximately twelve feet apart. Both the air force and the FBI stated that the encounter did happen, and they had no reason to believe that it was a hoax. However, they were unable to provide an explanation as to what the object or the humanoid beings were. Quintanilla said of the sighting, "There is no doubt that Lonnie Zamora saw an object that left quite an impression on him. There is also no question about Zamora's reliability. He is a serious police officer, a pillar of his church, and a man well versed in recognizing airborne vehicles in his area. He is puzzled by what he saw, and frankly, so are we. This is the best-documented case on record, and still we have been unable, in spite of thorough investigation, to find the vehicle or other stimulus that scared Zamora to the point of panic."[93]

The soil samples that were given to Hynek revealed interesting factors. The analysis compared the components of the burned soil to regular soil, and the results showed that the burned soil did not contain any foreign materials. This means that there were no propellants of any kind or an unusual radiation level. Four years after the sighting in 1968, Dr. James McDonald, an American physicist and UFO researcher, was able to locate the person who had carried out the laboratory analysis on the soil samples, Mary Mayes. Mayes stated that the analysis on the soil sample showed that there

---

93. National Investigations Committee on Aerial Phenomena, *The UFO Evidence.*

were two organic substances that could not be identified. This implies that the components in the sample were unnatural, contradicting what the air force had concluded. It also proved that the official report published by the air force did not disclose the full details of the analysis and the investigation.

Interestingly, the day after the analysis was carried out, Mayes stated that she and her colleagues were visited by an air force official who took all of their notes and ordered them not to speak about the investigation or the analysis they had just performed.

Conclusion

Zamora's encounter with the unknown may seem to be the perfect case that proves that an extraterrestrial race has visited our planet. Although the air force did not provide an explanation as to what the UFO or the humanoid beings were, they stated that there was not enough evidence to definitely state that this was an encounter of the third kind. With that being said, Hynek himself had interviewed Zamora on numerous occasions and he himself believed that he was being truthful.

I firmly believe that this case is one of the most clear-cut cases that proves the presence of extraterrestrial intelligence. All the evidence and details prove just that. However, it is also evident that even when there is the evidence to support this claim, the air force still does not acknowledge the extraterrestrial hypothesis as a plausible one.

Chapter 25
The Kecksburg Crash

Date: December 9, 1965
Location: Kecksburg, Pennsylvania, United States

One of the most remarkable UFO cases occurred in early December 1965 in Kecksburg, Pennsylvania. This sighting consisted of hundreds of witnesses who not only reported seeing the object, but also the dramatic measures the military undertook to cover up the incident. At approximately 17:00, individuals in Ontario, Canada, reported seeing a bright fireball in the sky. Initially, many thought that this was a meteorite, however, at one point, the object changed its direction and started heading south toward Pennsylvania.

The first official report was made at 18:30 by a woman named Frances Kalp, who at the time, was at her home in Greensburg when her two children ran inside the house and told her that they had seen a "star on fire" crash into the woods.[94] As Kalp and her two children made their way toward the site of the crash, they were taken aback when they saw an oddly-shaped object in the middle of the woods.

---

94. Kevin D. Randle, *Crash: When UFOs Fall from the Sky: A History of Famous Incidents, Conspiracies, and Cover-Ups,* (Franklin Lakes, NJ: New Page Books, 2010), 208.

From half a mile away from the object, Kalp described it as being bright and in the shape of a "four-pointed star."[95]

At that point, seeing the area full of smoke, Kalp took her children back home and phoned *WHJB,* the local radio station in Greensburg, Pennsylvania, to report the incident. At the station, John Murphy, who was the news director, took her call and immediately forwarded her report to the Pennsylvania State Police. Within a couple of minutes, Murphy arrived at the scene, where he immediately noticed that the police had sealed the woods as they started their search for the crashed object. He also noted how they had Geiger counters to record radiation levels. After several minutes, the two officers who were leading the primary investigation, Carl Metz and Paul Shipco, returned to their vehicle and refused to tell Murphy whether they had found a crashed object or not. Given the fact that Kalp and her two children had seen the crashed object in the woods, Murphy found it quite suspicious that the officers refused to answer his question. When he continued pressing for answers, the officers told him to ask the army.

Murphy was not getting any answers from the officers and they even denied him asking further questions, which is why he decided to go to the state police headquarters in Greensburg to talk to the captain himself. When he arrived, he noticed that the building was full of air force personnel. When he did get the opportunity to talk to Captain Joseph Dussia, he asked for an official statement. Surprisingly, Dussia told him that after a thorough search, they failed to locate any object in the woods. Knowing he was not going to get any genuine answers, he left the building. On his way out, he recognized an officer who was part of the search team in the woods. Albeit the fact that just minutes earlier Dussia had told

---

95. Randle, *Crash: When UFOs Fall from the Sky,* 208.

Murphy that nothing had crashed, the police officer confirmed that they had identified and located an object that was pulsating a bright light.

At the crash site, several local residents, as well as television reporters, had now gathered looking for answers. Although the area was sealed for investigation, several individuals managed to enter the woods and got a closer look at the crashed object. One of the individuals was Stan Gordon, one of the leading independent researchers of the Kecksburg crash. Gordon, who started his own investigation that same day, interviewed hundreds of witnesses, one being Jim Romansky, a firefighter who had arrived at the scene shortly after the accident was reported. Romansky stated that the crashed object had "cut a furrow in the streambed and came to rest in a hollow where it was partially concealed."[96] Romansky also described the object as having the shape of an acorn and had a diameter of nine to twelve feet. It had a golden bronze color and at the bottom of it was a band that had hieroglyphic symbols carved on it. Perhaps the most crucial characteristic of the object, which proved that it was not a terrestrial aircraft, was the fact that Romansky and his colleagues failed to locate an engine or any windows, doors, or wings.

As the night set in and people started leaving the site, Bill Weaver, another witness who had come in close proximity to the object, reported seeing military men dressed in white overalls carrying a huge box into the woods. It was at that moment that Weaver was spotted by an army official who instructed him to leave the area. Project Blue Book reports show that the investigation was terminated at around 01:00 when a military flatbed truck arrived at the scene. After a few minutes, individuals stated that

---

96. Randle, *Crash: When UFOs Fall from the Sky*, 212.

they had seen military vehicles escorting the truck. At the back of the truck was an object covered by a large tarp. What was so secretive that the air force had to cover? What was so secretive that the truck had to be escorted by multiple military vehicles?

The Aftermath

Once the truck left the area, the military personnel began to leave as well. However, the following day, details of the incident started to emerge. Several witnesses from different states started discovering metallic fragments on their properties. The material was similar to aluminum foil. However, this was dismissed by the air force as being chaff from aircraft that were carrying out military exercises over the area.

Several other witnesses came forward too, one of whom was Mary Keto, a local resident of Greensburg who had seen a "hovering fireball just above the tree line with blue smoke coming up."[97] Other eyewitnesses included firefighters who were the first to arrive at the scene. An unnamed firefighter stated that although they found several fires in the woods, they were unable to locate what had caused it. Newspapers published articles with headlines such as "'Unidentified Flying Object Falls Near Kecksburg" found in the Greensburg, Pennsylvannia, *Tribune-Review* and "Army, Police Seal Off Woods in UFO Probe" in the *Boston Record American*. It was clear amongst the individuals who were at the site that an extraterrestrial object had crashed in the woods. This was also supported by the military's reaction to the crash. If the object that had crashed was a meteorite, it would have been quite odd for the military to take such drastic

---

97. Randle, *Crash: When UFOs Fall from the Sky*, 208.

measures to conceal the fact that a meteor had crashed. After all, it would have been a natural phenomenon.

An Official Explanation

The first explanation that was provided by Project Blue Book stated that the crashed object was a meteorite. This theory immediately contradicts the explanation of the Pennsylvania state police, which originally stated that no objects were located at the crash site. However, even if it was the case that an object had crashed, it most certainly was not a meteorite. Ivan Sanderson, a biologist, carried out his own investigation. He interviewed several witnesses and compiled a detailed account of all the reported sightings. From the statements, Sanderson concluded that the object had traveled in a clear trajectory, from the northwest to the southeast. It remained visible for around six minutes, which means that it was travelling at one thousand miles per hour. If these calculations and details are accurate, this makes the object too slow to be a meteorite.

Moreover, the general description of the object does not match up with that of a meteorite. If one takes a look at the general crash site of a meteorite, one would notice that there would be a massive crater. Not only was this missing, but individuals reported seeing a fully compact acorn-shaped object. The object, which was golden bronze in color, had hieroglyphic symbols carved on its lower half. We must also ask why such a drastic response was taken by the military if it was simply a meteorite that had crashed. Why was the crash site sealed and treated as top-secret if it was simply a natural phenomenon?

In 2005, NASA stated that they had analyzed metal fragments that were collected from the Kecksburg crash site. The analysis showed that the metal was from Cosmos 96, a Russian satellite.

The space agency stated that the satellite had re-entered the earth's atmosphere and broke up; crashing into the woods in Kecksburg. Conveniently, when investigators started asking questions, NASA stated that they had lost all records relating to the investigation and analysis. The most recent publication states that this possibility is an unlikely one. The publication states the following: "Investigations of photographs and sightings of the fireball indicated its path through the atmosphere was probably too steep to be consistent with a spacecraft re-entering from Earth orbit and was more likely a meteor in a prograde orbit from the vicinity of the asteroid belt, and probably ended its flight over western Lake Erie. U.S. Uncertainties in the orbital information and reentry coordinates and time make it difficult to determine definitively if the fireball could have been the Cosmos 96 spacecraft."[98]

Conclusion

As with every other UFO case, the government did not offer a conclusive explanation. The two explanations that were theorized contradicted the statements that were given by the police department on the day. Apart from that, even if we do consider the meteorite hypothesis, the details provided by the witnesses do not match up with that of a meteor. Although this case remains unsolved and open, the facts speak for themselves. One thing we can conclusively say is that the air force did not want the public to find out what had truly crashed in the forest.

---

98. National Aeronautics and Space Administration, "Cosmos 96," NASA Space Science Data Coordinated Archive, accessed September 14, 2020, https://nssdc.gsfc.nasa.gov/nmc/spacecraft/display.action?id=1965-094A.

Chapter 26

Encounter in
the Rendlesham Forest

Date: December 26 and 28, 1980
Location: Rendlesham, England

The Rendlesham UFO encounter is known to be one of the most acclaimed cases in the United Kingdom. On two separate occasions, unidentified lights were observed in the Rendlesham woods near the Royal Air Force Woodbridge station. The reason why this case is so significant in UFO history is due to the compelling amount of evidence, including physical traces at the landing site, witness statements by air force officials, a tape recording of the investigation, and an official memo that was written to the Ministry of Defense. All witnesses were high-level air force officials, making this encounter one of the most credible cases in the study of UFO phenomena.

Bright Lights in the Woods

The first sighting was made on December 26, 1980. In this part of the chapter, we shall examine the witness statements that were signed and provided by five Royal Air Force officials who witnessed the phenomenon. Some statements are more detailed than others, however, what follows are the accounts of the air force personnel who encountered an unidentified flying objects in the Rendlesham forest.

Airman First Class John Burroughs

The first individual who reported seeing strange lights in the sky was Airman First Class John Burroughs, who was on patrol at the east side of the air force base. At around three in the morning, Burroughs' attention was caught by two bright red and blue lights in the sky. The red light was above the blue one and both were flickering on and off. Never having seen the lights at the base, Burroughs decided to drive toward them to get a better look. After a couple of seconds, as he was driving toward their location, he observed a third white light, which was so bright that it illuminated the nearby forest.

Having observed three separate unidentified lights, Burroughs started driving back toward the station to inform Lieutenant Fred Buran, the shift commander on duty. Throughout the drive back to the station, he kept his eyes on the three lights, which by now were in the middle of the woods. Buran, thinking that an aircraft had crashed in the woods, instructed Burroughs, Staff Sergeant Jim Penniston, Airman Edward Cabansag, and Master Sergeant J.D. Chandler to investigate the site and try to locate what had been emitting the bright lights.

Burroughs, together with Penniston and Cabansag, entered the wood to investigate, whereas Chandler monitored the communication and relayed the information back to Sergeant John Coffey, who managed security at the base. Burroughs, together with the two other air force officials, could identify that the lights were in the middle of the woods. In his witness statement, Burroughs stated that the entire woods were lit up and they started hearing "strange noises like a woman screaming."[99] He also noted that the animals at the nearby farms were reacting to the object.

The red and blue lights, which were now in the middle of the woods, started moving erratically toward the open field adjacent to the woods. When the officials reached the fence that separated the woods from the field, they noticed that the lights were now in the sky. Although many skeptics argue that the lights were a misidentification of a nearby lighthouse, Burroughs made the distinction between the two sets of lights. He stated that the lights they were pursuing were significantly brighter than the beacon and were also maneuvering in a way a lighthouse beacon could not.

Having not identified the lights after approximately fifty minutes, Buran instructed the officials to return to their original duties. As they were making their way back to the base, Burroughs and his colleagues observed a blue light to their left, which went out of sight as they continued the drive back to the station.

Lieutenant Fred Buran

Buran was the commanding shift operator on duty on the night of the encounter. Buran stated that at around three in the morning on December 26, 1980, he was notified by Burroughs that strange blue and red lights had been observed in the sky. The sighting was also confirmed by Penniston, who reported seeing the lights in the sky.

Thinking that an aircraft had crashed in the woods, Buran instructed Burroughs, Penniston, and Cabansag to go into the woods and investigate. In his witness statement, Buran noted that the patrol team had gotten very close to the lights, particularly Penniston, who described the lights as being mechanical in nature

---

99. John Burroughs written statement, undated, http://www.ianridpath.com /ufo/rendlesham2c.htm.

and having a triangular shape. The next details Buran provided in his witness statement were that he had terminated the search after fifty-four minutes and instructed the officers to return to their original duties. He also noted that Penniston had seemed particularly distraught from the incident. He also noted that he believed that the men had encountered something unnatural in the woods. In a statement submitted to the United States Air Force, Buran wrote, "After talking with [Penniston] face-to-face concerning the incident, I am convinced that he saw something out of the realm of explanation for him at the time. I would like to state at this time that Sergeant Penniston is a totally reliable and mature individual. He was not overly excited, nor do I think he is subject to overreaction or misinterpretation of circumstances. Later that morning, after conversing with Captain Mike Verano, the day shift commander, I discovered that there had been several other sightings."[100]

Airman Edward Cabansag

Cabansag stated that on December 26, 1980, the Suffolk police department had reported seeing strange lights past the east gate of the base. Together with Burroughs and Penniston, Cabansag entered the woods to investigate the unidentified lights. He stated that the entire time the three of them were in the woods they were able to see blue, red, white and yellow lights. Perhaps one of the most important aspects of this report is that Cabansag stated that the yellow light was the beacon light coming from the lighthouse and the three men has distinguished it from the other set of unidentified lights. He also stated that the lights were flickering in a specific pattern.

---

100. Fred Buran, written statement to United States Air Force, January 2, 1981, http://www.ianridpath.com/ufo/rendlesham2c.htm.

As the patrol team were one hundred meters from the edge of the forest, the lights made a quick movement and disappeared instantaneously. The investigation was terminated after fifty minutes or so.

Master Sergeant J.D. Chandler

On that same December day at three in the morning, Chandler was monitoring a radio transmission from Burroughs, who stated that he had observed strange lights in the wooded area at the east side of the base. Chandler stated that Penniston was directed to go to the east gate. Upon his arrival, he too had seen the lights in the sky.

After a few minutes, Penniston requested Chandler's presence at the site. As Penniston, Burroughs, and Cabansag entered the woods, Chandler remained next to the vehicle to report any developments back to the base's security team. During the radio transmissions, Chandler noted that Penniston was approximately fifty meters away from an object, and described the object as being mechanical in nature. Apart from its distinct features, he noted that it was emitting a noise that had made the animals in the nearby farm go berserk.

Penniston, Burroughs, and Cabansag continued to pursue the object and as they reached the end of the field, they were able to locate a lighthouse emitting a beacon of light. In his witness report, Chandler stated that Penniston was able to distinguish the beacon from the unidentified lights they had been pursuing in the woods. In his concluding remarks, Chandler stated, "After talking to the three of them, I was sure that they had observed something unusual. At no time did I observe anything from the time I arrived at RAF Woodbridge."[101]

Staff Sergeant Jim Penniston

Penniston reported that he had received orders to go to the east side as mysterious lights were reportedly seen in the forest. When he arrived at the east gate, he noticed a large yellow glowing light above the trees. In the center of the lights was a pulsating, flickering red light, as well as a continuous blue light.

When they proceeded past the gate, the light was so strong that it had lit up a thirty-meter area. At that point, Penniston was able to positively identify the object as being mechanical in nature. He also reported that the object had moved backwards in a zig-zag manner before they lost sight of it. As the men were ordered back to base, Penniston noticed a blue streaking light to his left, which only lasted for a couple of seconds.

Interestingly enough, unlike the other witness reports, Penniston does not mention seeing the lighthouse, which all the other officials included in their witness reports. Moreover, it is odd that although Penniston was the one who got the closest to the object, his report did not provide a detailed description of the unidentified object itself.

———

Later on that day, at around 10:30, a number of air force officials returned to the woods where the sighting was made. There, they noticed three small depressions in a triangular pattern. It was also reported that there were burn marks and broken branches

---

101. J. D. Chandler, written statement to United States Air Force, January 2, 1981, http://www.ianridpath.com/ufo/rendlesham2c.htm.

on the nearby trees. In the book *UFO Crash Landing?* author Jenny Randles includes an interview with a forester who lived nearby the site. The forester stated the following: "I noticed that the pine trees well above the ground were broken as if something heavy had fallen through from the sky. Branches were also torn off lower down. There were signs of scorching and burning on the forest floor and a series of indentations that indicated that something solid had come down there. There was also evidence that an object may even have been dragged along the ground to remove it from the area."[102]

The air force personnel also informed the local authorities of the findings. In a letter sent to Ian Ridpath, the first journalist to investigate the incident, the chief constable of the Suffolk police force stated that the force had received two reports. The first report was received at 04:11 on December 26, when the object was first seen in the woods and the second at 10:30 when the air force personnel located the indentations in the ground. The following is an excerpt from the letter, dated November 23, 1983: "A further report was received at 10.30 am on December 26, 1980 from a staff member at RAF Bentwaters indicating that a place had been found where a craft of some sort could have landed. An officer attended and the area involved did bear three marks of an indeterminate pattern. The marks were apparently of no depth and the officer attending thought they could have been made by an animal."[103]

---

102. Jenny Randles, *UFO Crash Landing? Friend of Foe?: The Full Story of the Rendlesham Forest Close Encounter*, (London: Blandford, 1998), 183.

103. Chief Constable of Suffolk Constabulary, letter, November 23, 1983, http://www.ianridpath.com/ufo/police.htm..

Monitoring Nuclear Arsenal?

Since the sighting in 1980, an important piece of information that provides more insight into the sighting has been kept from the public. It wasn't until 2010 that Lieutenant Halt disclosed that the Air Force Base contained twenty-five bunkers full of lightweight powerful nuclear bombs, ready, in the case of a Soviet invasion. The Bentwaters Air Force Base housed more nuclear bombs than any other military installation in Europe.

On the day of the sighting, it was reported that the strange lights flew over the nuclear storage site, possibly indicating that the visitors were interested in the nuclear arsenal being stored at the base. As we have seen in Chapter 18, it is evident that there is a correlation between UFO sightings and nuclear storage sites. Could it be that these beings visited the most heavily armed air force base in Europe as a way to monitor the nuclear arsenal mankind was in possession of?

Halt's Recording

In the early hours of December 28, 1980, Lieutenant Colonel Charles Halt was at the Royal Air Force Woodbridge base when his colleague informed him that the unidentified lights were spotted once again in the woods. Together with Lieutenant Bruce Englund and Sergeant Monroe Nevels, Halt made his way into the woods to investigate the sighting. The investigation was recorded by Halt on a microcassette recorder, and included radiation readings of the landing site and the identification of the triangular depressions. The recording also included the officials' reactions as they observed the unidentified object firsthand while investigating the woods.

The recording starts with Halt, Englund and Nevels locating the three indentations in the ground. They also started recording the radiation levels using a Geiger counter. Although the counter did not pick up any radiation levels at any of the three indentations, half a millirem was picked up at the center. While these are minor readings, it is interesting to note that the Geiger counter did not pick up any radiation levels at any other locations apart from the center of the depressions.

As Halt, Englund, and Nevels continued on with their investigation, soil samples were taken from the area, however, the analysis of such samples was never declassified and disclosed to the public. Halt mentioned there was a "round abrasion on the tree about three and a half, four inches in diameter."[104] Englund also pointed out the fact that a number of nearby trees were significantly damaged on the side facing the landing site. Shortly thereafter, Englund can be heard on the recording saying that he had seen a bright light in the woods. Halt noticed it immediately too, and he described it as being a small, intense red light.

Although many skeptics, such as astronomy writer and editor Ian Ridpath, have argued that this light could have been the lighthouse, this idea is debunked as Halt and his colleagues reported that the light broke off into different lights and started moving erratically. Halt described one of the lights as "an eye winking at you; moving from side to side."[105] He also noted that when he put a starlight scope (which is an image intensifier) on it, he noticed that it had a hollow but dark center.

---

104. "Transcript of Col. Halt's Tape," http://www.ianridpath.com/ufo /halttape2.htm.

105. "Transcript of Col. Halt's Tape," http://www.ianridpath.com/ufo /halttape2.htm.

When the three men reached the end of the field, they noticed five different lights had emerged in the sky. The lights had an oval shape and they were emitting a bright red color. Directly to their north, Halt noticed that there were two distinct objects in the shape of a half moon "dancing about with colored lights on them."[106] They were estimated to be ten miles out. Halt later explained that the lights remained visible in the sky for a total of two or three hours.

The tape ends by Halt and the two other air force personnel audibly shocked by a beam of light coming down to the ground from one of the above lights. Halt reported that, up until four in the morning, there was still an unidentified light moving erratically above Woodbridge.

The Halt Memo

In 1983, a memorandum written by Halt to the United Kingdom's Ministry of Defense was released under the United States Freedom of Information Act. Dated January 13, 1981, the memorandum recounts the encounter of the unidentified lights seen in the Rendlesham woods on December 26 and 28, 1980. The memo reads as follows:

******

1. Early in the morning of December 27, 1980 (approximately 0300L) two USAF security police patrolmen saw unusual lights outside the back gate at RAF Woodbridge. Thinking an aircraft might have crashed or been forced down, they called for permission to go outside the gate to investigate. The on-duty flight

---

106. "Transcript of of Col. Halt's Tape," http://www.ianridpath.com/ufo/halttape2.htm.

chief responded and allowed three patrolmen to proceed on foot. The individuals reported seeing a strange glowing object in the forest. The object was described as being metallic in appearance and triangular in shape, approximately two to three meters across the base and approximately two meters high. It illuminated the entire forest with a white light. The object itself had a pulsing red light on top and a bank(s) of blue lights underneath. The object was hovering or on legs. As the patrolmen approached the object, it maneuvered through the trees and disappeared. At this time the animals on a nearby farm went into a frenzy. The object was briefly sighted approximately an hour later near the back gate.

2. The next day, three depressions 1.5 inches deep and 7 inches in diameter were found where the object had been sighted on the ground. The following night (December 29, 1980) the area was checked for radiation. Beta/gamma readings of 0.1 milliroentgens were recorded with peak readings in the three depressions and near the center of the triangle formed by the depressions. A nearby tree had moderate (0.05–0.07) readings on the side of the tree toward the depressions.

3. Later in the night a red sun-like light was seen through the trees. It moved about and pulsed. At one point it appeared to throw off glowing particles and then broke into five separate white objects and then disappeared. Immediately thereafter, three star-like objects were noticed in the sky, two objects to the north and one to the south, all of which were about ten degrees off the horizon. The objects moved rapidly in sharp, angular movements and displayed red, green and blue lights. The objects to the north appeared to be elliptical through an 8-12 power lens. They then turned to full circles. The objects to the north remained in

the sky for an hour or more. The object to the south was visible for two or three hours and beamed down a stream of light from time to time. Numerous individuals, including the undersigned, witnessed the activities in paragraphs 2 and 3.

Charles I. Halt, Lt Col, USAF
Deputy Base Commander[107]

★★★★★★

Subsequent Health Problems

Many individuals who come into close contact with an unidentified and potentially extraterrestrial aircraft have reported health problems after the encounter. For Airman John Burroughs, the ensuing months and years were afflicted with mysterious and unprecedent health issues.

Shortly after the encounter at the Rendlesham forest, Burroughs started developing symptoms that resembled radiation exposure. Unfortunately, this was only the beginning of what would be years of fighting with authorities to acquire the treatment and financial aid Burroughs needed. In 2011, as part of his routine medical examination, the doctors were surprised when they found that Burroughs' mitral valve had failed, causing a heart murmur. Things took an even stranger twist when the doctors were unable to access Burroughs' medical records. Each time they asked the Air Force for access, they were informed that his files were classified. The air force even went on to state that Airman Burroughs was not employed at the time of the UFO sighting and was only enrolled in 1982, two years after the encounter.

---

107. Charles I Halt, memorandum to United Kingdom's Ministry of Defense, January 13, 1981, http://www.ianridpath.com/ufo/appendix.htm.

It took years of legal proceedings for Burroughs to acquire the veteran's disability benefits. In 2012, with the help of Cheryl Bennett, the former aide of Senator John McCain was able to prove that Burroughs' health deterioration was a result of the radiation present in the forest during the night of the encounter. Two documents in particular showed that the site at which the unidentified aircraft was sighted had high levels of radiation. This revelation is what got the US Veterans Association and Department of Defense to pay for the medical treatment.

Conclusion

Before going over the possible explanations for these two sightings, I will provide a condensed summary of what happened on the twenty-sixth and the twenty-eighth of December.

The First Sighting

At 03:00, Airman Burroughs reported seeing blue, red, and white lights in the sky at the east side of the RAF Woodbridge base. The lights were observed by four other air force personnel: Buran, Penniston, Cabansag and Chandler. As they entered the area, the lights were seen in the middle of the woods, which then started moving erratically backwards toward the open field. After the rapid movement the lights disappeared, however, they were identified shortly after in the sky. When the field was inspected in the morning, three indentations were located on the ground, supposedly where the object had landed.

The Second Sighting

The second sighting was made by Halt, Englund, and Nevels as they were investigating the woods. During the investigation they were able to locate the three indentations in the ground, which were assorted in a triangular shape. In the middle of the triangle, the Geiger counter picked up a higher radiation reading. A bright red light was seen in the middle of the woods that broke off into different balls of lights, which made erratic movements before disappearing shortly thereafter. A total of five bright lights were then located in the sky for a period of two to three hours. Two of the lights were described as having a half-moon shape, and at one point, a beam of light came down to the ground from one of the light sources.

The details and reports were made by high-level Air Force personnel. The high credibility of these individuals is what makes this case so compelling and convincing. However, were the unidentified lights simply a misidentification of the beacon light coming from the lighthouse or was it an extraterrestrial aircraft?

The former explanation is what makes the most sense to many skeptics such as Ian Ridpath. Amongst many other researchers, Ridpath argues that the lights seen in the forest were coming from the nearby Orford Ness lighthouse. However, does this explanation match up with the reports given by the witnesses? As we can see from the witness reports, on December 26, the lights were first seen by Burroughs at the east side of the base. Burroughs reported seeing red and blue lights, which do not match up with the color of the yellow beacon light. Moreover, this theory does not explain the five separate lights seen in the sky, nor the erratic movements the objects carried out.

If one takes into account Halt's investigation, this explanation does not seem to suffice either. Firstly, three indentation marks were located on the ground and a radiation reading was picked up at the center. This would not have been caused by a beacon light coming from a lighthouse. Moreover, this hypothesis does not explain what the red light in the forest was, nor the numerous lights that it dispersed into.

However, what I believe is one of the most important factors of this case is Halt's memorandum to the Ministry of Defense. I find it hard to believe that Halt, as well as his colleagues, would have been unable to differentiate a beacon of light coming from a lighthouse to what seemed to be a mechanical object, as Penniston described. Moreover, the encounter in the Rendlesham forest must have had a big enough impact on Halt for him to report it to the Ministry of Defense, potentially undermining his status and position in the air force.

Part 3
Military Pursuits

Military pilots have been witnessing strange lights and strange objects in the sky since the beginning of aviation. Many pilots have come face-to-face with the unknown and have also pursued such objects, only to find out that these aircraft are infinitely more advanced and superior than any military aircraft. As we shall see, in some cases, individuals have also lost their lives or have simply disappeared off the face of the Earth as they were chasing a UFO.

The following cases prove just how serious the UFO phenomenon is. The truth of the matter is that even though the air force disregards UFO reports and attributes the same explanations to the sightings, military jets are often scrambled and ordered to intercept. When an object infiltrates a country's airspace, this is deemed a threat. The object could easily be a foreign aircraft about to bomb the country, or even a missile. The characteristics of the objects pursued by military aircraft—from their unusual shapes, to their lack of wings and exhaust plumes—prove that the objects could not have been manufactured on Earth. Moreover, these objects' maneuverability and capabilities also prove that they are interplanetary in origin. They simply do not abide by the laws of physics and aerodynamics that every terrestrial aircraft is bound by.

Although military pilots may expect to encounter other fighter jets in the sky, it is unlikely that they would have contemplated coming face to face with an extraterrestrial aircraft. As we shall see in the following chapters, there have been numerous instances in which military pilots have shared the sky with an unknown and more capable and advanced aircraft. Some have lived to tell the story, others have not.

Chapter 27

The Foo Fighters

Date: 1944
Location: Worldwide

Throughout World War II, pilots reported seeing strange lights and objects in the sky. Such reports were so common that pilots started referring to these lights as "foo fighters." The phenomenon was also witnessed by radar plotters, who would track unidentified targets on their radars and refer to them as "bogeys." These blips would exceed seven hundred miles per hour, which made the operators think that these targets were supersonic Japanese aircraft. However, the Japanese were not in possession of such technology at the time.

In an article published by the *St. Louis Post Dispatch*, Lieutenant Donald Meiers stated that he had come across three types of foo fighters, "red balls of fire that fly along at wing tip; a vertical row of three balls of fire that fly in front of the planes, and a group of about fifteen lights that appear off in the distance—like a Christmas tree up in the air and flicker on and off."[108]

As we have seen in the previous chapters, it is not uncommon for UFOs to be spotted around military facilities. These UFOs, or

---

108. "Mysterious 'Foo Fighters,' Balls of Fire, Trail U.S. Night Flyers," *St. Louis Post Dispatch*, January 2, 1945.

foo fighters as they were called, seemed to have a particular interest in the global war happening at the time and mankind's self-destructive behaviors.

Foo Fighters at the Battle of Normandy

Starting in June 1944, the number of UFO reports made by aircraft pilots and army officials increased drastically. One of the earliest sightings of a foo fighter was made during the Battle of Normandy. Gunner Edward Breckel was on board the U.S.S. George E. Badger, which was anchored at Omaha Beach. Watching the skies from the deck of the vessel, Breckel noticed a dark cigar-shaped object cross the sky just five miles away. Breckel noted that the aircraft was at a low altitude, approximately fifteen feet above sea level, traveling a very smooth and circular course. The shape and characteristics of the object were very distinct; having no wings, windows or an apparent engine or fuselage. The object remained visible for three minutes before disappearing over the horizon.

In the last week of June 1944, a small cargo vessel was approaching Palmyra, a small island eight hundred miles off Hawaii. The executive officer of the vessel, Edward Ludwig, reported that the vessel had received a message from the Palmyra naval authorities asking for their assistance, as a navy patrol plane had been lost at sea. For hours, Ludwig and his colleagues cruised the body of water, however, they could not locate a single scrap of debris or an oil slick. Twenty-four hours later, the vessel was anchored at Palmyra. This is where the events took an even stranger twist.

As the night set in, Ludwig was on the ship's bridge on watch when he noticed a bright light high up in the sky. At first, he thought that this was a shooting star, but the light then began to get larger in size and began descending toward the vessel. Wishfully thinking that this was the navy patrol plane returning, Ludwig grabbed his binoculars to get a better look, but to his surprise he noticed that the bright light had a round shape and was hovering silently above the vessel. For the next half hour, the object remained above the vessel, drifting silently and smoothly across the sky.

The following morning, Ludwig made a report to the naval lieutenant. He assumed that the UFO's sighting was pertinent to the aircraft's disappearance. Could it have been that the bright spherical light Ludwig had observed was a Japanese aircraft that had shot down the navy patrol plane? This did not make sense to Ludwig and the lieutenant, as they would have located debris. Further confirmations showed that there were no Japanese aircraft in the airspace at the time of the sighting, leaving Ludwig and the lieutenant to wonder what the unidentified flying object could have been. Was it one of the "flying saucers" many pilots had reported seeing in the sky?

The Sightings

The first official foo fighter sighting was made on November 23, 1944, at around 22:00, by Lieutenant Edward Schlueter, Lieutenant Donald Meiers, and Lieutenant Fred Ringwald. The three lieutenants had just left the air force base in Dijon, France, on board a Bristol Beaufighter of the 415th Night Fighter, with the intention of flying over Rhine, Germany. The sky was visibly clear and the lighting inside the cockpit was turned off to enhance their night vision. The pilot on board was Schlueter, whilst Meiers served as the aircraft's radar operator and Ringwald as the intelligence officer and observer of the aircraft.

At one point during the flight, Ringwald noticed lights on the right side, which Schlueter assumed were lights coming from the hills. After a few minutes, the lights started getting closer to the aircraft, which is when the lieutenants on board noticed a row of eight or ten lights starting to emerge. The lights were similar to orange balls of fire and were moving at an incredible speed. In a matter of seconds, the lights veered to the left side and started imitating every turn and maneuver the Beaufighter executed. There was only one explanation: that the enemies were about to unleash an attack. To the three lieutenants' surprise, the aircraft remained in the sky, maneuvering and imitating the fighter jet's every move, only to disappear after a few minutes. Meiers later recounted the story to the *St. Louis Post Dispatch*: "When I first saw the things, I had the horrible thought that a German on the ground was ready to press a button and explode them. But they didn't explode or attack us, they just seem to follow us like will-o-the-wisps."[109]

———

In August of 1944, Captain Alvah Reida was stationed at Kharagapur in India in the 468th Bomb Group. On August 10 around midnight, a total of fifty fighter jets were to fly over Palembang and drop bombs over the Indonesian city. At intervals of two minutes, each plane would fly over the city, drop a bomb and then drop a photo flash bomb to photograph the damage.

Reida was piloting the last plane, flying at an altitude of fourteen thousand feet. As Reida and the rest of the squadron were flying back to base, about twenty minutes into the flight, his copilot informed him that an unidentified bright object was flying at an incredible speed, just five hundred yards off the wing. In his official witness report, Reida described the object as follows: "At that distance it appeared as a spherical object, probably five or six feet

109. "Mysterious 'Foo Fighters,' Balls of Fire, Trail U.S. Night Flyers," *St. Louis Post Dispatch*, January 2, 1945.

in diameter, of a very bright and intense red or orange color. It seemed to have a halo effect."[110]

Having just bombed a city, Reida and his copilot assumed that this object was being radio controlled and sent to shoot down the fighter jets. Going immediately into action, Reida constantly changed direction, at times making sharp ninety degree turns and ascending and descending by two thousand feet. Just like the previous report, the unidentified flying object imitated every move for eight whole minutes. It managed to copy each and every maneuver and turn, always maintaining a five hundred-yard distance. After eight minutes, the object made a sharp ninety-degree turn and accelerated rapidly, disappearing into the overcast above.

––––––

One way of keeping records during wartime was through war diaries. Each diary entry refers to the administration and the execution of an operation, which is later used as a reference by the military to improve its training and tactics, as well as to keep an official record of operations. A diary entry written by the 415th Night Fighter Squadron stationed at the Ochey Air Force Base in France, dated December 2, 1944, makes reference to a foo fighter sighting, which reads as follows: "More Foo-Fighters were in the air last night. The Ops. Report says: 'In vicinity of Hagenau saw two lights coming. Toward A/C from ground. After reaching the altitude of the A/C they leveled off and flew on the tail of Beau for two minutes. And they peeled up and turned away. Eighth mission—sighted two orange lights. One light sighted at ten thousand the other climbed until it disappeared."[111]

110. National Investigations Committee on Aerial Phenomena, *The UFO Evidence*

111. "War Diary 415th Night Fighters Squadron Ochey Air Base, France December 1944," CUFON, entry 23, http://www.cufon.org/cufon/foo.htm.

———

The most well-known foo fighter sighting took place on December 22, 1944. In an article published in the *American Legion Magazine* in 1945, Lieutenant David McFalls and Lieutenant Ned Baker provided a detailed account of their encounters with the unknown.

The two lieutenants were flying at an altitude of ten thousand feet over Hagenau in Germany. It was around 06:00 when Baker noticed two bright lights ascending from the ground. The lights appeared to be large orange glowing balls of light, and upon reaching the altitude of the aircraft, they remained at their tail, mirroring every move. For two whole minutes, Baker and McFalls made sharp turns. However, each time they maneuvered, the objects would keep up, until they steered off and accelerated toward the opposite direction. In their statements, both Baker and McFalls were convinced that whatever the bright objects were, they were being piloted by an intelligent being who had perfect control of the aircraft.

McFalls and Baker's encounter with the unknown did not end there. Just the following day, the two men were once again flying at ten thousand feet when they witnessed a singular bright spherical object "shooting straight up, which suddenly changed to a view of an aircraft doing a wing-over, going into a dive and disappearing."[112] If these aircraft were terrestrial, then they were most definitely being controlled remotely. The maneuverability and speed could not have been carried out or withstood by a human being.

---

112. Jo Chamberlin, "The Foo Fighter Mystery," *The American Legion Magazine*, December 1945, 44.

Explanations

St. Elmo's Fire

Although the foo fighter sightings remain unexplained to this day, a number of explanations have been proposed. The first theory we will analyze is the one provided by the Condon Committee. In the Condon Report, Martin Altschuler, a research assistant for the National Center for Atmospheric Research, stated that the foo fighter sightings were St. Elmo's fire or ball lightning: "The primary difference between ball lightning and St. Elmo's fire is that St. Elmo's fire remains near a conductor. It has been observed to move along wires and aircraft surfaces, sometimes pulsating. Foo-fighters are probably a manifestation of St. Elmo's fire."[113]

This explanation may seem credible and conclusive, most especially if one is not familiar with the reports made or with the characteristics of St. Elmo's fire. The following are characteristics that were common amongst all foo fighter sightings:

1. The UFOs were spherical and had a bright orange glow.
2. The UFOs appeared from nowhere and disappeared into thin air.
3. The UFOs mirrored every move carried out by the fighter jets.
4. All pilots who encountered a foo fighter were convinced that the aircraft was either being piloted by an intelligent conscious being, or was controlled remotely.

When we compare these characteristics to St. Elmo's fire, there is a clear and evident discrepancy. The latter consists of luminous plasma that is usually a bright blue or violet. In no case has

---

113. Condon Committee Report, January 1968, 173.

it been reported that a St. Elmo's fire ascended from the ground and carried out maneuvers identical to that of a fighter jet. Another substantial discrepancy is the general shape and color of the foo fighters, which had a spherical shape and a bright orange glow. It is also unheard of that any weather phenomenon follows fighter-jets for eight straight minutes, disappearing into thin air shortly thereafter.

Nazi Technology

"Floating Mystery Ball is New Nazi Air Weapon" was one of many headlines published in 1944 and 1945 attributing the foo fighter sightings to advanced Nazi technology. This particular article, published in the *New York Times* on December 14,1944, goes on to say that "the new device, apparently an air defense weapon resembles the huge glaze balls that adorn Christmas trees."[114]

This hypothesis is supported by the fact that many of the reported foo fighter cases were made at the same time the Germans began launching V-1 flying bombs. The V-1 bomb, also known as the Nazi flying bombs, consisted of a warhead that weighed more than four thousand pounds and was twenty-seven feet long. The cruise missile was launched from French and Dutch coast facilities and had a range of 160 miles. The V-1 flying bombs were designed specifically to bomb London.

The question is, could the foo fighters have been V-1 bombs? Many newspapers and pilots believed so, however, there are no official military records to support this theory. Apart from that, it is important to note that all witnesses reported that the unidentified objects mirrored every maneuver the fighter jet performed.

---

114. "Floating Mystery Ball Is New Nazi Air Weapon," *New York Times*, December 14, 1944, https://www.nytimes.com/1944/12/14/archives/floating -mystery-ball-is-new-nazi-air-weapon.html.

Although the V-1 bombs were controlled using inertial navigation systems, these missiles did not have the maneuverability the foo fighters seemed to possess. We must also consider the fact that the V-1 engine could be heard from over ten miles away and also had a very apparent exhaust plume that would have been visible from a long distance.

After eight minutes of imitating every maneuver the fighter jet carried out, the foo fighters would simply vanish into thin air. Naturally, if these unidentified objects were the V-1 bombs, this would not have occurred. The bombs would have remained visible in the sky until they gradually went out of sight or until they impacted on the ground. Reports also stated that, prior to their disappearance, the foo fighters would make sharp ninety-degree turns. In September of 1944, the Germans launched the V-2 rocket, which flew on a ballistic arc of more than fifty miles in altitude. These missiles were far superior than their predecessor, as they were almost impossible to shoot down. However, this theory has the same limitations as the V-1 explanation. In actual fact, the V-2 rockets had less maneuverability and were significantly louder and larger.

In reality, we cannot say that the foo fighters were definitely not Nazi aircraft or missiles. We cannot come to a definite conclusion due to the lack of evidence. However, from the reports made by the witnesses, this theory does not sufficiently explain the numerous sightings.

Interplanetary Flying Objects

The final explanation we will examine is the idea that the foo fighters were extraterrestrial in nature. They were aircraft that were either remotely controlled or were being piloted by an intelligent being. This explanation seems to make the most sense when we take into consideration the behavior and the characteristics of these UFOs.

Firstly, the general appearance is coherent to other UFO reports. The spherical shape and glowing light are perhaps one of the most common characteristics of a UFO. Apart from that, if we consider the previous chapters, interplanetary flying objects usually appear from nowhere and disappear in the same fashion. There is no gradual disappearance and the maneuvers carried out are erratic. The fact that the foo fighters mirrored every move of the fighter jet is also a very common characteristic. As we have seen in chapter 12, the UFOs reported over Kaikoura maneuvered in a similar manner; they mirrored every maneuver the aircraft carried out, and this characteristic will remain a common occurrence in the subsequent chapters.

The main reason why this explanation is the most plausible one is due to the fact that there were no known terrestrial aircraft or missiles that could maneuver the way these unidentified aircraft did. Moreover, they displayed characteristics that terrestrial aircraft simply could not possess, such as the absence of an exhaust plume and the lack of wings and engines. This seemed to be a sentiment shared by the pilots as well: "It was said that the foo fighters might be a new kind of flare. A flare, said the 415th [fighter squadron], does not dive, peel off, or turn. Were they to frighten or confuse Allied pilots? Well, if so, they were not succeeding—and yet the lights continued to appear."[115]

---

115. Chamberlin, "The Foo Fighter Mystery," 44.

Chapter 28
Chiles' and Whitted's
Encounter with the Unknown

Date: July 24, 1948
Location: Montgomery, Alabama, United States

The Chiles and Whitted UFO sighting is one of the cases that forced the United States Air Force to initiate an investigation into the numerous UFO reports that were being made. This case has enough evidence that the conclusion the air force's Project Sign came to was that the reported object was interplanetary.

On July 24, 1948, pilot Clarence Chiles and copilot John Whitted were on board the Eastern Airlines DC-3 aircraft, en route to Atlanta from Houston. Both pilots had military experience, Chiles having logged over 8,500 hours. The time was around 02:45 and the aircraft was flying southwest of Montgomery at an altitude of five thousand feet when Chiles noticed a bright light dead ahead. Initially, the two pilots thought that the light was the exhaust from an aircraft that was flying ahead of them. However, they then noticed that whatever was in front of them was disk-shaped and approaching their aircraft at an incredible speed.

The disk-shaped object was flying at such a great speed that it reached their position instantly, with both pilots expecting a collision to happen at any second. Luckily enough, Chiles and Whitted were taken aback as they saw the bright light fly tightly overhead, just seven hundred feet above their aircraft and just barely avoiding a crash. As the light flew overhead, Chiles made a sharp left turn and as the two looked back at the object, they saw it halt and start a steep vertical climb as it disappeared out of sight. The ability of the object to halt so suddenly from such a velocity and to start such a steep vertical climb was incomprehensible. On board the flight, only one other passenger had seen the object streak past the aircraft. The unnamed individual described the object as a "strange, eerie streak of light, very intense."[116] The light was so intense, and everything had happened so quickly that he was unable to make out any other details.

A few minutes after Chiles and Whitted's sighting, a crew chief at Robins Air Force Base in Georgia reported seeing a bright light pass over the base at an incredible speed. Three days later, a third individual came forward. The individual had stated that he was flying commercially over Virginia, North Carolina, when at the same time of Chiles and Whitted's encounter, he saw what looked like a bright shooting star fly rapidly through the sky.

Witness Statements

American physicist Dr. James McDonald interviewed both witnesses separately and the two pilots gave a similar witness statements. Chiles and Whitted both stated that the object could not have been a terrestrial aircraft; its maneuverability and abilities could not have possibly been withstood by a human.

The cigar-shaped aircraft was the size of a B-29 bomber—approximately 99 feet long—but was twice as thick. There were

---

116. Ruppelt, "The Report," 40.

no visible engines or wings, but both Chiles and Whitted described a row of windows that had a bright blue light (similar to burning magnesium) glowing inside. Once the object flew overhead and they looked back at it, they saw that it also had a "bright trail of orange, red flame" shooting out of its end. Beneath the aircraft was also a glowing blue light.

Although the object was enormous in size, it was exceptionally maneuverable. What I find so compelling about this case is the fact that the object was able to maneuver so accurately over the DC-3. The maneuverability and capability prove that the object was being piloted by a highly intelligent being who possessed spatial awareness.

The unidentified flying object was seen by at least three other independent eyewitnesses. The most important eyewitness statement that corroborates and verifies Chiles' and Whitted's story is the one made by the crew chief at Robins Air Force Base in Georgia. If we take a look at the location of the DC-3 at the time of the sighting, given that the UFO passed over the aircraft, it would have passed over Macon, Georgia, which is just two hundred miles away from the air force base.

The Investigation

At the time of the sighting, Project Sign was investigating all UFO reports. This case was highly credible; it had multiple independent witnesses from different locations whose statements substantiated one another. There was no other plausible explanation other than the extraterrestrial hypothesis. No terrestrial aircraft could carry out such maneuvers, and no human being could have endured the G forces.

The investigators at Project Sign wrote up a report titled the "Estimate of Situation," which explained how the object witnessed by Chiles and Whitted was interplanetary. This was the only hypothesis that made sense. The report, which was sent to Air Force Chief of Staff Hoyt Vandenberg, was highly classified. Although the preliminary investigation stated that all evidence showed that the UFO was extraterrestrial, Vandenberg agreed with the conclusion that Dr. J. Allen Hynek had come to. Hynek stated that what Chiles and Whitted had seen was not an interplanetary flying object but a bright meteorite. This statement was endorsed by Dr. Donald Menzel, another astronomer and notable UFO skeptic.

It must be noted that all three individuals who attempted to debunk the extraterrestrial hypothesis were all prominent UFO skeptics, who went to extreme lengths to try and disprove any cases that prove the existence and presence of extraterrestrial life.

Conclusion

Under no circumstances can a meteor possess the characteristics of the reported UFO, or maneuver the same way the object did. It is evident that Vandenberg's own biases influenced the conclusion of the report.

In 1968, Dr. James McDonald spoke in front of the United States Congress and explained how the majority of UFO reports had been poorly investigated and prematurely dismissed. In his concluding statement, McDonald stated the following: "To conclude, then, my position is that UFOs are entirely real, and we do not know what they are because we have laughed them out of court. The possibility that these are extraterrestrial devices, that we are dealing with surveillance from some advanced technology is a possibility I take very seriously."[117]

117. James McDonald, United States House of Representatives hearing, U.S. Government Printing Office, 1968.

Chapter 29

The Gorman Dogfight

Date: October 1, 1949
Location: Fargo, North Dakota, United States

Just a couple of days after the *Estimate of the Situation* was sent to Air Force Chief of Staff Hoyt Vandenberg, another compelling UFO sighting was reported. It was October 1, 1949, in North Dakota. Although just twenty-five years of age, George Gorman was a second lieutenant in the North Dakota Air National Guard and had also served as a veteran fighter pilot during the Second World War. Gorman, together with his colleagues, had just participated in a cross-country mission on board a F-51 Mustang. At around 20:30 Gorman and his colleagues decided to land at Hector Airport in Fargo.

Given that the weather conditions were optimal for a night flight, Gorman decided to keep flying in the area for a few more minutes. It was around 21:00 when Gorman requested permission to land. Given that a Piper Club aircraft was in the area, Gorman had to wait for the aircraft to land first. He was able to make visual contact with the Piper, however, in the distance he also noticed a second aircraft in the sky. Flying from east to west, Gorman saw an intense bright white light, which, at first, he thought was a taillight from another aircraft.

When contacting the Hector Airport Air Traffic Control, George was informed that the only two aircraft in the nearby distance were his own F-51 and the Piper Club, which was now descending to land. As the light got closer to his F-51, he noticed that it was simply a ball of light, without any wings or exhaust plume. It was roughly six to eight inches in diameter and its presence was confirmed by the pilot and passenger on board the Piper Club aircraft. Unable to offer any explanation for what the light was, Gorman made a left turn and decided to pursue the object himself.

He quickly noticed that the ball of light was infinitely faster than his aircraft and the only way that was he was going to be able to get closer to the unidentified aircraft was by making turns to cut the distance. Flying at four hundred miles per hour, Gorman pushed the F-51 to its limits and he noticed that the light, which was straight ahead, pulled a sharp turn and rapidly accelerated toward Gorman. Collision was imminent and Gorman was expecting the worst. However, just like the Chiles and Whitted encounter, the UFO made a sharp turn and just barely avoided his aircraft. Mirroring the turn, Gorman continued his pursuit. In his report, he noted that he had temporarily blacked out due to the excessive speed. As the light accelerated farther away from the F-51, its brightness increased, becoming more intense.

Gorman was now chasing the UFO, which was thousands of feet away. For the second time, the object slowed down and started accelerating toward his aircraft once again. This time, the aircraft broke off into a vertical climb before it reached the F-51. Gorman attempted to mirror the same climb, but his aircraft could not handle such a steep gradient. The F-51 started stalling once it reached fourteen thousand feet but the bright light was still at least two thousand feet above.

At this point, the chase was occurring over the airport and air traffic control operator L.D. Jensen was witnessing the entire encounter through his binoculars. The light descended until it leveled at the same altitude of the F-51, and as it did so, it started accelerating toward his plane, for what now was the third head-on approach. Once again, the object broke off into a vertical climb before it reached his aircraft. However, this time, it continued the climb until it disappeared out of sight. Unable to locate the light, Gorman was forced to break off the pursuit at 21:27.

"I am convinced that there was definite thought behind its maneuvers," Gorman said. "I am further convinced that the object was governed by the laws of inertia because its acceleration was rapid but not immediate and although it was able to turn fairly tight at considerable speed, it still followed a natural curve. When I attempted to turn with the object, I blacked out temporarily due to excessive speed. I am in fairly good physical condition and I do not believe there are many, if any pilots, who could withstand the turn and speed effected by the object and remain conscious. The object was not only able to out-turn and out-speed my aircraft...but was able to attain a far steeper climb and was able to maintain a constant rate of climb far in excess of my aircraft."[118]

The Investigation

Within a few hours after the sighting, investigators from Project Sign arrived at Fargo and interviewed Gorman, the two pilots on board the Piper Club and the two radio control operators who had witnessed the encounter.

---

118. Curtis Peebles, *Watch the Skies! A Chronicle of the Flying Saucer Myth*, (Washington, DC: Smithsonian Institution Press, 1994), 26.

The investigators checked the F-51 for an unusual radioactive level and the Geiger counter did indeed show that Gorman's aircraft had a higher radioactive level than the other F-51 aircraft. The high radioactive levels indicated that the UFO was atomic-powered, which ruled out the possibility of the object being a weather balloon or any aircraft. For a second time, the radars were checked, and the investigators confirmed that there had been no registered aircraft or weather balloons in the vicinity at the time of the sighting. Thus far in the investigation, it was becoming apparent that this case involved an extraterrestrial aircraft. Just like the Chiles and Whitted sighting, there were no other plausible explanations.

A few days after the initial investigation, Air Force Chief of Staff, General Hoyt Vandenberg rejected the idea of the object being extraterrestrial in nature and instructed another department to carry out a second investigation. As the months went by, the investigation was passed from one organization to another; no one could come up with a conclusive explanation. At the end of the year, an explanation was finally deduced. The UFO Gorman had pursued was a light weather balloon that had been released from Fargo at 20:50. The high radioactive levels were a result of the F-51 flying at a high altitude that resulted in the aircraft being hit with more cosmic rays.

The National Weather Service verified this statement and stated that the weather balloon was released from the weather station and traveled with the wind's direction, which was westward. After ten minutes in the air, the balloon reached Hector Airport where the two radio control operators reported seeing the UFO. The official report stated that the maneuvers the UFO had carried out were illusions. The report also suggested that the light could have been confused for a bright Jupiter, even though at the time of the sighting it was in the southwestern sky and would have been practically impossible for Gorman to mistake it for a moving aircraft.

Conclusion

It is still unclear how a weather balloon or a planet could have been mistaken for a moving aircraft. Once again, Vandenberg's own biases influenced the objectivity of the investigation. For over half an hour, Gorman chased an object that could not have been anything other than an interplanetary object. No terrestrial aircraft could possibly execute the same maneuvers the unidentified object had.

Even though this case is a perfect example of an encounter with an extraterrestrial aircraft, the air force refused to even consider such a hypothesis; perhaps because by acknowledging such a thing would mean the public would become aware that the military is not as powerful and in control as everyone believes. How can any government acknowledge the fact that there is a race out there that is infinitely more advanced and superior? Wouldn't that affect the control the governments have over the people? Could it be that acknowledging such a thing would make the military seem somewhat powerless when compared to these extraterrestrial beings? Would acknowledging such a possibility affect the power and control the government has over its civilians? As UFO researcher Stanton Friedman stated, "nationalism is the only game in town."

Chapter 30
UFOs Outmaneuver F-61

Date: October 15, 1948
Location: Fukuoka, Japan

Just like George Gorman's case, the following case includes a cat-and-mouse chase between a fighter jet and an unidentified flying object. This time, the UFO was tracked on airborne radar and six interception attempts were made. On one occasion, visual contact was also made with the UFO. This case was one of the very first cases in which the pursued UFO was tracked on radar. As stated in the introduction of this book, when a UFO report includes radar evidence, it makes the case tremendously more credible. Author and former head of Project Blue Book Edward J Ruppelt said of radar and UFO cases: "Then [in 1948] radar came into the picture. For months the anti-saucer factions had been pointing their fingers at the lack of radar reports, saying, "If they exist, why don't they show up on radarscopes?" When they showed up on radarscopes, the UFO won some converts."[119]

It was October 15, 1948 and an F-61 Black Widow fighter was patrolling the skies of Fukuoka, Japan, as part of a usual routine mission. Piloting the F-61 was Lieutenant Oliver Hemphill Jr. with Second Lieutenant Barton Halter as a radio observer. At

---

119. Ruppelt, "The Report," 45.

around 23:05, Halter began picking up an unknown target on his radar, which was five miles straight ahead and slightly below their aircraft. In an attempt to gain visual contact with the object, Hemphill increased the speed to 220 miles per hour, gaining on it. At first, the lieutenants thought that the aircraft must have been a military aircraft from base, but this thought was quickly dissolved.

In a matter of seconds, Halter noticed that the position of the target had changed, and it was now above their aircraft, closing the distance between them. In an instant, the target executed a dive beneath the fighter jet. Pursuing the object, Hemphill followed by mirroring the nose dive.. In a split second, the target performed a second dive and sped away, even though the F-61 had descended 3,500 feet a minute at three hundred miles per hour. How could any terrestrial aircraft outpace and outmaneuver the F-61, disappearing in a split second? The lieutenants knew full well that no human being would have been able to endure the stressors caused by such a maneuver.

Communicating back with their base, the ground control station confirmed that there were no military or commercial aircraft in the sky. With that being said, on board the fighter jet, Halter picked up another target on radar that was moving at such an incredible speed that it had outdistanced their aircraft immediately. After a couple of seconds, Hemphill made the first and only visual sighting with the UFO. To the starboard position, Hemphill noticed a strange object that had a short and stubby body, similar to a rifle bullet. He also noticed how it did not have any wings or an exhaust plume.

Hemphill immediately made a sharp right turn, but by the time the aircraft carried out the turn, the bullet-shaped UFO had already sped away and had traveled at least ten miles, leaving their aircraft behind. Just a second after the object disappeared, another target was picked up on radar and had passed overhead. Within a few seconds, the fifth interception was made when a target appeared nine miles ahead, traveling at two hundred miles per hour. The fighter jet was traveling at 220 miles per hour and as they closed in at twelve thousand feet, the UFO accelerated and covered over ten miles in just twenty seconds, which means that it must have been traveling at at least 1,800 miles per hour.

"I had an excelled silhouette of the target thrown against a very reflective undercast by a full moon," Hemphill recalled. "I realized at this time that it did not look like any type of aircraft I was familiar with, so I immediately contacted my Ground Control Station and asked for information regarding any aircraft flying in the area. The Ground Control Station informed me there were no other aircraft in the area. I informed them what I had seen and was in contact with them from then on."[120]

The Unidentified Flying Object

Hemphill and Halter made a total of six radar interceptions on the object but just one visual sighting. Although it is assumed that all six interceptions were made of the same UFO, it could have been the case that there were numerous unidentified flying objects in the sky. The visual sighting was made on the third interception, in which Hemphill located an unfamiliar aircraft in the shape of a rifle bullet.

The cat-and-mouse chase lasted for less than ten minutes, in which the speed of the UFO ranged from two hundred miles per hour to over 1,800 miles per hour. Each time the F-61 tried to close down the distance, the UFO would respond by making a rapid acceleration, leaving the aircraft behind. In his witness report, Halter

---

120. Hynek, *The UFO Experience: A Scientific Inquiry*, 136.

stated they must have been shown "a new type of aircraft by some agency unknown to us."[121]

Dr. J. Allen Hynek, one of the air force's consultants, stated that the object must have been equipped with some sort of radar warning equipment, as it seemed to have been aware of the F-61's whereabout at all times, and responded accordingly to the jet's position in space.

Conclusion

As Ruppelt stated, for many years, skeptics had argued that if extraterrestrials did visit our planet then they would show up on radar. Now that there have been numerous cases that include radar evidence, it is still insufficient to prove to skeptics that extraterrestrials do visit our planet.

Although this case is officially listed as unidentified, the only explanation that suffices is the extraterrestrial hypothesis. The object's appearance, together with its maneuverability and radar evidence makes this encounter one of the most convincing and compelling cases.

---

121. Project Blue Book report, page 23, http://www.nicap.org/docs /481015japan_docs.pdf.

Chapter 31
The Death of Thomas Mantell

Date: January 7, 1948
Location: Franklin, Kentucky, United States

Individuals like Gorman, Chiles, and Whitted, to name a few, have lived to tell their stories of coming face-to-face with the unknown. The following encounter is unlike any other. I firmly believe that this case shows just how serious the phenomenon is. Individuals have lost their lives pursuing unidentified flying objects they encountered during their flights. One such individual is Thomas Mantell, who on January 7, 1948, lost his life when pursuing a UFO.

The Incident

Thomas Mantell was a twenty-five-year-old air force officer and a Second World War veteran. Mantell was awarded the Distinguished Flying Cross and Air Medal for his service. With over two thousand hours of flying experience, Mantell was an F-51D Mustang pilot for the Kentucky Air National Guard.

On January 7, 1948, at 13:15, Technical Sergeant Quinton Blackwell, the radio control operator at Godman Air Force Base outside Louisville, Kentucky, received a call from the Kentucky State Highway Patrol informing him that they had spotted an unusual aircraft in the sky. The highway patrol wanted to know if there were any military exercises underway or if there were any military aircraft in the sky. The base confirmed that there were no military aircraft or exercises happening at that current moment. The air force base contacted the flight service at Wright-Patterson Air Force Base, which confirmed that there were no military aircraft in the area.

Within twenty minutes, the highway patrol started receiving numerous calls from individuals reporting the same sighting. The calls were made predominately from the west side of Louisville. All reports described a strange circular object with a diameter of roughly three hundred feet. The sky was cloudless, making the object very easy to spot. Around 13:45, the tower operators at Godman Air Force Base made a visual sighting themselves. The two operators could certainly surmise that the object was not a weather balloon. They then forwarded the report to flight operations, where Colonel Guy Hix ordered four F-51 fighter jets to intercept. Captain Thomas Mantell was the flight leader of the squadron. Given that they had just returned from a flight mission, one of the fighter jets was running low on fuel and thus had to abandon the mission.

The remaining three aircraft, which were piloted by Mantell, Lieutenant Albert Clements and Lieutenant Buford Hammond, continued on their mission to identify what the circular aircraft was. Mantell was leading the pursuit, and at an altitude of ten thousand feet, he made visual contact with the object, which he described to be tremendous in size and having a metallic shiny surface. The object initiated a vertical climb and Mantell followed, even though his aircraft was not equipped with enough oxygen levels. Shortly into the pursuit, the object outpaced all three fighter jets and the two other wingmen frantically attempted to communicate with Mantell, who, at that point, was still pursuing the UFO.

All three aircraft were running low on fuel and oxygen levels. Continuing the pursuit, Mantell started a vertical climb and had gone out of sight—even at fifteen thousand feet, Clements and Hammond were unable to locate Mantell or the disk-shaped object. Climbing a further seven thousand feet, they were still unable to locate any aircraft. At that point they were putting their lives on the line. Clements and Hammond eventually had to return to base, leaving Mantell behind. The last transmission message that Mantell had made to the radio operators was the following: "It's above me and I'm gaining on it. I'm going to twenty thousand feet."[122]

Unfortunately, that was the last anyone had heard from Mantell. Once the wingmen landed at Sandiford Field, they refueled the aircraft and one of them returned to the sky in an attempt to locate Mantell. For hours, the airman patrolled the sky, but his efforts were futile. It was around 19:20 when radio towers from all around the Midwest started making reports of a circular unidentified object flying in the sky. Over a dozen reports were made, all similar in nature and all describing the same UFO.

Back at Kentucky, Mantell's last transmission was made at 15:15 and a search team was immediately sent out to investigate the surrounding areas, attempting to locate any debris that would have indicated that Mantell had crashed. It was shortly after 17:00 when the search team located Mantell's F-51 outside a farm near Franklin, Kentucky. Scattered over half a mile, the search team located the wreckage, as well as Mantell's body inside the broken cockpit. His wristwatch had stopped at 15:18, indicating his time of death.

The death of Mantell shocked everyone. At that period of time, nobody was really taking the UFO phenomenon seriously;

---

122. Ruppelt, "The Report," 32.

many had mocked individuals who came forward and spoke about their encounters, but this case was the turning point. Just a few hours after the accident, two individuals named William Mayes and Glenn Mayes signed an affidavit, in which they stated that they had seen Mantell's aircraft in the sky, circling toward the ground. The two individuals also stated that the aircraft had made a loud noise as it exploded before reaching the ground.

The Investigation

Within a couple of hours after the crash, the air force started receiving queries asking about Mantell's accident. The officers at Project Sign were pressured to come up with an answer fast, and this is when the Venus explanation was put forward. Even before an investigation was made, officers at Project Sign stated that Mantell had mistaken the UFO for a bright Venus. Naturally, this explanation was not well-received. It took them over a year to release an official report on the case, which stated that the UFO was not a bright Venus, but was a weather balloon. Edward J. Ruppelt stated the following in regard to the UFO that Mantell had pursued: "It was said that the UFO might have been Venus, or it could have been a balloon. Maybe two balloons. It probably was Venus except that this is doubtful because Venus was too dim to be seen in the afternoon."[123]

The idea that an experienced lieutenant had lost his life because he was chasing a bright planet, or a weather balloon was not accepted by many and it did not take long for this explanation to be completely disparaged.

At the time of the UFO sighting (15:00), Venus would have been located southwest of Godman whereas the UFO was report-

---

123. Ruppelt, "The Report," 34.

edly seen southwest of Godman. It is the case that the UFO was roughly at the same location where Venus was, however, Venus would not have been bright enough at 15:00 to be visible in the sky, let alone for an experienced pilot to mistake it for an aircraft and chase it down.

We must also take into consideration that the UFO carried out a steep vertical climb. As far as I know, celestial bodies remain in a stationary position in the sky, and this in itself disproves the theory. The Venus explanation was a flawed one and Dr. J. Allen Hynek himself had known this, which is when the latter explanation was provided.

The second explanation stated that the UFO was a Skyhook weather balloon, which is a meteorological weather balloon with a diameter of approximately 100 feet. These weather balloons would be released in the sky to collect more accurate information regarding the weather. Each time a weather balloon is released in the sky there are always records that indicate the location of where the balloon was released and at what time. Ruppelt was unconvinced by this theory and he himself had gone through the entire air force and navy records, but he was unable to find any reports.

"Somewhere in the archives of the air force or the navy, there are records that will show whether or not a balloon was launched from Clinton County Air Force Base in Ohio on January 7, 1948," wrote Ruppelt. "I never could find these records. People who were working with the early Skyhook projects 'remember' operating out of Clinton Country Air Force Base in 1947 but refuse to be pinned down to a January 7 flight. 'Maybe,' they said. The Mantell incident is the same old UFO Jigsaw puzzle."[124]

---

124. Ruppelt, "The Report," 39.

Conclusion

Although it truly was a tragedy that Thomas Mantell lost his life, this case shows what has been stated numerous times throughout this book: UFOs pose a threat not only to the country's national security, but also to the pilots who encounter these unidentified objects in the sky.

It is also unclear why the air force stated that the UFO was a weather balloon, given that weather balloons are nonpowered and Mantell was traveling at least 400 miles per hour. In what circumstances would a nonpowered weather balloon overtake a fighter-jet and outmaneuver it?

Chapter 32
T-33 Chases UFO over Sandy Hook

Date: September 10 and 11, 1951
Location: Monmouth, New Jersey, and Sandy Hook,
Connecticut, United States

Over a span of two days, unidentified objects were tracked on military radar and visual contact was also made by a pilot flying a Lockheed T-33 aircraft. The case begins on the morning of September 10, 1951 at the Fort Monmouth radar facility center. Private First-Class Eugent Clark was giving a demonstration for a number of visiting officers on a AN/MPG-1 radar set. Unfortunately for Clark, the demonstration did not go as smoothly as he had planned.

At around 11:18, Clark started picking up an unidentified target on his radar scope, which was flying along the coast line and was presenting an unusually high radar return. The target was flying at an unusually low altitude and was travelling at such a high speed that the automatic setting on the radar could not keep up with it. The AN/MPG-1 radar had the ability to track targets travelling up to 700 miles per hour. The target then crossed the entire coast line in an instant and disappeared near the Sandy Hook coastal peninsula. At the time of the radar sighting, Lieutenant Wilbert Rogers was airborne, piloting a Lockheed T-33 jet trainer with Major Edward Ballard Jr. sitting in the rear seat.

En route to Mitchell Air Force Base in New York, the T-33 was at an altitude of twenty thousand feet, flying over Point Pleasant in New Jersey at 450 miles per hour. The time was around 11:35, just seventeen minutes after the radar sighting had been made back at Fort Monmouth, when Ballard noticed a disk-shaped object flying below their T-33 aircraft. Ballard pointed the sighting out to Rogers who immediately noticed the flying object. The two estimated that the object had a diameter of thirty to fifty feet and had a flat surface without any visible windows or exhaust plumes; it was also not leaving any trails behind, it was simply gliding through the air at an incredible speed. The object was estimated to be traveling at least nine hundred miles per hour. In an attempt to keep up with it, Rogers increased the aircraft's speed up to 550 miles per hour and descended to seventeen thousand feet. Even at this speed, the object was well ahead of them.

The disk-shaped object had crossed the coast in mere seconds. Rogers attempted to mirror the trajectory of the object, however, it disappeared out of sight in a matter of seconds. In an article published in *The Canberra Times* on September 12, 1951, Rogers stated the following: "I don't know if it was a flying saucer, but it sure was something I've never seen before. This could not have been a balloon because it was descending, and no balloon goes that fast."

A few hours after the object disappeared, a second radar sighting was made. At 15:15, the commanding officer at Fort Monmouth started tracking an unidentified blip on radar, which was moving slowly at an altitude of ninety-three thousand feet. Although the object could not be identified, records show that a weather balloon was released at around the same time, leading many to assume that it was the target captured on radar. The following day, September 11, more radar sightings were made at Fort Monmouth. At 10:50, two separate radar scopes picked up an unidentified object at an altitude of thirty-one thousand feet, traveling well over seven hundred miles per hour. Once again, the automatic tracking on both sets of radars could not keep up with the target.

Switching to manual tracking, the radar operators attempted to lock down with the object, however, it was simply too fast. The high velocity made it virtually impossible for them to keep up with it. Just two hours later, at 13:30, another target was picked up on radar. This time, the object was moving erratically at an altitude of six thousand feet, and then even proceeded to remain in a stationary position, signifying that the object must have been hovering. Although the object was close to the radar facility, the radar operators were unable to locate any aircraft outside their windows. Within a few seconds, the target began a vertical climb. The elevation was performed at such an incredible rate that the operators suspected that the target had performed a vertical rise.

The Unidentified Flying Object

In a letter sent to the commanding general at the Wright-Patterson Air Force Base dated September 12, 1951, Lieutenant Wilbert Rogers described the encounter as follows:

★★★★★★

a. The unidentified object, which was sighted at about 11:35 DST Monday, September 10, was round and flat in shape. The size of the unconventional object is estimated to be the size of a fighter or light bomber, thirty to fifty feet in diameter. Only one object was sighted, and no exhaust or trail was observed at any time. […] Only one time was the object seen edgewise and it appeared definitely discus-shaped; the rest of the time it was in a port turn, disappearing as it went out to sea.

b. Time of observation was between 11:35 and 11:40 DST. Duration of the observation was about two minutes.

c. The manner of observation was visual. The object was sighted from an Air Force T-33, which was on a routine training flight from Dover Air Force Base. The T-33 was cruising at twenty thousand feet making good about 450 miles per hour when the object was sighted at least twelve thousand feet below at eleven o'clock position. After making a gradual 120-degree descending turn to seventeen thousand feet the T-33 was going over 500 miles per hour when the object disappeared out to sea.

d. The observers were above and due south of the object when it was first sighted. Observer plane was over Point Pleasant and the object was over Sandy Hook, N.J. when it was first sighted. The object flew southwest over Red Bank and started a gradual port turn to about 120 degrees, crossing just south of Point Pleasant and disappearing out to sea.

e. The observers were 1st Lt. Wilbert S. Rogers and Ballard, Jr. Both men are experienced fighter pilots.

f. Weather ceiling for Mitchell Air Force Base at 1:30, September 10 was twenty thousand feet and seven mile visibility. Pilot reports CAVU at point of sighting object.

g. No meteorological conditions that might account for the sighting existed.

h. No photographs were possible.

i. Observer turned to chase the object but could not stay with it

j. Local aircraft airborne during the observation is unknown.

★★★★★★

The Investigation

The two sightings were investigated under Project Grudge, the predecessor of the air force's Project Blue Book. Lieutenant Henry Metscher, one of the lead investigators of Project Grudge, had come up with several explanations for the four sightings. The official conclusions that Project Grudge came to are as follows:

1. The unidentified aircraft reported by the T-33 pilots was probably a balloon launched by the Evans Signal Laboratory a few minutes before the T-33 arrived in the area.

2. The 11:10 EDST radar sighting on September 10, 1951, was not necessarily a very high-speed aircraft. Its speed was judged only by the operator's inability to use aided tracking and this was possibly due to the operator being excited, and not the high speed of the aircraft.

3. The 15:15 EDST radar sighting on September 10, 1951, was a weather balloon.

4. The 10:50 EDST radar sighting on September 11, 1951, was a weather balloon.

5. The 13:30 EDST radar sighting on September 11, 1951, remains unknown but it was very possible that it was due to anomalous propagation and/or the student radar operators' thoughts that there was a great deal of activity of unusual objects in the area.

Weather Balloon or Flying Saucer?

Project Grudge had attributed the sightings to a pair of weather balloons that were released from Evans Signal Laboratory at 11:12 on September 10. The facility in question is in close proximity to Fort Monmouth, however, were these weather balloons the same object Lieutenant Rogers and Major Ballard had seen in the sky? Were these weather balloons the same targets that the radar operators had tracked on four separate occasions?

The visual sighting was made at around 11:35 over Point Pleasant. In the twenty-three-minute difference between the time when the balloons were released (11:12) and the time of the sighting, a typical radiosonde weather balloon would have reached an altitude of seventeen thousand to eighteen thousand feet. If we consider the weather conditions on the day, given the upper winds, the weather balloon would have traveled to the northeast toward Sea Bright, whereas the UFO traveled southwest over Red Bank. Moreover, Rogers and Ballard stated that the object had made a sharp 120-degree turn, before speeding out to sea at an incredible velocity (it most definitely exceeded 700 miles per hour, which is unduly faster than the velocity of a weather balloon). We must also consider the fact that the airmen described the object as having a disk-shape and a flat surface, this naturally does not match up with the characteristics of a typical weather balloon. Another factor that proves that the UFO in question was not a weather balloon is the fact that, given the altitude the UFO was at, the weather balloon would have had a diameter of fifteen feet (as opposed to the thirty to fifty feet in diameter the UFO reportedly had).

Conclusion

So, with all the information presented, was the UFO a weather balloon? Ruppelt, who would later lead Project Blue Book, did not believe so. He stated that there was no comparison between the reported disk-shaped UFO and the released weather balloons. There are too many factors that simply disprove this hypothesis. Although Project Grudge refused to acknowledge so, neither Ruppelt nor Metscher were able to explain what the unidentified flying object was: "Lieutenant Metscher took over and, riding on his Fort Monmouth victory, tried to show how the pilots had seen the balloon. He got the same thing I did—nothing"[125]

125. Ruppelt, "The Report," 114.

Chapter 33
Colonel Gordon Cooper's Encounters with the Unknown

Colonel Gordon Cooper was a United States Air Force pilot, an aerospace engineer, and one of the astronauts involved in NASA's Project Mercury, which was the first human spaceflight program with the goal of sending humans to space and returning them safely back to Earth. Cooper also flew as command pilot of the Gemini mission, logging a total of 222 hours in space and over seven thousand hours in the sky.

Apart from having a memorable career in the air force and with the space agency NASA, Cooper was also an avid believer in extraterrestrial life. In his autobiography *Leap of Faith*, Cooper wrote, "Ever since I looked up at the stars as a boy, I've felt that there had to be some interesting forms of life out in space for us to discover and get acquainted with."[126] Cooper reported seeing multiple UFOs when flying over West Germany in 1951, and also reported that a UFO landed on a dry lake bed at Edwards Air Force Base in Southern California.

---

126. Cooper and Henderson, *Leap of Faith*, 89.

UFOs Over West Germany

In 1950, Cooper was assigned to the 525th Fighter bomber Squadron, stationed at Neubiberg Air Force Base in West Germany, but it was not until 1951 that Cooper had his first UFO sighting. At the time, several other Air Force pilots had reported seeing strange objects in the sky. Many pilots had been reporting seeing foo fighters in the sky and bogies on their radar. "I don't believe in fairy tales, but when I got into flying and military aviation, I heard other pilots describe too many unexplained examples of UFOs sighted around Earth to rule out the possibility that some forms of life exist beyond our own world," wrote Cooper.[127]

On one day in particular, Cooper recalled that he and his comrades had received an alert that an unidentified flying object was in the sky. Immediately, Cooper jumped into an F-86 fighter jet and took off in an attempt to intercept the unidentified aircraft. Cooper had reached an altitude of forty-five thousand feet and radar showed that the UFO was still hundreds of feet above, also traveling at a much greater speed. During the encounter, Cooper managed to get a visual on the object, which he described as "metallic silver and saucer-shaped." The saucer-shaped aircraft was also vastly different to a weather balloon or the Soviet Union MiG-5 fighter jet Cooper had initially thought it was.

For the following three days, Cooper and his squadron reported seeing several unidentified objects flying over the base. On one night, Cooper recalled seeing as many as sixteen objects flying in formation at once. It was clear to Cooper that these flying objects were extraterrestrial. Each time they attempted to intercept, the unidentified aircraft outmaneuvered the fighter jets effortlessly. After several failed attempts, Cooper and the rest of the squadron

---

127. Cooper and Henderson, *Leap of Faith*, 89.

would simply just look up at the sky through their binoculars in awe, watching the saucer-shaped aircraft carry out erratic maneuvers at incredible speeds.

The UFO Landing

Cooper's experience with the unknown did not end in 1951. Six years after the initial sighting, Cooper was stationed at Edwards Air Force Base in southern California and was part of the Experimental Flight Test Engineering Division.

On May 3, 1957, Cooper was part of a project that included filming a precision landing using an Askania camera, which would automatically take pictures, one frame per second, as the aircraft made its landing on the dry lake bed. Part of Cooper's team were cameramen James Bittick and Jack Gettys. After the crew had set up the apparatus and several hours had gone by, Bittick and Gettys rushed into Cooper's office and told him that they had caught a "strange-looking saucer" on film.[128] The saucer-shaped aircraft flew overhead for a couple of seconds as three landing gear extended. The UFO proceeded to make a smooth landing on the dry lake bed, just fifty yards away from Bittick and Gettys. The two cameramen described the object as being similar to an inverted plate. It was silver in color and had a diameter of approximately thirty feet. The object did not emit any noise throughout the landing, and as the two men approached it to get closer pictures, the saucer ascended and started a vertical climb and disappeared out of sight, completely silent.

When Bittick and Gettys showed Cooper the footage, he made an official report to the Pentagon, which instructed him to develop the film and send it over to Washington, DC. The film quality was

---

128. Cooper and Henderson, *Leap of Faith*, 93.

exceptional and was undeniable proof of an extraterrestrial aircraft landing at an air force base. With that being said, the investigation did not go as Cooper was expecting. With all the evidence he had, Cooper was expecting a follow-up or an investigation of some sort. Once Cooper sent the footage over, he never saw it again, nor was he contacted. Nobody mentioned the sighting to him or the two cameramen ever again; it was as though nothing had ever happened.

Letter to the United Nations

The lack of interest and investigation proved to Cooper that either the phenomenon was not being studied at all, or else there was a cover-up and the government was concealing facts from the public. After he retired, Cooper made several efforts and urged the government agencies to disclose any information they had regarding the phenomenon. Cooper also wrote a letter to the United Nations, in which he addressed the lack of interest (or rather lack of disclosure) and stated that there should be more transparency when it comes to the phenomenon:

> I wanted to convey to you my views on our extra-terrestrial visitors popularly referred to as 'UFO's', and suggest what might be done to properly deal with them. I believe that these extra-terrestrial vehicles and their crews are visiting this planet from other planets, which obviously are a little more technically advanced than we are here on earth. I feel that we need to have a top level, coordinated program to scientifically collect and analyze data from all over earth concerning any type of encounter, and to determine how best to interface with these visitors in a friendly fashion. We may first have to show them that we have learned to resolve our

problems by peaceful means, rather than warfare, before we are accepted as fully qualified universal team members. This acceptance would have tremendous possibilities of advancing our world in all areas. Certainly, then it would seem that the UN has a vested interest in handling this subject properly and expeditiously.

I should point out that I am not an experienced UFO professional researcher. I have not yet had the privilege of flying a UFO, nor of meeting the crew of one. I do feel that I am somewhat qualified to discuss them since I have been into the fringes of the vast areas in which they travel. Also, I did have occasion in 1951 to have two days of observation of many flights of them, of different sizes, flying in fighter formation, generally from east to west over Europe. They were at a higher altitude than we could reach with our jet fighters of that time.

I would also like to point out that most astronauts are very reluctant to even discuss UFO's due to the great numbers of people who have indiscriminately sold fake stories and forged documents abusing their names and reputations without hesitation. Those few astronauts who have continued to have a participation in the UFO field have had to do so very cautiously. There are several of us who do believe in UFO's and who have had occasion to see a UFO on the ground, or from an airplane. There was only one occasion from space that may have been a UFO.

If the UN agrees to pursue this project, and to lend their credibility to it, perhaps many more well qualified people will agree to step forth and provide help and information.[129]

---

129. Gordon Cooper, letter to the United Nations, November 9, 1978.

Conclusion

Cooper's story is only one of many. There have been hundreds of military officials who have reported seeing unidentified flying objects in the sky, only for their report to be completely disregarded and dismissed. As we have seen so far in this book and as we shall continue to see, in most cases, it is evident that these UFOS are interplanetary. Their maneuverability and characteristics are superior to the military's fighter jets and this in itself is worrisome. On several occasions, military pilots have shared the skies with advanced beings that could potentially cause them harm, putting their lives at risk. This phenomenon is a serious one that should not be ignored, and the government should certainly not shy away from addressing the issue. As Cooper stated, it is about time that the public is made aware of what is in the sky and of capabilities these beings possess.

Chapter 34
Gloucestershire Air Force Base UFO Encounter

Date: October 21, 1952
Location: Gloucestershire, England

Royal Air Force Base Little Rissington is located in Gloucestershire, a county in south England. At the time, this air force base was the home of the air force's main institution for training future military pilots. On October 21, 1952, Lieutenant Michael Swiney, together with his student Lieutenant David Crofts, experienced perhaps the most thrilling training flight.

On that day, Swiney and Crofts took off from Little Rissington Air Force Base on board a Gloster Meteor fighter jet for what they thought was going to be another ordinary training flight. The fighter jet had just traversed through a thick layer of clouds at fifteen thousand feet when Crofts saw three saucer-shaped objects straight ahead. At first, Crofts thought that they were parachutes, but he then noticed how perfectly circular they were and how they just hovered in the sky.

Swiney instructed Crofts to climb to thirty thousand feet and as he did so, the three saucer-shaped objects mirrored the climb and crossed from the left side of the aircraft to the right side. For over ten minutes, Swiney and Crofts observed the three UFOs and their unconventional characteristics, such as the absence of wings, exhaust plume, and visible propulsion system. Throughout the entire ten minutes, the disk-shaped aircraft remained in the sky, at the same altitude as the fighter jet, before they took off and vanished. At that point, Swiney called off the training flight and instructed Croft to fly back to base.

"It was something supernatural, perhaps, and when I landed someone told me I looked as if I had seen a ghost. I immediately thought of course, of saucers, because that's actually what they looked like. They were not leaving a condensation trail as I knew we were. They were circular and appeared to be stationary. We continued to climb to twice that height [to thirty thousand feet] and as we did so they did in fact change position. They took on a slightly different perspective. For example the higher we got they lost their circular shape and took on more of a 'flat plate' appearance—like when you hold a tea-saucer above your head and look at it, and then bring it down to your eye-level, it loses the circular shape and becomes a flat plate."[130]

It was the height of the Cold War and the officers at Little Rissington immediately forwarded the report to the fighter command at Royal Air Force Stanmore Park in London. Orders were given for two Meteor F.8 fighter jets to be scrambled and patrol the sky. In that hour, several air force bases all around south England started tracking unidentified targets on their radar. At Staverton, the radar operators managed to track three unidentified targets, which were all traveling at a tremendous speed, faster than any military fighter jet. The targets were also being picked up by the airborne radar.

---

130. David Clarke, "Operation Mainbrace UFOs," Dr. David Clarke Folklore and Journalism, accessed July 17, 2020, https://drdavidclarke.co.uk/secret-files /operation-mainbrace-ufos/.

Interestingly enough, on one occasion, the targets on radar were in close proximity to the Meteor F.8 jets and as the pilots started closing down on the distance, the targets simply disappeared off the radar, at an estimated one thousand miles per hour. The second they disappeared, the air force base in Wiltshire detected three unidentified targets that had entered the airspace at three thousand miles per hour. Once again, here we have a case in which the reported UFOs broke the sound barrier without producing a sonic boom, implying that the aircraft must have been traveling through a vacuum.

Fifty years after the incident, Terry Barefoot, a Royal Air Force signal officer, came forward and contacted David Clarke, an investigative journalist, who researched this incident and several other UFO sightings in the United Kingdom. Barefoot stated that on the day of the sighting, he was on duty at Rudloe Manor, which is an underground complex containing a plotting control room in which the air force monitored all aircraft movements happening over the south of England. Barefoot recalled the exact moment in which he and his colleagues witnessed what he could only describe as extraordinary: "The radar station called up saying that three objects had entered our airspace, going at a fantastic speed, approximately three thousand miles per hour. We had nothing that went that fast, and neither had the Russians or the Americans."[131]

The Investigation

Back at the little Rissington Air Force Base, upon their landing, Swiney and Croft were met by the wing commander, who instructed them to go to their cabin and to not talk to anyone until they were interviewed the following day. They were instructed to

---

131. Clarke, "Operation Mainbrace UFOs."

not leave their room at all costs; even the meals were brought to them. The following morning, an Air Ministry intelligence officer interviewed the two separately. The reports were immediately transported to the deputy directorate of intelligence in London. Coincidentally, all the records and files for this case have been lost or destroyed and there was no further follow-up or investigation.

Conclusion

This case goes to show that the cover-up regarding the phenomenon is worldwide. Although the majority of the reported UFO cases have occurred over the United States, this case shows that even in other countries, the phenomenon is disregarded and hidden from the public eye. The three saucer-shaped objects that Swiney and Croft encountered were undoubtedly extraterrestrial in origin. It is impossible for any vehicle of any kind to operate without an exhaust plume. Furthermore, the absence of a visible propulsion system, and the fact that these UFOs had exceeded the speed of sound without producing a sonic boom, confirms that these interplanetary flying objects do not abide by the general laws of physics and aerodynamics every terrestrial aircraft is bound by. "I had then been flying for about nine years and I had seen many funny reflections, refractions through windscreens and lots of other things, but this was nothing of the sort. We tried very hard to explain away what we were looking at but there was no way we could do that. There was something there, there is absolutely no doubt about it. It was NOT a reflection."[132]

---

132. Clarke, "Operation Mainbrace UFOs."

Chapter 35

Radar-Visual Sightings Prove Extraterrestrial Presence

Date: August 5, 1953
Location: Rapid City, South Dakota, United States

The following case is one of the few cases even the skeptics at Project Blue Book could not disregard and dismiss. It was two in the morning when Edward J. Ruppelt received a call from Airman First Class Max Futch, who at the time was at the United States Air Force's Air Technical Intelligence Center. On the call, Futch told Ruppelt, "Captain, you know that for a year I've read every flying saucer report that's come in and that I never really believed in the things. But you should read this wire."[133]

Futch had always downplayed the extraterrestrial hypothesis and he never took UFO reports seriously. On this day however, Ruppelt sensed the urgency and panic in his voice.

Ruppelt hurried to the Intelligence Center where he had officials from the Pentagon on the phone, asking about the several reports that were being made describing a flying saucer infiltrating American airspace. The incident was occurring in South Dakota where, at around 20:05, a woman at Black Hawk (which is around seven miles from Rapid City) had seen a bright light hovering at a

---

133. Ruppelt, *The Report*, 232.

very low altitude. The woman immediately called the local ground observer police, which forwarded the report to the Ellsworth Air Force Base just outside of Rapid City. For the next several minutes, the radar operators at the base tracked two unidentified targets at the same location where the woman had reported seeing the bright light. The operators described the objects as being well-defined and solid, which made them unlikely to be a weather target.

On radar, the objects were at sixteen thousand feet and began picking up their speed as they started approaching Rapid City. Every individual in the room was fixated on the radar scope. As two men ran outside to try and locate the moving target, they saw a large bright red light sweeping across the sky completely silently. At the time of the sighting, there was already an F-84 fighter jet in the sky, and thus, the pilot instructed to pursue and intercept the UFO. After a few moments, four targets started showing up on the radar, and this was only the beginning of one of the most eerie nights the involved personnel would experience.

On the airborne radar, the pilot was tracking four separate blips, but he was only able to locate one bright light outside his cockpit windows. He put the F-84 on full throttle in an attempt to close down the distance and get as close as he possibly could to the bright light. He described how as the light increased in its speed so did its brightness, which he described to be "brighter than the brightest star."[134] The pilot kept at its tail and each time he would try to close down the distance and get three miles from it, the object would make a rapid acceleration. Throughout the entire encounter, the object had maintained the three-mile distance. After several minutes of chasing down the bright light, the jet was

---

134. Project Blue Book,227, https://web.archive.org/web/20070221115954 /http://www.nicap.org/images/ellsdoc2.gif.

running low on fuel and the pilot had to abort the mission and return back to base. What he did not expect, however, was for the light to follow him back.

As the pilot started flying back to base, he noticed that the bright light was now just fifteen miles behind, now keeping at the F-84's tail. The tables had completely turned and now the fighter jet was the one being pursued. At the base, another F-84 was already warming up and ready to take off, and luckily the first jet was able to make a safe landing. With another fighter jet in the sky, the pursuit continued. The red light illuminated the entire sky and the pilot was able to spot it right away. Once again, as the pilot attempted to close down the distance, the object responded and initiated a vertical climb, climbing to twenty-six thousand feet.

The pilot mirrored the vertical climb, but in an instant, the object made a nose dive, going exactly below his fighter jet. Just like a cat chasing down a mouse, the pilot made the same dive, and as he gained speed, the UFO responded, and, once again, as he reached the three mile distance from the object, it accelerated, leaving the fighter jet behind. The pilot, completely bewildered at what he was experiencing, wanted to confirm that the light was not a reflection. He turned off all the lights inside the cockpit, but the light remained in the sky. He swerved the plane to the side to make sure it wasn't a reflection from the ground, but once again, the light remained in the sky. The last explanation he could think of was that it was a celestial body, however, the light was moving in relation to the three stars; it hadn't remained in a stationary position. In actual fact, it had carried out maneuvers and was responding according to the F-84's position in space, proving that whoever was piloting the aircraft possessed spatial awareness.

The nearby Weather Bureau station at the Rapid City Municipal Airport were immediately contacted and asked whether a weather balloon had been released. They did confirm that a weather balloon had been released at 20:00, however, it had moved south from the Municipal Airport, which put it outside the area where the encounter had taken place, leaving this case unsolved. Ruppelt wrote of the investigation: "The sighting was thoroughly investigated, and I could devote pages of detail on how we looked into every facet of the incident; but it will suffice to say that in every facet we looked into we saw nothing. Nothing but a big question mark asking what it was."[135]

Conclusion

One of the main reasons why this case is one of the most significant ones in UFO history is due to the fact that no other explanation except for the extraterrestrial hypothesis holds true. There is no other hypothesis that can explain what the object in the sky, or what the targets on the radar, could have been.

The most interesting aspect of this encounter is the awareness the beings piloting the aircraft seemed to possess. The fact that the UFO responded according to the maneuvers the fighter-jet carried out proves that whoever was piloting that light possessed great spatial awareness, implying that these beings must be conscious beings.

---

135. Ruppelt, *The Report*, 235.

Chapter 36

The Disappearance of Felix Moncla and Robert Wilson

Date: November 23, 1953
Location: Upper Michigan, United States

Another tragic case related to the UFO phenomenon is the disappearance of Lieutenant Felix Moncla and Lieutenant Robert Wilson. These two men are presumed to be dead, disappearing as they were pursuing an unidentified flying object. Although we do not know the full details of what happened during the encounter, it does seem that the UFO played a part in their disappearance. What makes this case even more bizarre is that unlike the death of Thomas Mantell, no debris or wreckage was found to indicate that the fighter jet they were flying had crashed.

As we have seen so far in this book, it is not uncommon for radar operators to track unidentified targets on radar. Naturally, when an unidentified object does infiltrate a nation's airspace without authorization, this is deemed a threat to national security.

November 23, 1953, was a day like no other for Moncla and Wilson. The sun had set, and the moon was illuminating the sky. Although there were scattered clouds here and there, the visibility was generally clear. At Truax Air Force Base in Wisconsin, the radar controllers started tracking an unidentified object on their radar, which was carrying out erratic maneuvers that distinguished it from conventional or military aircraft. The report was forwarded to Kinross Air Force Base (later renamed Kinchloe Air Force Base), located near Sault St. Marie, Michigan, where an F-89C Scorpion jet was scrambled to locate and identify the target. On board the Scorpion jet was Moncla, with Wilson in the rear seat serving as radar operator. The target was flying over Lake Superior and was being tracked by ground and airborne radar. Given that the two lieutenants disappeared during the encounter, it is unclear whether they had made visual contact with the object. All the information we have on this case was from the developments happening at the air force base.

The radar showed that with each turn the Scorpion jet made, the UFO followed, mirroring every move but maintaining a distance from the jet. Moncla and Wilson were exceeding five hundred miles per hour, but the UFO was faster, making it impossible for the lieutenants to close down on the object. For half an hour, the radar operators just watched the Scorpion jet chase after this unidentified flying object, until the unexpected happened.

After half an hour, the radar operators noticed that Moncla and Wilson were closing down the distance between their fighter jet and the UFO. The two blips started getting closer and closer. At an altitude of eight thousand feet, the two blips had merged into one, and although the radar operators were expecting them to separate once again, both targets simply disappeared, not to be seen again. Multiple attempts were made to communicate with Moncla and Wilson, but to no avail; no one heard from either of them again. A search and rescue team was immediately sent out to inspect the lake and surrounding areas.

The Investigation

The search and rescue team were unable to locate any wreckage or bodies. To this day, Wilson and Moncla are missing, presumably dead. Nobody knows what truly happened during the encounter, although it is evident that the UFO they were pursuing was responsible for their disappearance.

The incident was first investigated by air-safety experts, who confirmed that the weather conditions could not have caused the fighter jet to crash. With that, the air force was being pressed for answers, answers they did not have. Eventually, the air force stated that the UFO they were chasing was a Royal Canadian Air Force C-47 aircraft. The air force stated further that Moncla and Wilson had suffered from vertigo, which caused them to crash the F-89 jet into the lake. What they failed to explain, however, was why the fighter jet would intercept a Canadian aircraft to start with. Moreover, if the Scorpion jet had crashed into the river, why weren't the search and rescue team able to locate the wreckage?

Over the years, UFO researchers have said that there was no Canadian aircraft in the sky. This information comes from a letter that was sent to NICAP by the chief of air staff at the Department of the National Defense in Ottawa. The letter reads as follows: "A check of the Royal Canadian Air Force records has revealed no report of an incident involving an RCAF aircraft in the Lake Superior area on the above date. May we point out that if an aircraft fails to answer a radio request to identify itself, it would normally be assumed that its radios are not functioning, or that the aircraft has suffered a complete electrical failure."[136]

---

136. National Investigations Committee on Aerial Phenomena, *The UFO Evidence*, 114.

This statement has been misinterpreted and misconstrued in UFO literature for several years. Although the letter states that there are no records that show a Canadian aircraft was involved in an accident on the night in question, this does not mean that there wasn't a C-47 in the sky. The letter simply states that no aircraft was involved in an accident. As a matter of fact, UFO researcher Gord Heath managed to find records that show a C-47 aircraft did indeed fly over Lake Superior at the time of Moncla and Wilson's disappearance. The Accident Investigation Report used the code "VC-912" as the identification code for the aircraft. Over the years, Heath has acquired the flight records for the 412 Transport Squadron, which operated the C-47. Over time, he managed to locate the crew members on board, one being Gerald Fosberg, the pilot on board the C-47 aircraft. In his correspondence with Heath, Fosber stated, "I remember the flight reasonably well, and just checked my log books to confirm the date. It was a night flight. We were probably at seven thousand or nine thousand feet over a solid cloud deck below and absolutely clear sky above. Somewhere near Sault Ste. Marie, and north of Kinross AFB, I think a ground station (can't remember whether it was American or Canadian) asked us if we had seen another aircraft's lights in our area. I do think I recall them saying at that time that the USAF had scrambled an interceptor and they had lost contact with it. We replied that we had not seen anything. A few days later I received a phone call from somebody at Kinross who was carrying out an investigation on a missing aircraft. I could only tell them that we had seen nothing. That was the last I ever heard of the incident."[137]

---

137. Heath Gord, correspondence, http://www.ufobc.ca/kinross /openingQuestions/whatCausedAlert.html.

With that being said, Fosberg did confirm that the C-47 he was piloting was not the target being pursued by Moncla and Wilson. He also stated that he was unable to visually locate the Scorpion jet outside his cockpit window. Naturally, if we look at the details of the case, prior to the disappearance, the two blips merged into one, which meant that Wilson and Moncla were closing in on the target. If the C-47 and the Scorpion jet were that close in proximity, the pilot would have been able to visually locate the fighter jet effortlessly.

Secondly, it was also reported that Wilson and Moncla were flying at least five hundred miles per hour, and yet, the UFO was still somehow ahead of them. Given that the C-47 aircraft has a top speed of two hundred fifty miles per hour, this makes it impossible for it to have been the target. The third, and most obvious detail that disproves the theory is the fact that the two blips had merged into one and then disappeared. If the C-47 was the object being pursued, then the aircraft would have reemerged once again on radar.

Conclusion

The disappearance of Moncla and Wilson leave us with several unanswered questions. The lack of answers makes one wonder whether the UFO was interplanetary in nature and if these beings had malicious intentions. If they did, for what reason? If it was not an extraterrestrial aircraft, then why did the air force state that the UFO was a Canadian aircraft when it wasn't? Was this explanation simply a scapegoat?

The only facts we do know about the case that suggest that the UFO was interplanetary are the following:

- Although the C-47 aircraft was in the sky, it was not the UFO being tracked on radar nor the aircraft being pursued by Moncla and Wilson.
- No wreckage or bodies were found in the lake or the surrounding areas.
- The UFO traveled well over five hundred miles per hour, making it faster than any fighter jet at the time.

All these factors support the theory that many UFO researchers believe: the UFO was responsible for Moncla and Wilson's disappearance. All the factors discussed in this chapters cannot be simply attributed to mere coincidences.

Chapter 37
Finland's Infamous UFO Case

Date: April 12, 1969
Location: Pori, Finland

The following case deals with the only UFO sighting that has been formally acknowledged by the Finnish Air Force to this day. On April 12,1969, pilot Juoko Kuronen was taxiing his aircraft, preparing to take off for an orienteering flight over Pori, Finland. Prior to his departure, Kuronen reported that he had heard a conversation over radio between the air traffic control operator and Tarmo Tukeva, a combat pilot who was airborne at the time.

According to the conversation, it seemed as though there were seven unidentified objects in the sky. Given that the seven unidentified objects were being tracked on radar, the air traffic control operator instructed Tukeva to try and identify the seven UFOs and intercept if necessary. At an altitude of approximately ten thousand feet, Tukeva made visual contact with the objects, however, the objects were not weather balloons as he initially presumed, nor were they anything he had seen previously in the sky.

Flying in formation were seven disk-shaped bright yellow objects. The presence of the objects was confirmed by three independent radars: Tukeva's, Kuronen's, and the ground radar. As Tukeva started approaching the objects, he noticed that the disk-shaped objects began accelerating toward the north at an incredible speed, out-pacing his fighter jet. Within a couple of minutes, the objects started showing on radars in Vaasa, which is 200 kilometers away from Pori. This means that the object must have been traveling well over the speed a terrestrial aircraft can travel at (if one assumes that the objects follow the general laws of physics, they must have been traveling well over ten thousand miles per hour). It must be pointed out that once again, no sonic boom was heard even though the object had broken the sound barrier.

It has not been disclosed whether an official investigation was carried out or not. However, a couple of months after the incident, Kuronen was named the head of Lappeenrata Airport. Throughout the years, he has been asked numerous times what he thought of the incident and whether he thought the objects were interplanetary or not. In an interview with a local news station in 2009, Kuronen said, "I cannot explain the observation in any way, and hardly anyone can ever do that."[138]

---

138. "The UFO Sighting in Pori Still Speaks," UUTISET, last modified July 12, 2009, https://yle.fi/uutiset/3-5971507.

Chapter 38
Extraterrestrial Aircraft Malfunctions Fighter Jet

Date: September 19, 1976
Location: Tehran, Iran

The following case is admittedly the case that made me start researching and studying the UFO phenomenon. The details unequivocally prove that the reported UFOs are extraterrestrial in nature, and their displayed capabilities are truly astonishing.

The incident began shortly after midnight on September 19, 1976. What started as a routine night for the Iranian Air Force command post in Tehran turned out to be one of the most horrifying encounters any air force pilot could ever experience. At around 00:30, the officer at the command post started receiving several calls in succession from locals who reported seeing a bright light in the sky. The light was described as being "a helicopter with a shining light."[139] Since there were no helicopters in the area, the officer immediately notified General Nader Yousefi, the senior officer on duty.

At first Yousefi dismissed the reports as misidentification of a bright star. However, the reports kept coming in. Given the

139. "Iranian Air Force Jets Scrambled," NICAP, November 1976, http://www
.nicap.org/reports/760919tehran_NICAP.pdf.

amount of reports being made, Yousefi started observing the sky himself in an attempt to locate the bright light. As soon as he stepped outside, he immediately noticed that the object was significantly larger and brighter than any star in the sky, and was also carrying out erratic maneuvers. The alarms were immediately raised. There were no known helicopters or aircraft in the area, which only left Yousefi to assume that a foreign aircraft was infiltrating the country's airspace.

The first F-4 Phantom II jet was scrambled from Hamadan Air Force Base at 01:30. The pilot on board was Captain Mohammed Azizkhani, who immediately made visual contact with the unidentified object, which was seventy miles ahead of his aircraft. As Azizkhani started closing down on the object, the second he was forty miles from the target, his fighter jet malfunctioned and lost all communication with the base. When Azizkhani broke off the pursuit and started heading back to base due to the malfunctioning, the jet regained all of its functioning. Due to the harsh brightness of the object, Azizkhani was unable to estimate its size or its definite shape.

Once Azizkhani returned to the base, a second F-4 fighter jet was scrambled just ten minutes later, piloted by Lieutenant Parvis Jafari and Lieutenant Jalal Damirian. Exceeding seven hundred miles per hour, Jafari started closing in on the object. However, the UFO immediately proceeded to rapidly accelerate, maintaining the distance. The rapid acceleration was confirmed both by the airborne radar and the radar at the air force base. For several minutes, Jafari attempted to reduce the distance, yet it seemed impossible to penetrate the forty-mile distance between the F-4 and the UFO. The lieutenant also noted that the object had changed from being an intensely bright white light to a flashing strobe-like light, arranged in a rectangular pattern. The lights alternated from blue to green to red to orange. The alteration was happening so quickly that all four lights were visible at once.

Now flying over the south of Tehran, a small object detached from the UFO and started accelerating toward the F-4 at an incredible speed. The jet was equipped with AIM-9 missiles, and because the object was approaching their aircraft at a rapid rate, Jafari deemed this a threat and attempted to launch the missile toward the UFO. However, as he was about to execute, the communication and weapon control systems were disabled simultaneously. The fighter jet had suffered a sudden power loss.

Completely unarmed and unable to communicate with the base, Jafari made a sharp nose dive in an attempt to avoid the object. However, as he made the dive, the UFO responded by mirroring the maneuver. The object continued trailing just three kilometers behind the fighter jet. Luckily for Jafari and Damirian, the object then changed its course and disappeared as it reattached to the main UFO they were first pursuing. Could it be that the UFO retreated and changed course after it no longer deemed the F-4 a threat?

This, however, was not the end of the night for the lieutenants. As the smaller UFO reattached to the main UFO (which I shall refer to as the "mothership" to avoid confusion), the communication and weapon control systems were restored and Jafari was able to resume the pursuit. The mothership was still moving at an incredible speed, infinitely faster than their fighter jet. Once again, a second unidentified object detached from the mothership and began accelerating toward the ground at a tremendous speed. Naturally, given that the object was free-falling, Jafari and Damirian were expecting some sort of crash or explosion. Instead, the object simply halted the drop instantaneously and came to a rest on the ground, making a perfect landing. As the mothership sped away out of sight, the resting object remained stationary on the ground, so intensely bright that it lit up a three kilometer radius. In an attempt to get a better look at the object, Jafari started to descent toward it.

Interestingly, as the F-4 started getting closer to the object, the onboard systems started malfunctioning once again, only to resume functioning once the fighter jet retreated from the landed object. Shortly thereafter, the light emitted from the unidentified object went out and the lieutenants were unable to locate it any further. The lieutenants took note of the exact location and then returned to the base.

Flying back to base, both Jafari and Damirian struggled with their vision due to the intensity of the light the object had been emitting. Prior to approaching the landing strip, a cylindrical-shaped object, which was roughly the size of a fighter jet, with bright lights on each end and a flashing light in its center, appeared from nowhere, several feet above their aircraft. The fly over was also witnessed by multiple personnel on the ground.

The following day, Jafari and Damirian boarded a helicopter and flew back to where the unidentified object had landed. There were no traces on the ground, but the area was checked for abnormal radiation levels. As the helicopter left the landing site, its communication radio started picking up a significant beeper signal. The signal was being received just above an isolated farm, and when they asked the residents if they had experienced anything unusual the previous night, they informed them that they had heard a loud sound and noticed bright lights coming from the landing site's direction.

The Investigation

On November 12, 2007, Jafari took to the stands during a press conference in Washington, DC and recounted his experience with the unknown. In his speech, Jafari stated that the day after the encounter he was interviewed by an American colonel in detail. The United States Department of Defense declared the following in the evaluation report:

★★★★★★

"An outstanding report. This case is a classic, which meets all the criteria necessary for a valid study of the UFO phenomenon:

a. The object was seen by multiple witnesses from different locations (i.e., Shamiran, Mehrabad, and the dry lake bed) and viewpoints (both airborne and from the ground).

b. The credibility of many of the witnesses was high (an air force general, qualified aircrews, and experienced tower operators).

c. Visual sightings were confirmed by radar.

d. Similar electromagnetic effects (EME) were reported by three separate aircraft.

e. There were physiological effects on some crew members (i.e., loss of night vision due to the brightness of the object).

f. An inordinate amount of maneuverability was displayed by the UFOs."[140]

★★★★★★

As stated in the beginning of this chapter, it is evident that the unidentified flying objects in the Iranian sky were extraterrestrial

---

140. Major Roland B. Evans, Defense Intelligence Agency Defense Information Evaluation Report IR No.6846013976, September 22, 1976.

in origin. There are not many cases that are as clear-cut as this one, and this case proves just how superior extraterrestrial beings are and how advanced their technology is. When an aircraft has the capability to completely disarm a fighter jet, it truly makes one wonder what else these beings are capable of.

Governments have the responsibility to study these reports. Isn't it futile for a military to protect their nation from other countries if they cannot even fathom the capabilities of these beings? Shouldn't governments focus on trying to understand the advanced technology these beings are in possession of as opposed to spending billions on warfare?

Chapter 39
The Disappearance
of Frederick Valentich

Date: October 21, 1978
Location: Bass Strait, Australia

Frederick Valentich was a twenty-year-old Australian pilot who, at the time, had just about one hundred fifty hours of flying time. Valentich had obtained a class four instrument rating, which allowed him to fly at night as long as the weather conditions were favorable for him to maintain visual separation from other aircraft and the terrain. Valentich was also a member of the Royal Australian Air Force Air Training Corps, and he was planning to pursue a career in aviation. Previously, Valentich had failed to pass commercial license examinations, and had failed to enlist into the Royal Australian Air Force due to his poor academic qualifications.

Regardless of his academic performances, we must keep in mind that Valentich was not incapable of operating an aircraft. The 150 flying hours prove that he most certainly knew how to operate an aircraft.

On October 21, 1978, Frederick Valentich was planning to fly from Moorabbin to King Island and then return. He had arranged to pick up some of his friends from King Island, and thus he took four life jackets on board the aircraft as a precaution. Prior to his departure, Valentich attended a meteorological debriefing and also submitted a flight plan, as was required.

At 18:10, the Cessna 182L Valentich would fly was refueled and departed at 18:19. Shortly after the departure, Valentich established a two-way radio communication with the Melbourne Flight Service Unit, and things were going smoothly until 19:06. There was no air traffic in the vicinity, and flying at an altitude of 4,500 feet, weather conditions were optimal.

As Valentich was flying over Bass Strait, he noticed there was another aircraft in the sky, which started approaching his aircraft. No aircraft were registered on his radar, and thus he contacted the Melbourne Air Traffic Control for clarification. Once he got a better look at the object, which was just one thousand feet above his aircraft, he noticed that it had unusual characteristics and it did not resemble any conventional aircraft he knew of. The object was disk-shaped, had four bright lights that were as bright as landing lights, and it was significantly large.

At 19:10, Valentich reported to the air traffic control operator that the object was hovering above his aircraft. He noticed that it had a green light and appeared to have a metallic surface. Within a couple of seconds, the object started approaching Valentich from the southwest, and, simultaneously, his engine began to idle roughly. Shortly after 19:12, the radio control operator lost contact with Valentich. Search and rescue operation procedures were initiated at 19:33, when Valentich failed to land at King Island.

For four days an extensive air, sea, and land search was carried out, but no traces were found to indicate that the aircraft had crashed. The investigation was terminated on October 25, 1978, and Valentich is still missing to this day, presumably dead.

Communication with Air Traffic Control

The following is the transcript of the entire conversation between Valentich (listed by his registration code VH-DSJ) and the Melbourne Flight Service Unit, as recorded in the Department of Transportation's Aircraft Investigation Summary Report.

19:06:14—VH-DSJ: Melbourne, this is Delta Sierra Juliet. Is there any known traffic below five thousand?

19:06:23—MFSU: Delta Sierra Juliet, no known traffic.

19:06:26—VH-DSJ: Delta Sierra Juliet. I am—seems to be a large aircraft below five thousand.

19:06:46—MFSU: Delta Sierra Juliet. What type of aircraft is it?

19:06:50—VH-DSJ: Delta Sierra Juliet. I cannot affirm. It is four bright, it seems to me, like landing lights.

19:07:04—MFSU: Delta Sierra Juliet.

19:07:32—VH-DSJ: Melbourne, this is Delta Sierra Juliet. The aircraft has just passed over me at least a thousand feet above.

19:07:43—MFSU: Delta Sierra Juliet. Roger and it is a large aircraft confirm.

19:07:47—VH-DSJ: Er, unknown due to the speed it's traveling. Is there any air force air craft in the vicinity?

19:07:57—MFSU: Delta Sierra Juliet. No known aircraft in the vicinity.

19:08:18—VH-DSJ: Melbourne. It's approaching now from due east toward me.

19:08:28—MFSU: Delta Sierra Juliet.

19:08:49—VH-DSJ: Delta Sierra Juliet. It seems to me that he's playing some sort of game. He's flying over me two to three times at a time at speeds I could not identify.

19:09:02—MFSU: Delta Sierra Juliet. Roger. What is your actual level?

19:09:06—VH-DSJ: My level is four and a half thousand four five zero zero.

19:09:11—MFSU: Delta Sierra Juliet and confirm that you cannot identify the aircraft.

19:09:14—VH-DSJ: Affirmative.

19:09:18—MFSU: Delta Sierra Juliet. Roger. Standby.

19:09:28—VH-DSJ: Melbourne Delta Sierra Juliet. It's not an aircraft. It is…(open microphone for two seconds)

19:09:46—MFSU: Delta Sierra Juliet. Can you describe the, er, aircraft?

19:09:52—VH-DSJ: Delta Sierra Juliet as it's flying past it's a long shape. Cannot identify more than…(open microphone for three seconds) before me right now Melbourne.

19:10:07—MFSU: Delta Sierra Juliet. Roger and how large would the, er, object be?

19:10:20—VH-DSJ: Delta Sierra Juliet Melbourne. It seems like it's stationary. What I'm doing right now is orbiting and the thing is just orbiting on top of me. Also, it's got a green light and sort of metallic like it's all shiny on the outside.

19:10:43—MFSU: Delta Sierra Juliet.

19:10:48—VH-DSJ: Delta Sierra Juliet (open microphone for five seconds). It's just vanished.

19:10:57—MFSU: Delta Sierra Juliet.

19:11:03—VH-DSJ: Melbourne would you know what kind of aircraft I've got? Is it military aircraft?

19:11:08—MFSU: Delta Sierra Juliet confirm the er aircraft just vanished.

19:11:14—VH-DSJ: Say again.

19:11:17—MFSU: Delta Sierra Juliet is the aircraft still with you?

19:11:23—VH-DSJ: Delta Sierra Juliet approaching from the southwest.

19:11:37—MFSU: Delta Sierra Juliet.

19:11:52—VH-DSJ: Delta Sierra Juliet the engine is rough idling. I've got it set at twenty-three, twenty-four. and the thing is (coughing).

19:12:04—MFSU: Delta Sierra Juliet. Roger what are your intentions?

19:12:09—VH-DSJ: My intentions are, ah, to go to King Island, ah, Melbourne that strange aircraft is hovering on top of me again. It's hovering and it's not an aircraft.

19:12:22—MFSU: Delta Sierra Juliet.

19:12:28—VH-DSJ: (Seventeen seconds of open microphone.)

19:12:49—MFSU: Delta Sierra Juliet, Melbourne.

After seventeen seconds of silence, an unidentified metallic scratching noise was heard. All contact was then lost.

Did the Cessna Crash?

One of the possibilities to consider is the fact that Valentich could have crashed the aircraft, leading to his death. When the radar control operator lost contact with Valentich, he was flying over Bass Strait, which is a body of water that separates Tasmania from Australia.

Bass Strait is a relatively shallow sea, with an average depth of fifty to seventy meters. If it was the case that the Cessna had crashed into the water, the wreckage would have probably been carried a long distance due to the ocean's current. However, the

Cessna aircraft has a relatively low mass aluminum structure, which would have prevented it from sinking quickly.

When we also take into consideration the depth of the water, this would have made it even more likely that the search and rescue team would have located the wreckage. Although we cannot rule out this hypothesis, the lack of wreckage located by the search and rescue team makes this theory an unlikely one.

Was the UFO Extraterrestrial?

Because the object that was hovering above Valentich's aircraft was not tracked on radar and was unidentified, we must explore the possibility that it could have been extraterrestrial.

Valentich described the UFO as having a long shape, four bright lights (as bright as a landing strip) and one green light. The object was also somehow manipulating the function of the Cessna, as the aircraft started idling roughly as the object hovered above. Interestingly enough, on the night of Valentich's disappearance, several eyewitnesses in the surrounding areas reported seeing a green colored light moving erratically in the sky. UFO researcher Paul Norman was able to identify several eyewitnesses and their testimonies are crucial to this case.

One witness, who went by the pseudonym Ken Hansen, stated that as he, his wife, and two nieces traveled to Hansen's house, all four of them saw a small light in the sky and a large green light traveling at a slightly higher altitude. Hansen stated that during the drive, their niece was the first to spot the green light in the sky. As he slowed down to get a better look, he was also able to locate the lights of Valentich's Cessna. The sighting lasted for a minute before both sets of lights disappeared. However, Hansen did not think much of it and continued on the drive back home.

Although there is no way we can verify the authenticity of this report, twenty other individuals did report seeing a strange green light in the sky in the vicinity of Bass Strait. Was this green light the same light that was described by Valentich? Did this green light play a part in his disappearance?

The investigation report states that "the reason for the disappearance of the aircraft has not been determined."[141] If we do consider the characteristics of the object, as described by Valentich and the other witnesses who reported seeing the green light, the extraterrestrial hypothesis becomes the most plausible one. If the Cessna had truly crashed, then the search and rescue team would certainly have found the wreckage when considering how shallow the sea is.

Although to this day we do not know what happened to Valentich or his Cessna, it is a fact that something bizarre happened in the Australian sky on October 21, 1978. It is also evident that the reported unidentified flying object did play a part in Valentich's disappearance. When we have cases such as this one and the disappearance of Moncla and Wilson, the reality starts setting in; the reality being that sometimes a UFO sighting is not simply seeing strange lights in the sky. As we have seen, several individuals have lost their lives as they were chasing the unknown.

---

141. Commonwealth of Austrailia Department of Transport, "Aircraft Accident Investigation Summary Report: VH-DSJ Cape Otway to King Island 21 October 1978 – Aircraft Missing [Valentich]," reference number V116/783/1047, https://recordsearch.naa.gov.au/SearchNRetrieve/Interface/ViewImage.aspx?B=10491375.

Chapter 40
UFO Causes Aircraft to Make Emergency Landing

Date: November 11, 1979
Location: Valencia, Spain

What was supposed to be an ordinary commercial flight turned into the most infamous UFO case in Spain. A commercial aircraft was forced to make an emergency landing after multiple unidentified flying objects were observed in close proximity to the aircraft. TAE Supercaravelle Flight JK-297 was en route to Las Palmas in the Canary Islands from Salzburg, Austria. On board the aircraft was Commander Francisco Javier Lerdo de Tejada, copilot Jose Ramon Zuazu Nagore, flight mechanic Francisco Javier Rodrigues and a total of 109 passengers.

The time was 23:05 when things took a bizarre turn. Flying at an altitude of twenty-three thousand feet, Rodrigues, the flight mechanic, noticed two intense red lights straight ahead of the aircraft. Rodrigues immediately notified Tejada and Nagore, who were also able to locate them. The crew described the objects as not having a solid body, they were simply intense lights, which were moving closer and closer to the aircraft. Tejada decided to ascend the aircraft to prevent any collision from happening, and as he did so, the two UFOs mirrored the same climb, just five hundred meters away.

269

The Air Transit Control in Barcelona was unable to identify the two aircraft, and the only target air transit did have on radar was Flight JK-297. Every maneuver the aircraft carried out was mirrored by the lights. It was evident that whoever was piloting these strange aircraft was aware of the aircraft's position in space and time. Due to the lack of information and identification, the crew decided to make an emergency landing at Manises Airport in Valencia. Prior to landing at 23:45, the crew at the airport noticed strange bright red lights, and, thinking that it was an unregistered aircraft having trouble landing, the crew lit up the emergency lights on the runway.

At the Los Llanos Air Force Base in Albacete, the chief of service of the air command of the Spanish Air Defense instructed a military jet to be scrambled. Receiving the order, Captain Fernando Camara took off from the base at 00:40 on board an F-1 Mirage in an attempt to locate and identify the two red lights, which multiple individuals had now seen. The visibility was exceptional, and it did not take Camara long to locate the red lights from afar. Although he had made visual sighting with the objects, he was unable to close the distance. It seemed as though no matter how fast the Mirage was going, the UFOs responded by increasing their speed in order to maintain the distance. Camara described the objects in a similar manner; he stated that they did not have a solid body, they were simply balls of intense light. Camara's encounter with the unknown became even stranger as his radio communication started getting interference. Furthermore, his aircraft warning system was alerting him that the Mirage was being constantly locked-on (which occurs when another aircraft is locking on to the aircraft on its radar).

After an hour and a half of pursuing the two red lights, Camara had to abandon the mission, as his aircraft was running low on fuel.

The Investigation

Unsurprisingly, as it is with the majority of UFO reports, the authorities played down the seriousness of the encounter and provided explanations that did not match with the reports and observations made. The authorities stated that the two intense red lights, which were observed by the crew members on board Flight JK-297, were bright flash blazes from combustion towers at a chemical industry complex. When it came to the visual sightings made from the ground, the report stated that they were stars and the personnel had misidentified them as UFOs due to their overexcitement.

The UFOs, which were seen by Camara, were unrelated to the lights that were reported earlier by the crew on board Flight JK-297. Since Camara described the lights as being undefined and distant, the report attributed this sighting to celestial bodies once again. The investigation further claimed the Mirage's electronic malfunctioning was caused by the U.S Sixth Fleet, which at the time was using powerful electronic warfare equipment. Camara, however, did not accept this explanation. He stated that he was flying significantly farther from the Six Fleet's position and he was positively sure that the lights were not celestial bodies. They were maneuvering relative to his fighter jet's position, which disproved the theory. To further support their explanations, the authorities stated that Tejada was psychologically vulnerable because he was going through personal issues at the time, and this vulnerability played a part in the UFO sighting.

Although this case is officially closed, we still do not know what Tejada and the rest of the witnesses reported seeing. It could not have been the case that the red lights were emitted from the industry complex, nor could they have been celestial bodies. Lights from a tower would not have maneuvered, they would have simply remained in a stationary position. This explanation also disproves the "bright planets and stars" theory.

Conclusion

Although we cannot decisively state what these lights were, it is important to question how maneuvering lights could have been mistaken for stationary celestial bodies. This conclusion becomes less plausible when we take into consideration that one of the witnesses was Captain Camara, an experienced military pilot.

Chapter 41
The Night of UFOs

Date: May 19, 1986
Location: São Paulo, Brazil

With over twenty unidentified flying objects in the sky, the following case is one of the most significant and extraordinary cases to date. Throughout the entire night of May 19, 1986, UFOs were seen in the sky over São Paulo, and fighter jets chased them down. The following day, a press conference was held that was broadcast on television. In it, the Brazilian Air Force fully acknowledged the events and stated that they could not explain what the unidentified objects had been.

The night of May 19, 1986 remains, to this day, a very significant date for UFO researchers. The night of UFOs began to unfold at about 18:30. The control tower staff at São Jose dos Campos airport in São Paulo noticed two bright lights in the sky just above the runway. They estimated the lights to be roughly ten miles away, and the radio control operators were also able to track three unidentified objects on their radar scope. All three unidentified aircraft were in the sky without any preapproved flight plans, which meant that the air force had to intervene.

In an hour, the three objects on radar increased to eight targets, all of which were flying at an incredible speed. It was not until 21:10 that the first visual sighting was made, when Commander

Alcir Pereira da Silva was piloting an Embrare Xingu aircraft. For thirty minutes, da Silva reported seeing a "dancing point of light" in the distance.[142] The intense light remained in the distance, drifting in the sky. Although its presence was confirmed by the ground radar, the radar operators were unable to explain what the target was, which is why he da Silva decided to pursue the UFO himself. As he got closer to the object, he started noticing that the light was a bright reddish orange light. He was unable to make out whether it had a definite shape or not. As he started flying toward it, the object started disappearing, only to reappear in different locations in the sky.

The encounter was happening just over the airport and da Silva requested permission to land. However, as he started the descent, he noticed that the bright light was straight ahead and flying toward his position. Although the object was moving slowly, da Silva was forced to postpone the landing, and as he did so, the light disappeared out of the sky. Da Silva now had to circle the airport for a few minutes until he was able to land, and on the second attempt the same incident played out. As he started his descent and was approaching the landing strip, the UFO reappeared, the light so bright that it illuminated the entire sky. Once again, he was forced to postpone his landing, however, this time, he decided to attempt and pursue the UFO once again.

The radio control operators were able to track both the Xingu aircraft and the unidentified flying object da Silva was pursuing on radar. Each time da Silva would try and close down on the object, it would simply disappear, only to reappear in a completely different location. It was now 21:30 and the Xingu was running low on fuel. For a third time, da Silva requested to land, and as he started

---

142. Good, *Above Top Secret*, 427.

approaching the runway, three bright lights appeared just below his aircraft. Da Silva was now communicating with the air traffic control operators, but luckily enough, the three bright lights made a sharp ninety-degree turn and accelerated toward the mountains of Serra do Mar.

For half an hour, da Silva not only had pursued the three lights, but had also been chased by them. The description and characteristics undoubtedly prove that these objects were extraterrestrial in nature. However, this was only the beginning of the night.

Military Jets Scrambled

Back at the Air Traffic Control Center, the Integrated Air Defense had now gone on full alert, as the eight unidentified targets had saturated their radars, not only causing a disruption to the air traffic, but also causing a potential threat to national security. It was shortly after 22:00 that three F-5E Tiger jets were scrambled from Santa Cruz Air Force Base, as well as three Mirage III jets from Anápolis Air Force Base.

Captain Armindo Viriato, the pilot on board one of the Mirage fighter jets, started tracking an unidentified target on his radar at around 22:55, and although the object was just ten kilometers away, he was unable to make visual contact with it. Viriato was flying well over 850 miles per hour, and yet the unidentified object was still somehow managing to outpace him. On the radar the object was carrying out erratic maneuvers, flying from side-to-side until it disappeared.

On board one of the F-5E fighter jets, Lieutenant Kleber Marinho spotted a bright light outside his cockpit window. The light was so bright that it illuminated the entire night sky, and its colors alternated from red to white to green and back to red. Regardless of how fast he pushed the fighter jet, the bright light managed to maintain its distance, making his attempts at closing down on it futile. It was as though he was chasing a point in infinity. Regardless of how fast he was going, the UFO was infinitely faster.

One of the most interesting and terrifying accounts of the night comes from Captain Marcio Jordão. Jordão reported that as he was flying over São José dos Campos, he started picking up thirteen targets on his radar, just twenty miles ahead. The sky was perfectly clear, and yet he was unable to visually locate any aircraft outside his windows. The objects kept getting closer and closer and the captain recalled the terrifying moment when he noticed that his aircraft was completely surrounded by thirteen targets. On one side there were seven targets and on the other were six. He didn't know whether these UFOs would shoot down his aircraft or not. He was completely defenseless and helpless.

After a few seconds, the objects made a sudden 180-degree turn, and when Jordão maneuvered his aircraft to continue his pursuit, the objects disappeared off the radar. He estimated the objects to have been flying at least 621 miles per hour when they made the sharp turn and he stated that no aircraft or human can even withstand such a turn. "No plane I know can make turns like that at one thousand kilometers an hour," recounted Jordão.[143]

The entire sighting lasted for three hours. The following day, a press conference was issued in which the air minister addressed the situation to the public.

The Press Conference

In the press conference, several witnesses recounted the previous night's encounter with the unknown. The Minister of Aeronautics

---

143. Good, *Above Top Secret*, 428.

Moreira Lima also spoke about the events, stating that the sightings, which many had witnessed, and the objects ,which the pilots pursued, were not a result of a meteorological phenomenon. In the press conference, Lima confessed how the air force did not have any answers to what the UFOs were. "Every time a UFO is detected, obviously there is a very efficient process to verify if it was an airplane flying, and if there was an approved flying plan," Lima said, "But when it is proved that it is something different, the military aircraft are called in. What happened is that radar detected many UFOs at the area of São Paulo, São José dos Campos and Rio de Janeiro. For many minutes, our craft were followed by these objects. One craft had seven objects by one side and six by the other. Radar is not subject to optical illusions. Radar echoes are due to solid objects, or massive clouds, which were not present that night."[144]

The UFO sightings over São Paulo are one of those few cases where only one explanation makes sense. The turn of events could not have possibly been anything other than an encounter with extraterrestrials. Nothing can account for the capabilities and of the reported UFOs.

What makes this case so pivotal in the study of UFOs is the transparency the Brazilian Air Force adopted. The fact that the authorities stated that they simply could not explain what many had seen, as opposed to saying that the UFOs were either weather balloons or bright stars or planets, is certainly applaudable. Perhaps if every UFO case is treated with such importance and the public was made aware of how serious the phenomenon is, then people would be able to handle the truth and understand what we are sharing our skies with.

---

144. Ministry of Aeronautics press conference, May 23, 1986.

Chapter 42

GIMBAL UFO

Date and location: Classified

The year 2017 was possibly the most important year for the study of UFO phenomenon. To the Stars Academy of Arts and Science, a public benefit aerospace, science, and entertainment company, released three declassified videos that show military aircraft chasing unidentified flying objects. The first footage we will examine was taken by navy jets from the U.S.S. Theodore Roosevelt aircraft carrier, and is known as the "GIMBAL" footage. The thirty-four second footage shows an unidentified flying object carrying out unusual maneuvers that could not have been performed by a terrestrial aircraft.

The Footage

The name GIMBAL comes from a type of suspension of the same name, which allows an object to rotate about a single axis. This is most likely attributed to the movements the object was able to execute. The footage itself was captured by an F/A-28 Super Hornet using Raytheon AN/ASQ-228 Advanced Targeting Forward-Looking Infrared. This is the most advanced sensor and tracking radar system any nation can be in possession of.

Unlike the Tic Tac UFO in the Nimitz incident (see chapter 44), we do not have a lot of background information on this footage, and the date and location are still classified. Before analyzing the footage and the UFO, the following is the transcript of the conversation between the two pilots who encountered the extraterrestrial aircraft. We must keep in mind that these pilots are not only highly skilled, but they are also the best of the best. For years, these pilots have been trained to distinguish aircraft by their shape, altitude, and speed, and then forced to decide whether the aircraft constitutes a threat based on the analysis. Although military pilots are also trained to manage the stress they might experience when airborne, it is evident that these two pilots cannot comprehend what they are witnessing before their very own eyes.

Pilot 1: It's a fucking drone, bro.

Pilot 2: There's a whole fleet of them. Look on the ASA.

Pilot 1: My gosh!

Pilot 2: They're all going against the wind. The wind is 120 knots out of the west.

Pilot 2: Look at that thing dude!

Pilot 2: That's not a (inaudible) is it?

Pilot 1: That is an (inaudible).

Pilot 1: Look at that thing! It's rotating!

From the audio of the footage, it is clear that the pilots had never experience a similar encounter; the excitement and thrill can be heard in their voices. The footage itself is made of infrared images, which alternate between white and black. The items that are black indicate that they are colder than their background, whereas the items that are white indicate that they are warmer than their background.

At the beginning of the footage the UFO is white, traveling at 383 miles per hour at an altitude of 25,010 feet. Although we can only see the one disk-shaped object in the sky, from the transcript we can gather that there were multiple ones. The object then switched to black, indicating that there was a drop in temperature. The object itself had an oval shape with a bump on its top and bottom. The most important characteristics of the UFO are the lack of exhaust plumes and wings, and the fact that it performed a 180-degree angle rotation whilst perpendicular to the horizontal plane. This maneuver shows that the object does not follow the known aerodynamic principles every terrestrial aircraft is bound by.

Speaking to UFO researcher Luis Elizondo for the first time about the incident was Lieutenant Ryan Graves, who is an active duty Navy fighter pilot. Graves told Elizondo that as they were preparing for deployment to the Middle East, several pilots reported seeing strange objects in the sky. The footage released by To the Stars Academy is simply a shorter and lower resolution video of what Graves and his colleagues were shown later that day on board the U.S.S. Roosevelt. The GIMBAL UFO visible in the declassified footage was accompanied by five other unidentified aircraft flying in formation. This explains why one of the pilots says "there's a whole fleet of them."

Interestingly enough, in March 2015, prior to their deployment to the Arabian Gulf, the UFOs had not been observed by the military personnel for a period of time. It was only once the Roosevelt was deployed to the Arabian Gulf that the UFOs reappeared over the Middle East. Is this a modern account of the foo fighter sightings pilots had witnessed during the Second World War? For what reason did these unidentified aircraft suddenly reappear as the Americans were deployed to the Middle East? It is evident that whoever was piloting the aircraft was aware of the military's presence. Could it be that this global presence is a way for these beings to monitor our actions and military decisions to destroy other countries? We must then ask ourselves, for what reason are these beings interested in mankind's self-destructive behaviors? Could it be that they are interested in preserving life on this planet?

Chapter 43

Go Fast!

Date and location: Classified

Given the incredible speed of the UFO seen in the footage, the second footage released by To the Stars Academy, which we shall examine, is known as the "Go Fast" UFO. This footage was taken just weeks apart from the GIMBAL UFO footage by the same navy jets from the U.S.S. Theodore Roosevelt aircraft carrier. Just like the GIMBAL UFO, the footage was obtained by To the Stars Academy through the Freedom of Information Act and was recorded from the Raytheon AN/ASQ- 228 Advanced Targeting Forward-Looking Infrared, which the F/A-18 Super Hornets are equipped with.

The Footage

Flying at an altitude of twenty-five thousand feet, the Super Hornet was traveling at three hundred miles per hour above the ocean, which is clearly visible in the video. In a split second, a white dot enters the frame at a rapid speed and crosses from the right side to the left in a second. The unidentified flying object was traveling at such a rapid velocity that the radar could not even keep up with it. As a matter of fact, the operator only managed to lock down on the object after three attempts. On the third attempt, the radar operator managed to lock on to it so that the automatic tracking system could keep the object centered in frame. In the footage we can also hear the excitement and thrill of the pilots as they are witnessing the majestic UFO.

Pilot 1: Whoa! Got it!

Pilot 2: Hahaha! Wohoo!

Pilot 1: What the fuck is that thing?

Pilot 2: Did you box a moving target?

Pilot 1: No, it's in auto track.

Pilot 2: Oh okay.

Pilot 1: Oh my gosh dude.

Pilot 2: Wow! What is that man?

Pilot 1: Look at that flying!

The conversational exchange between the two pilots shows just how bizarre and unusual this encounter was. The visible characteristics of the object are certainly unconventional; from the lack of wings, visible engines or an exhaust plume, to the tremendous speed the object was traveling. What is interesting to note is the lack of familiarity the pilots have of the object. To become a fighter pilot and fly a Super Hornet takes several years of training and experience. Apart from that, pilots must be familiar with any aircraft they might encounter in the sky. It is only this familiarity that will help them distinguish what is a threat and what is not.

The characteristics and maneuverability of the UFO without a doubt could not have been executed by a terrestrial aircraft. This footage is further proof that extraterrestrials do exist and are certainly infinitely more technologically advanced than us, nor are they bound by the general laws that terrestrial aircraft are.

Chapter 44

The Tic Tac UFO

Date: November 14, 2004

The third and perhaps most fascinating footage is known as the "Tic Tac" UFO. This footage was recorded back in November 2004 but was only released in 2017 by To the Stars Academy. The "Tic Tac" UFO footage is considered by many to be the ultimate proof that extraterrestrials exist, and that they are in possession of technology that is far superior to anything we have on earth.

On November 10, 2004, Navy Chief Petty Officer Kevin Day, on board the U.S.S. Princeton, started noticing numerous targets on the radar. As many as one hundred targets appeared, all traveling south toward southern California. The objects were at an altitude of twenty-eight thousand feet and were traveling at just 120 miles per hour. It is incredibly unusual for any aircraft to travel at such a low speed when at that altitude. Several other vessels were tracking the same targets on their radar and these sightings continued throughout the week.

The actual footage, which To the Stars Academy released, captured the visual sighting and pursuit, which occurred on November 14, 2004. At around 09:00, the same events started playing out; numerous unidentified targets started appearing on the radar. At the time, there was an F/A-18 Hornet and two F/A-18E/F Super

Hornets flying in the area and thus, the operations officer on board the U.S.S. Princeton asked them to intercept the unidentified object, which was being tracked on radar. On board the lead Hornet was Commander David Fravor, and flying as wingman on the second Hornet was Lieutenant Jim Slaight.

On the day of the visual sighting, the visibility was clear. The radar showed that the object had made a drastic drop in altitude in a significantly and inconceivably short time, which would have been impossible for any human to withstand. In just one second, the object dropped from twenty-eight thousand feet to sea level, which simply could not have been performed by a terrestrial aircraft; such a drop would have turned any human into paste.

The sonar team on board the U.S.S. Louisville, which was patrolling just below the surface, simultaneously reported that an unidentified object had plunged into the ocean, exceeding seventy knots, which is twice as fast as the navy's fastest submarine.

Flying above the vector, given that the object was at sea level, Fravor looked out the cockpit windows at the sea, where he noticed a large area of churning water, as though a Boeing aircraft had just crashed into it. In an instant, the object appeared just fifty feet above sea level and Fravor immediately noticed the Tic Tac-shaped UFO moving erratically at an insurmountable speed. The object itself was approximately ten to fourteen meters long and, once again, it had no visible wings, engines, or exhaust plumes.

Fravor plunged the jet toward the UFO, and as he did so, it started moving in the opposite direction. The UFO now started ascending along a curved path. Fravor kept pursuing the object, however, in less than two seconds the UFO accelerated and disappeared out of sight. Given that the UFO was now out of sight,

Fravor and Slaight started flying to their rendezvous point, which was approximately sixty miles away.

A few minutes into their journey to the predesignated location, the U.S.S. Princeton informed Fravor and Slaight that the UFO had now reappeared at the rendezvous point. If the general laws of physics are applied, given that the object had traveled sixty miles in just a couple of seconds, the UFO must have been traveling at a greater speed than 1,190 miles per hour, which is the maximum speed of the Hornet fighter jet.

The Declassified Infrared Footage

On December 16, 2017, To the Stars Academy released the infrared footage, which was filmed from the F/A-18 Super Hornet. Each fighter jet is equipped with a Raytheon AN/ASQ-228 Advanced Targeting Forward Looking Infrared camera, the most sophisticated and advanced technology the military is in possession of. Before going into the analysis of the footage, many skeptics have argued that the footage is not authentic. The authenticity is no longer debatable. On April 29, 2020, the Pentagon acknowledged the videos and stated that they are truly genuine. Apart from that, each of the three videos include a chain-of-custody documentation, further cementing their authenticity.

Although just two minutes and forty-five seconds long, the footage shows the advanced capability of the object, which, without a doubt, proves its extraterrestrial origin. The general shape of the object is similar to that of a Tic Tac, lacking wings and an exhaust plume. As stated in previous chapters, an exhaust plume is a major component of any motor object. Without one, the engine would simply malfunction since the gases from the combustion of fuel would not be discharged out of the engine.

A few seconds into the footage, the object makes a sharp acceleration, which the radar sensor cannot keep up with. One other aspect that proves that the object was of an extraterrestrial origin is the fact that no sonic booms were heard even though the object had exceeded the speed of sound. Fravor estimated the object to be traveling at a speed greater than Mach 5 (which means that it exceeded the speed of sound by five times). Since no sonic boom was heard, the object must have been traveling through a vacuum. Once again, as has been stated in previous chapters, no terrestrial aircraft can travel in a vacuum.

The following is part of an in-depth interview published by To the Stars Academy of Arts & Sciences with Fravor, in which he recounts his experience in a great amount of detail. Fravor stated that the plan originally was to do air defense exercises, but then their plans had changed. He said, "The U.S.S. Princeton, their controller calls us up and tells us we're going to cancel the air defense exercise and we have real-world tasking.

"So, as we're flying, we start looking around because of our merged plots, now you're into a visual arena you're not as much worried about your radar [...] I look out the right side and I see something in the water, and it looks like about the size of a 737 in the water, pointing east. So, he's pointing east so it would be on the right hand side of the airplane, just forward of the wing line is this little white object that looks like a Tic Tac, and it's moving around erratically. There's no rotor wash, which you see from a helicopter. It's just this odd object. I'm like, 'That's interesting.' I said, 'Well, I'm going to go check it out.' So, about the 9 o'clock [position], between nine and ten, I started an uneasy descent, and I'm watching this thing and it's just kind of randomly moving around this vehicle, and it's basically moving around like it was checking it out.

"So, as we passed through about the 12 o'clock position, and we're descending, it kind of recognizes that we're there and it starts to mirror. It's probably around three thousand feet below us and about a mile across the circle. It's about the size of an F-18 so forty-seven feet long but it has no wings. I don't see any exhaust plume. So, as I come across, I'm a little above him and I go, 'Well, the only way I might get this is to do an aggressive out-of-plane maneuver.' So, I dump the nose and I go from the 9 o'clock through the vertical down to go across to the 3 o'clock.

"As I get down to about sixty degrees, nose a little through the bottom, it starts to accelerate. It has an incredible rate of acceleration and it takes off and it goes south. It takes off like nothing I have ever seen. It's literally one minute it's there and the next minute it's like poof, it's gone. So, I come up on the radio and I said, 'Hey, let's spin around and go back to see what was in the water.' So, right there it's kind of below us and there's nothing in the water. I call up the Princeton and I said, 'Hey, do you guys have all of this?' I was talking back and forth to the controller and we got into more detail. We have been tracking these things, they've been dropping from eighty thousand feet and they come straight down. They hang out at about twenty thousand feet. They don't monitor, they just sit there. We have had nothing airborne, and when they're done, they go back straight up, and they disappear.

"So, we start going back to the cap and the Princeton controller calls us up and says, 'You're never going to believe this. That thing, is that your cap (the target that was sixty miles away)? It's hanging out right where you're supposed to be.'"[145]

Jim Slaight, the wingman on board the second Hornet, made similar comments in an interview for the television program *Contact*. He, too, was surprised by the objects' capabilities and was adamant that this object could not have been piloted by a human being. As a matter of fact, there was no chance that the object was terrestrial in origin. No nation or military could be in possession of such advanced technology, that defies the loaws of physics and aerodynamics. Moreover, no human being can even withstand the physical stress caused by such maneuvers.

In the interview Slaight said, "We went out there primarily to do individual ship training. I started noticing these really anomalous tracks, unlike nothing I'd ever seen before, and these objects were coming into my radar coverage. There were probably ten objects in the sky."

"In the back of my mind I was thinking I want to intercept one of these things and so I launched an intercept aircraft," Slaight said. "He started making the approach to this object and that's when everything changed. This thing did a barrel roll right around his aircraft, then went straight down to the surface of the ocean. He went following it down, and as soon as he went like that, this thing popped straight back out of the water, back up to twenty-eight thousand feet. It was completely quiet.

---

145. To the Stars Academy of Arts & Sciences, interview with Commander David Fravor, November 2017, https://thevault.tothestarsacademy.com/2004-uss-nimitz-pilot-interview/tag/David+Fravor.

"Something going that fast is going to sound like, 'Boom boom boom boom boom.' It's going to have a whole bunch of sonic booms. There were no sonic booms."[146]

When asked about the technology the Tic Tac UFO possessed, Slaight explained how the (approximately forty-seven-foot long) object did not have any wings or any propulsion system. He commented on how the object was capable of traveling several miles in just a matter of seconds, and that such an acceleration would turn any human being into "mush." Slaight stated that there was no possible way a human being would be able to withstand that type of G force. "I think the human body can withstand about eight Gs," Slaight said. "This thing had about 1350 Gs. You would've been paste."[147]

Erased Communication

Whatever Fravor and several other military personnel had witnessed was most certainly not terrestrial. The situation became even more mysterious when on the same day of the incident, military personnel exited from a helicopter and requested all the data recordings of the day. Gary Voorhis, the computer technician on board the U.S.S. Princeton was requested to hand over all the data recording tapes without an explanation, a procedure that is not the norm.

Conclusion

After decades of silence and denying the existence of extraterrestrials and their aircraft, the Pentagon has finally acknowledged that

---

146. *Contact*, "Alien Evidence," Bill Howard, Sarah Wetherbee, Jason Wolf, executive producers, aired August 7, 2019 on Discovery.

147. *Contact*, "Alien Evidence," Bill Howard, Sarah Wetherbee, Jason Wolf, executive producers, aired August 7, 2019 on Discovery.

not only does it take the UFO phenomenon seriously, but also that fighter pilots have had numerous encounters with these unidentified aircraft. The three UFOs that are shown in the footage released by To the Stars Academy are undoubtedly extraterrestrial in origin. Although this is a big claim, it is not made lightly.

UFO research Luis Elizondo and his team at To the Stars Academy outline five observables, which are characteristics and behaviors that conventional aircraft cannot possess or perform. The first observable is the antigravity lift that is evident in all three aircraft shown in the declassified footages. The unidentified flying objects overcome Earth's gravity without a visible propulsion system and lack characteristics terrestrial aricraft must possess, such as wings and exhaust plumes. The second observable is the instantaneous acceleration, which no human can survive the G forces of. The unidentified objects seen in the footages and in other cases we have analyzed in this book accelerate and change direction so fast that it would turn any human into paste. The G forces are simply insurmountable.

The third observable is hypersonic velocity, which is the ability of the aircraft to exceed the speed of sound without producing a sonic boom or without leaving a signature trail. This implies that the aircraft would be traveling in a vacuum, which is impossible for any terrestrial aircraft to do. Low observability or "cloaking" is the fourth observable. A constant factor throughout UFO sightings is the fact that observers rarely manage to get a clear picture of the aircraft. As a matter of fact, many witnesses report seeing balls of light or glowing objects in the sky.

The fifth and final observable is trans-medium traveling—when an aircraft has the ability to travel in different mediums, such as space, the atmosphere, and even water. In the Tic Tac incident, the object descended from thirty thousand feet and plunged into the ocean, traveling twice as fast as the navy's submarine.

With the declassification of these videos, we can now start asking questions related to the technology these beings possess. Are there any militaries that are in possession of such technology? (Perhaps they acquired the technology from a crash site.) Can humans even duplicate or come close to creating technology that has similar capabilities? If so, will this technology be used in wars, causing more destruction and deaths? Or will we use it proactively, such as to explore the possibility of interstellar travel?

Part 4

Government
Projects

The study of unidentified aerial phenomena can be traced back to the year 1948. From that year, every reported UFO case has been forwarded to the United States Air Force, where it is reviewed, and an explanation provided (even in cases where there simply wasn't an explanation). Before going into this section on government projects, I must point out that just because a UFO case was investigated does not mean that it was adequately done or that it was investigated objectively and without any biases. The majority of these government funded projects have been underfunded and have had a lack of resources, making it impossible for the air force to investigate the UFO reports sufficiently.

Throughout the following chapters, it will become more evident how the air force has disregarded one of the most significant UFO cases and simply provided the same generic explanation to the majority of the reports. Even when some cases simply could not be explained, the air force still provided an explanation even if it did not corroborate with the details of the sighting and witness statements. The extraterrestrial hypothesis itself was rarely even considered. In fact, it was never used to explain any of the cases thus far. To this day, the air force has never publicly stated that a UFO report was a result of an interplanetary flying object.

In this section, we shall examine every project that has been funded by the air force in order to investigate the reported UFO sightings.

Chapter 45
Project Sign

Project Sign was the first project initiated by the United States Air Force to investigate reports of unidentified flying objects. The project was initiated on January 22, 1948, and was terminated on December 30 of the same year.

In September of 1947, Commander Lieutenant General Nathan Twinning wrote to the commanding officer of the air force regarding the increase in UFO reports. In the memo, Twinning stated that the objects seemed to exhibit maneuvers and characteristics that were unconventional to any terrestrial aircraft, weather phenomenon, or weather balloons. He also emphasized the fact that the phenomenon is a real one and not a visionary or fictional one. The letter reads as follows:

* * * * * *

1. As requested by AC/AS-2 there is presented below the considered opinion of this command concerning the so-called "Flying Discs." This opinion is based on interrogation report data furnished by AC/AS-2 and preliminary studies by personnel of T-2 and Aircraft Laboratory, Engineering Division T-3. This opinion was arrived at in a conference between personnel from the Air Institute of Technology, Intelligence T-2, Office, Chief of Engineering Division,

and the Aircraft, Power Plant and Propeller Laboratories of Engineering Division T-3.

2. It is the opinion that:

    a. The phenomenon reported is something real and not visionary or fictitious.

    b. There are objects probably approximating the shape of a disc, of such appreciable size as to appear to be as large as man-made aircraft.

    c. There is a possibility that some of the incidents may be caused by natural phenomena, such as meteors.

    d. The reported operating characteristics, such as extreme rates of climb, maneuverability (particularly in roll), and action that must be considered evasive when sighted or contacted by friendly aircraft and radar, lend belief to the possibility that some of the objects are controlled either manually, automatically, or remotely.

    e. The apparent common description of the objects is as follows:

        1. Metallic or light reflecting surface.

        2. Absence of trail, except in a few instances when the object apparently was operating under high performance conditions.

        3. Circular or elliptical in shape, flat on bottom and domed on top.

        4. Several reports of well-kept formation flights varying from three to nine objects.

        5. Normally no associated sound, except in three instances a substantial rumbling roar was noted.

6. Level flight speeds normally above three hundred knots are estimated.

f. It is possible within the present U. S. knowledge—provided extensive detailed development is undertaken—to construct a piloted aircraft that has the general description of the object in sub-paragraph (e) above that would be capable of an approximate range of seven thousand miles at subsonic speeds.

g. Any developments in this country along the lines indicated would be extremely expensive, time consuming, and at the considerable expense of current projects and therefore, if directed, should be set up independently of existing projects.

h. Due consideration must be given the following:

1. The possibility that these objects are of domestic origin—the product of some high security project not known to AC/AS-2 or this Command.

2. The lack of physical evidence in the shape of crash recovered exhibits that would undeniably prove the existence of these objects

3. The possibility that some foreign nation has a form of propulsion possibly nuclear, which is outside of our domestic knowledge.

3. It is recommended that:

a. Headquarters, Army Air Forces issue a directive assigning a priority, security classification and code name for a detailed study of this matter to include the preparation of complete sets of all available and pertinent data that will then be made available to the army, navy, Atomic Energy Commission, JRDB, the Air Force Scientific Advisory Group, NACA, and the RAND and NEPA projects for comments and recommendations, with a preliminary report to be forwarded within fifteen days of receipt of the data and a detailed report thereafter every 30 days as the investigation develops. A complete interchange of data should be affected.

4. Awaiting a specific directive AMC will continue the investigation within its current resources in order to more closely define the nature of the phenomenon. Detailed Essential Elements of Information will be formulated immediately for transmittal thru channels.[148]

★★★★★★

The members of Project Sign investigated a total of 156 cases and out of those cases, only seven of them remained unidentified. This means that the members of the project could not come up with any sufficient explanation for these seven cases.

As I have stated in the beginning of the book, most sightings can easily be explained by natural phenomena or a misidentification of celestial bodies or aircraft. However, there is a portion of cases in which the reported objects or lights are interplanetary and extraterrestrial in origin. As has been outlined in the cases explored in this book, the reports usually depict the technological superiority of these UFOs to anything we have on Earth. The maneuverability, capabilities and general characteristics are unfathomable even to the highest-level officials.

Although Project Sign's final report acknowledged the existence of UFOs, it did conclude that there was not enough evidence

---

148. Air Materiel Command Wright-Patterson, "Unidentified Aerial Objects, Project Sign," February 1949, http://www.nicap.org/docs /SignRptFeb1949.pdf.

to confirm that the objects were extraterrestrial in origin. The board members of Project Sign did believe that these UFOs were interplanetary, which is why they wrote the *Estimate of the Situation*, a document that explained why the extraterrestrial hypothesis is the most plausible one. Albeit the fact that several military personnel believed that these objects were not terrestrial, General Hoyt Vandenberg, the Chief of Staff, found this explanation to be humorous and inaccurate.

The final conclusion that Project Sign came to (or rather Vandenberg) was that these objects were either natural weather phenomena, celestial bodies or misidentifications. As we shall see in this chapter, all government studies of UFOs negate the extraterrestrial hypothesis, even though several military personnel have had first-hand experience with the phenomenon.

The final document that Project Sign produced classified the UFO reports into four categories. The first category includes the typical flying saucers, which usually have a disk shape, a torpedo shape or a cigar shape. The second category includes balloon-shaped aircraft; the third includes spherical aircraft and the fourth includes balls of light. All four categories have one aspect in common and that is the way the objects maneuver. As we have seen in the UFO cases covered in this book, in all encounters it is evident that the UFOs do not follow the general laws of physics and aerodynamics, and do not seem to possess any of the limitations that terrestrial aircraft are bound by.

Chapter 46
Project Grudge

Project Grudge was initiated on February 11, 1949, and was terminated three years later in March of 1952. Although Project Grudge's investigations lasted three whole years, only one document was produced, which was over six hundred pages long. Shortly after the document was released in 1952, the air force terminated the project. Although the personnel who made up Project Grudge stated that they had an unbiased approach to the reports, the conclusions and explanations they provided showed otherwise. From the get-go, it appeared that the aim of Project Grudge was to debunk and ridicule the reported sightings and the witnesses.

Interestingly enough, the project even included a public relations campaign in which articles were posted, highlighting the fact that UFO sightings were hoaxes and attempts by people to gain fame. It is with no surprise that the Grudge report denied the extraterrestrial hypothesis, even though several reports contained convincing evidence were supposedly investigated. The conclusions Project Grudge came to are the following:

1. There is no evidence that objects reported upon are the result of an advanced scientific foreign development, and, therefore, they constitute no direct threat to the national security. In view of this, it is recommended that the investigation and study of reports of unidentified flying objects be reduced in scope.

2. All evidence and analyses indicate that reports of unidentified flying objects are the result of:

    a. Misinterpretation of various conventional objects.

    b. A mild form of mass hysteria of "war nerves."

    c. Individuals who fabricate such reports to perpetrate a hoax or to seek publicity.

    d. Psychopathological persons.

3. Planned release of unusual aerial objects coupled with the release of related psychological propaganda could cause mass hysteria:

    a. Employment of these methods by or against an enemy would yield similar results

The conclusions offered are certainly inadequate and inconclusive. The air force claimed that these objects did not pose a threat to national security, nor did they exhibit any characteristics that indicated that they were scientifically more advanced than terrestrial aircraft. This first statement in itself is inaccurate. The term UFO states that the object is unidentified. If an unidentified aircraft has infiltrated a country's airspace, isn't that considered a threat? Moreover, if an unidentified object outmaneuvers military fighter-jets, doesn't that imply that it is superior and more technologically advanced?

The second point the report made was that UFO sightings were a misidentification of conventional aircraft, a result of mass hysteria or a hoax. Although it is true that the majority of UFO sightings do have a natural explanation, the cases examined in this book cannot be as easily explained. As a matter of fact, all cases covered in this book cannot be sufficiently explained using traditional hypotheses (such as the weather balloon explanation and the bright stars/planets explanation). In cases such as The Battle of L.A in which thousands of individuals had observed multiple UFOs in the sky, it would be foolish to conclude that the sighting was a delusion. Moreover, claiming that all UFO reports are a result of those four explanations is most definitely generalization, as there are multiple reports made by credible individuals who did not gain anything from them reporting their sighting. Actually, the only thing they did gain was harassment and ridicule.

Once again, although the personnel involved in Project Grudge claimed to have had an unbiased and objective approach, the facts prove otherwise.

Chapter 47
The Robertson Panel

Following a wave of UFO sightings in 1952, the Central Intelligence Agency made a recommendation to the Intelligence Advisory Committee to create a scientific committee. This panel would carry out an independent investigation into the UFO cases that had initially been examined by Project Blue Book. The panel was led by physicist Howard Robertson, and included physicist and radar expert Luis Alvarez, nuclear missile expert Frederick Durant, nuclear physicist Samuel Goudsmit, astrophysicist Thornton Page, physicist Lloyd Berkner, and astronomer J. Allen Hynek.

Although the panel members only had four formal meetings (a total of twelve hours), they did manage to come up with conclusions that explained the UFO sightings. How the panel was able to solve the UFO phenomenon in just twelve hours is unbeknownst to me. Unsurprisingly, the conclusion that the panel came to was identical to the previous projects, making this project a complete waste of resources and a waste of an opportunity to truly study the phenomenon. The report stated, "The Panel members were in agreement with O/SI opinion that, although evidence of any direct threat from these sightings was wholly lacking, related dangers might well exist resulting from:

a. Misidentification of actual enemy artifacts by defense personnel.

b. Overloading of emergency reporting channels with "false" information ("noise to signal ratio" analogy—Berkner).

c. Subjectivity of public to mass hysteria and greater vulnerability to possible enemy psychological warfare."[149]

The personnel on the panel also made several recommendations to the national security agencies: "1. Pursuant to the request of the Assistant Director for Scientific Intelligence, the undersigned Panel of Scientific Consultants has met to evaluate any possible threat to national security posed by unidentified flying objects ("flying saucers"), and to make recommendations thereon. The panel has received the evidence as presented by cognizant intelligence agencies, primarily the Air Technical Intelligence Center, and has reviewed a selection of the best documented incidents.

2. As a result of its considerations, the panel concludes:

a. That the evidence presented on unidentified flying objects shows no indication that these phenomena constitute a direct physical threat to national security. We firmly believe that there is no residuum of cases that indicates phenomena that are attributable to foreign artifacts capable of hostile acts, and that there is no evidence that the phenomena indicates a need for the revision of current scientific concepts.

---

149. F. C. Durant, "Report of Meetings of Scientific Advisory Panel on Unidentified Flying Objects," Office of Scientific Intelligence, CIA, January 14–18, 1953, 17, https://rense.com//general96/JANUARY181953--2.pdf.

3. The panel further concludes:

    a. That the continued emphasis on the reporting of these phenomena does, in these parlous times, result in a threat to the orderly functioning of the protective organs of the body politic. We cite as examples the clogging of channels of communication by irrelevant reports, the danger of being led by continued false alarms to ignore real indications of hostile action, and the cultivation of a morbid national psychology in which skillful hostile propaganda could induce hysterical behavior and harmful distrust of duty constituted authority.

4. In order most effectively to strengthen the national facilities for the timely recognition and the appropriate handling of true indications of hostile action, and to minimize the concomitant dangers alluded to above, the panel recommends:

    a. That the national security agencies take immediate steps to strip the unidentified flying objects of the special status they have been given and the aura of mystery they have unfortunately acquired;

    b. That the national security agencies institute policies on intelligence, training, and public education designed to prepare the material defenses and the morale of the country to recognize most promptly and to react most effectively to true indications of hostile intent or action. We suggest that these aims may be achieved by an integrated program designed to reassure the public of the total lack of evidence of Inimical forces behind the phenomenon, to train personnel to recognize and reject false indications quickly and effectively, and to strengthen regular channels for the evaluation of and prompt reaction to true indications of hostile measures."[150]

Despite the fact that the sole purpose of the Robertson Panel was for there to be an independent investigation into the already reviewed cases, not only did the personnel come to the same conclusions as the previous studies had, but they also encouraged the national security agencies to disregard the UFO phenomenon altogether.

With hundreds of reports that prove that these objects are in possession of technology that is superior to anything the military is in possession of, the panel managed to explain all the UFO reports that had been made in just twelve hours. Up to this point in history, there still was not a single objective study of the phenomenon; actually, there was the opposite. The projects we have examined so far are all examples of the general approach the air force takes when it investigates UFO reports. In all circumstances, the members assigned to the projects have all been skeptics whose biased opinion and beliefs influenced the study and investigation. The Robertson Panel shows not only that the UFO reports were not being objectively studied, but also that a propaganda was being promoted to reduce the public's interest in the phenomenon.

---

150. Durant, "Report of Meetings of Scientific Advisory Panel on Unidentified Flying Objects," 27.

Chapter 48
The Condon Committee

From the year 1966 to 1968, the United States Air Force funded the University of Colorado to study the unidentified aerial phenomenon. The eighteen-month study was directed by Edward Condon, a nuclear physicist who played a major part in the development of radar and nuclear weapons. Similar to the Robertson Panel, the University of Colorado studied hundreds of UFO reports that had been previously investigated by Project Blue Book.

Although the objective of the study was to have an objective investigation, it was evident that this was simply another opportunity for UFO skeptics, such as Edward Condon himself, to deride the phenomenon. This was evident early on in the investigation. James McDonald, a senior physicist in the Department of Meteorology at the University of Arizona, had numerous meetings with Condon, and it was apparent to McDonald that Condon had already come to a conclusion even before any cases were reviewed. On one occasion during a meeting between the two, Condon had literally fallen asleep as McDonald was carrying out a briefing on significant UFO reports.

In July 1967, the credibility of the study was further tarnished when a letter was leaked to McDonald that showed the humiliating approach that Condon himself had adopted. The letter arrived in McDonald's hands by one of the committee's investigators who had a disagreement with the way Condon was approaching the study. The letter, which was written by chief assistant Robert Low, reads as follows: "The trick would be, I think, to describe the project so that, to the public, it would appear a totally objective study but, to the scientific community, would present the image of a group of nonbelievers trying their best to be objective but having an almost zero expectation of finding a saucer."[151]

It was no surprise when the committee published its report, titled *Scientific Study of Unidentified Flying Objects*, which completely ruled out the extraterrestrial hypothesis. The title itself is ironic, considering that the investigation was neither scientific nor objective. The conclusion the Condon Committee came to was the following: "Our general conclusion is that nothing has come from the study of UFOs in the past twenty-one years that has added to scientific knowledge. Careful consideration of the record as it is available to us leads us to conclude that further extensive study of UFOs probably cannot be justified in the expectation that science will be advanced thereby. It has been argued that this lack of contribution to science is due to the fact that very little scientific effort has been put on the subject. We do not agree. We feel that the reason that there has been very little scientific study of the subject is that those scientists who are most directly concerned, astronomers, atmospheric physicists, chemists, and psychologists, having had ample opportunity to look into the matter, have individually decided that UFO phenomena do not offer a fruitful field in which to look for major scientific discoveries."[152]

---

151. Jerome Clark, *The UFO Book: Encyclopedia of the Extraterrestrial*, (Detroit: Visible Ink Press, 1998), 594.

152. Condon Committee Report, Scientific Study of Unidentified Flying Objects, January 1968, 15.

The committee explained how the military was wasting its time and money when investigating UFO reports. Furthermore, Condon suggested that the phenomenon, and any future reports, be completely disregarded. The document also stated that the idea of the government having extraterrestrial vehicles or technology in its possession is "fantastic nonsense."

Once again, it is unfathomable how an investigation that only lasts eighteen months can explain and solve one of the most mysterious and perplexing phenomena. The only constructive aspect that came out of this study was the letter, which was leaked to McDonald, which proved once and for all how disgracefully these air force funded projects were approaching and investigating the UFO phenomenon.

Chapter 49
Project Blue Book

Project Blue Book is perhaps the most well known project the U.S. government has carried out when it comes to investigating unidentified flying objects. The project was initiated in March of 1952 and was terminated over a decade later in December of 1969, after the military stated that there was no benefit in investigating the phenomenon. Throughout the seventeen years, the members investigated a total of 12,618 UFO reports; 701 of which are to this day unexplained (or rather can only be explained by the extraterrestrial hypothesis).

The aim of Project Blue Book was twofold: the first aim was to scientifically and objectively study the UFO reports, and the second was to determine whether these unidentified flying objects, which thousands had seen in the sky, had posed a threat to national security or not. The project itself was terminated not because there was a drop in UFO reports, but because the Condon Committee had stated that studying UFO reports was wasting the military's resources. As a result of such a statement, the study was terminated even though there were over seven hundred cases still unsolved, and a significant number of reports that had enough evidence to prove the existence of extraterrestrial life.

Captain Edward Ruppelt was the first director of the project, and was the first individual to use the term "unidentified flying object." Ruppelt's stance on the phenomenon was an unbiased one, and he made sure that all members on the board would have the same approach. With the previous UFO studies having tarnished the phenomenon, Ruppelt's approach reinstated its importance. In 1956 Captain George Gregory took over as head director of Project Blue Book. The direction that Gregory led was the total opposite of Ruppelt's. The majority of UFO reports were not investigated. The ones that were investigated were given the same explanation: that the sighting was a misidentification of a meteor or of another natural phenomenon.

In an attempt to once again reinstate the objectivity of the study, Lieutenant Colonel Robert Friend was appointed the director of the project in 1958. Although Friend's approach was similar to Ruppelt's, there was an issue with a lack of resources that limited the investigation. Ironically enough, his era as the head director of the project came to an end due to the fact that Friend himself believed that the study was ineffective and practically useless given the lack of money and resources being provided to him. Project Blue Book's final years were under Major Hector Quintanilla's control. Once again, the study had a well-renowned UFO skeptic as its director.

In 1970, the project was terminated, and its final report stated: "No UFO reported, investigated, and evaluated by the air force has ever given any indication of threat to our national security. There has been no evidence submitted to or discovered by the Air Force that sightings categorized as "unidentified" represent technological developments or principles beyond the range of present-day scientific knowledge. There has been no evidence indicating the sightings categorized as "unidentified" are extraterrestrial vehicles."[153]

153. United States Air Force, USAF Fact Sheet 95–03, http://www.gutenberg.org/files/25674/25674-h/25674-h.htm.

It must be emphasized once again that just because a report is officially listed as unexplained does not mean that there is not a logical explanation. It is crystal clear by now that no Air Force funded project considered the extraterrestrial hypothesis to be a plausible one, and the conclusions that all projects came to had been predetermined. The lack of objectivity and openness made the studies a failure from the get-go.

With reference to the conclusion that Project Blue Book had come to, there are a number of flaws that will be outlined. The first is that there have been enough UFO reports that prove that extraterrestrials do exist. Although there is also a good amount of reports that can be explained through natural phenomena, there have been hundreds of UFO reports that prove the presence of an interplanetary object.

Secondly, as has already been stated, since we do not know the intentions of these beings, we cannot come to a definite conclusion and state that these UFOs do not pose a threat to mankind's safety. In reality, it would be quite foolish to assume that. The truth of the matter is that these beings are clearly in possession of advanced technology. If they ever decided to, they could wipe out mankind effortlessly.

Chapter 50
Advanced Aerospace Threat Identification Program

In December of 2017, the government stated that it had been officially investigating UFO reports since 2007; making it the most recent UFO study. With a budget of over twenty million dollars, the Advanced Aerospace Threat Identification Program (AATIP) was initiated by Senate Majority Leader Harry Reid in 2007 and was led by Luis Elizondo.

Elizondo claimed that, apart from investigating UFO reports, the government was in possession of metal alloys that were extraterrestrial in origin. In an interview with Alejandro Rojas, Elizondo stated that these metals have "strange isotopic values, indicating it is not from earth."[154] Elizondo also stated that this material was most definitely not terrestrial and couldn't have originated from technologically advanced countries such as Russia or China.

"The data we have been seeing is so advanced it is hard enough for us to replicate our observations with our understanding of quantum mechanics," Elizondo said. "But for this type of technology to be available when we first start seeing it, I think is beyond improbable, I'm not going to say impossible, but I think it is really, really unlikely to come from another country like Russia or China."

---

154. Alejandro Rojas, interview with Luis Elizondo, June 8, 2019.

Elizondo continued, "It leads to the next quest if it's not ours and not theirs, then whose is it? I don't know whose it is and that is why we are asking the questions and why we did what we did for the last 10 years and why we need to continue doing what we are doing because we need to ask those questions. We don't know who they belong to, we don't know who they are or what they are, but we know they are real."[155]

Elizondo resigned from the Pentagon in 2017 because he believed the government was concealing information regarding the UFO phenomenon,and was not properly investigating UFO reports. With that being said, Elizondo's journey to raise awareness on the phenomenon continued when he joined To the Stars Academy of Arts and Science, which is the company that released the GIMBAL, Tic Tac, and Go Fast videos showing military jets chasing UFOs. In his resignation letter, Elizondo claimed that the Department of Defense and other organizations within the military were not taking the phenomenon seriously, even though these objects posed a threat to national security. Elizondo's resignation letter stated: "Despite overwhelming evidence at both the unclassified and classified levels, certain individuals in the department remain staunchly opposed to further research on what could be a tactical threat to our pilots, sailors and soldiers, and perhaps even an existential threat to our national security....I humbly submit my resignation in hopes it will encourage you to ask the hard questions: "who else knows?", "what are their capabilities?" and "why aren't we spending more time and effort on this issue?"[156]

---

155. Alejandro Rojas, interview with Luis Elizondo, June 8, 2019.

156. Luis Elizondo, letter of resignation, October 4, 2017, https://www.history.com/news/unidentified-ufo-investigation-documents.

The reason why the project was terminated was due to the lack of finances. Interestingly enough, the same explanation was used for Project Blue Book. Tom Crosson, a spokesperson for the Pentagon, stated the following when asked about AATIP: "it was determined that there were other, higher priority issues that merited funding and it was in the best interest of the Department of Defense to make a change."[157]

Although AATIP was officially terminated in 2012, I firmly believe that the air force is still investigating the UFO phenomenon, and is spending millions of dollars on the study, but simply under a different name. When there is footage, such as the videos released by To the Stars Academy that clearly show an aircraft of extraterrestrial origin, it is difficult to believe that the air force simply disregards these reports and assumes that they do not pose a threat to national security. As a matter of fact, given that wars are started without any hesitation or for vain reasons, I firmly believe that the phenomenon is being studied profoundly, and attempts are being made for the military to obtain the technology that these beings possess, and is even attempting to duplicate and reverse engineer it.

---

157. Helen Cooper, interview with Thomas Crosston, *New York Times*, December 16, 2017.

Afterword

In May of 2020, the Pentagon publicly acknowledged the existence of the UFO phenomenon. With the declassification of the three videos released by To the Stars, Academy, the Pentagon has finally acknowledged that there have been numerous instances in which pilots have chased down unidentified flying objects, only for these unidentified aircraft to outmaneuver them and display characteristics that prove they could not have been man-made. Although this acknowledgment was only just recently made, the authorities have always deemed unidentified flying objects as a threat; hence why there was such a full-scale military response in the majority of the cases discussed in this book. With that being said, there have also been numerous cases in which the air force publicly dismissed or disregarded the reports. Naturally, this does not mean that the case was not properly investigated, it solely means that the case was played down for the public's interest.

The biggest take away you, as the reader, can get from this book is to understand just how advanced and powerful these visitors are. In all of the cases we have covered in this book, the reported UFOs have displayed characteristics that simply cannot be possessed by man-made aircraft. Moreover, these extraterrestrial aircraft defy the laws of physics. The technology that these beings are in possession of is incomprehensible and remarkable. The idea of manipulating gravity and having an antigravity propulsion system makes time travel possible, which explains how these beings can travel light-years in a lifetime. There are also other components that prove that these UFOs are extraterrestrial in origin, such as the absence of exhaust plumes and breaking the sound barrier without producing a sonic boom.

With this, however, comes a number of existential questions that we must ask. What are the intentions of these beings? What does it mean for the human race if these beings have malicious intentions? Although we can't know the answers to these questions at the moment, we must not bury our heads in the sand and deny that these beings exist and have been visiting our planet. We now live in a day and age where most people believe that we are not alone in the universe; the days in which disclosure will cause worldwide panic are over. We are living in a revolutionary time and with that, revolutionary changes must be made. Isn't it time for governments all over the world to declassify the information they have regarding extraterrestrial life and these interplanetary flying objects?

This book has covered cases from all over the world that prove the existence of extraterrestrial life. The one thing that can never be taken away from a human being is the knowledge one learns, and I hope that this book has been a tool for you to broaden your knowledge on the UFO phenomenon. I hope this book has ignited a fire in you to start asking questions and demanding answers. Always do your own investigating. I truly hope that as you look up at the starry sky, you realize that we are not alone. We never have been. Our planet is simply a speck in an ever-evolving universe. In a universe that is infinite, there are infinite possibilities.

Bibliography

Air Materiel Command Wright-Patterson Air Force Base. *Unidentified Aerial Objects Project Sign*. February 1949. http://www .nicap.org/docs/SignRptFeb1949.pdf.

———. *Unidentified Aerial Objects Project Grudge*. August 1949.

———. *Unidentified Aerial Objects Project Blue Book*. February 1969.

Ambinder, Marc. "Failure Shuts Down Squadron of Nuclear Missiles." *The Atlantic*. October 26, 2010. https://www.theatlantic .com/politics/archive/2010/10/failure-shuts-down-squadron -of-nuclear-missiles/65207/.

Amond, A., W. De Brouwer, P. Ferryn, and S. Meesen. "ERNAGE 1989: The Facts and Their Analysis." Comité belge d'étude des phénomenes, 2008. http://www.cobeps.org/pdf/ernage _report.pdf.

Author's interview with Stanton Friedman. 2017. Email.

Baker, Robert. Testimony at the Committee on Science and Astronautics Symposium on Unidentified Flying Objects, July 29, 1968. http://files.ncas.org/ufosymposium/baker .html#oralstmt.

Baure, Jean-Francois, David Clark, Paul Puller, and Martin Shough. "Unusual Atmospheric Phenomena Observed Near Channel

Islands, UK, 23 April 2007." *Journal of Scientific Exploration* 22, no.3, (2008): 291–308. https://web.archive.org/web/20110606212717/http://www.scientificexploration.org/journal/jse_22_3_baure.pdf.

Beloff, John. "Parapsychology: The Continuing Impasse." *Journal of Scientific Exploration* 1, no. 2, 1987, 191–196.

Berliner, Don and Stanton Friedman. Crash at Corona: The U.S. Military Retrieval and Cover-Up of a UFO. New York: Paraview, 2004.

Berlitz, Charles, and William L. Moore. *The Roswell Incident*. New York: Fine Communications, 1997.

"Best Known Finnish UFO Cases." Translated by Tapani Koivula and Anneli Sjöstedt. Suomen Ufotutkijat Fufora. Accessed August 20, 2019. https://www.fufora.fi/english/bestknowncases.php.

Binding, Lucia. "UFO Investigated in Ireland After Multiple Aircraft Sightings." *Sky News*, November 12, 2018. https://news.sky.com/story/ufo-investigated-in-ireland-after-multiple-aircraft-sightings-11552908.

Bloecher, Ted. *Report on the UFO Wave of 1947*. Washington, D.C.: National Investigations Committee on Aerial Phenomena, 1967.

Bowyer, Ray. "Channel Report." Interview by Nick Waite on ITV1 Channel TV. April 25, 2007.

———. Speech at the National Press Club. November 12, 2007.

Buran, Fred. Written statement to United States Air Force. January 2, 1981. http://www.ianridpath.com/ufo/rendlesham2c.htm.

Burns, Kevin, producer. "The Return," *Ancient Aliens*, May 25, 2010, A&E Television Networks.

Burroughs, John. Written statement. Undated. http://www
.ianridpath.com/ufo/rendlesham2c.htm.

Carlson, Peter. "50 Years Ago, Unidentified Flying Objects from
Way beyond the Beltway Seized the Capital's Imagination."
The Washington Post, June 21, 2002.

Carter, Jimmy. *Report to the International UFO Bureau.* 1969. http://
www.nicap.org/waves/CarterSightingRptOct1969.pdf.

Central Intelligence Agency. "The Investigation of UFOs." September 22, 1993. https://www.cia.gov/library
/center-for-the-study-of-intelligence/kent-csi/vol10no4/html
/v10i4a07p_0001.htm.

———. Memorandum from Assistant Director of the Office of
Scientific Intelligence to Director of Central Intelligence. "Flying Saucers." October 2, 1952. https://www.cia.gov/library
/readingroom/docs/DOC_0000015339.pdf.

———. Memorandum. "Flying Saucers." December 3, 1952.
https://www.cia.gov/library/readingroom/docs
/DOC_0000015345.pdf.

Chamberlin, Jo. "The Foo Fighter Mystery." *The American Legion
Magazine*, December 1945. https://archive.legion.org/.

Chandler, J.D. Written statement to United States Air Force.
January 2, 1981. http://www.ianridpath.com/ufo
/rendlesham2c.htm.

Chief Constable of Suffolk Constabulary. Letter. November, 23,
1983. http://www.ianridpath.com/ufo/police.htm.

Clarke, David. "Operation Mainbrace UFOs." Dr. David Clarke
Folklore and Journalism. Accessed July 17, 2020. https://
drdavidclarke.co.uk/secret-files/operation-mainbrace-ufos/.

———. *The UFO Files: The Inside Story of Real-Life Sightings.* Surrey,
UK: The National Archives. 2009.

Clarke, David and A. Roberts. *Out of the Shadows: UFOs, the Establishment and the Official Cover Up*. London: Piatkus, 2002.

Clark, Jerome. *The UFO Book: Encyclopedia of the Extraterrestrial*. Detroit: Visible Ink Press, 1998.

Clark, Jerome and Lucius Farish. "The Mysterious Foo Fighters of World War II." *UFO Annual 1977*, January 1, 1977.

CNN Larry King Live. "Debate Over Existence of UFOs." July 18, 2008. http://transcripts.cnn.com/TRANSCRIPTS/0807/18 /lkl.01.html.

Collins, Paul. "World War II UFO Scare." *FATE Magazine* 40, no. 7, issue 448. July 1987.

Commonwealth of Australia Department of Transport, "Aircraft Accident Investigation Summary Report: VH-DSJ Cape Otway to King Island 21 October 1978 – Aircraft Missing [Valentich]," reference number V116/783/1047, https:// recordsearch.naa.gov.au/SearchNRetrieve/Interface /ViewImage.aspx?B=10491375.

Condon Committee Report. Scientific Study of Unidentified Flying Objects. January 1968.

Contact. "Alien Evidence." Bill Howard, Sarah Wetherbee, Jason Wolf, executive producers. Aired August 7, 2019 on Discovery.

Cooper, Gordon and Bruce Henderson. *Leap of Faith: An Astronaut's Journey Into the Unknown*. New York: Harper Collins Publishers, 2000.

Cooper, Gordon. Letter to the United Nations. November 9, 1978.

Cooper, Helen. Interview with Thomas Crosson. *New York Times*, December 16, 2017.

Cory, Elizabeth. "UFO At O'Hare? Officials Say Weird Weather." *CBS News*, January 2, 2007.

Cox, Billy. "O'Hare Incident Worth Revisiting." *Herald-Tribune,* August 21, 2007. https://www.heraldtribune.com /news/20070821/ohare-incident-worth-revisiting.

Craven, Wesley Frank, and James Lea Cate. *The Army Air Forces in World War II.* Vol. I. Chicago: University of Chicago Press, 1948.

"Jättecigarr över St. Mellösa." *Dagens Nyheter,* May 24,1946.

Durrach Jr., H.B. and Robert Ginna. "Have We Visitors from Space?" *Life Magazine,* April 7, 1952.

Druffel, Ann. *Firestorm: Dr. James E. McDonalds Fight for UFO Science.* Columbus: Wild Flower, 2003.

Durant, F.C. "Report of Meetings of Scientific Advisory Panel on Unidentified Flying Objects," Office of Scientific Intelligence, CIA, January 14–18, 1953, 17, https://rense.com//general96 /JANUARY181953--2.pdf.

Elizondo, Luis. Letter of resignation. October 4, 2017. https:// www.history.com/news/unidentified-ufo-investigation -documents.

Evans, Major Roland B. Defense Intelligence Agency Defense Information Evaluation Report IR No.6846013976. September 22, 1976.

"Farmer Trent's Flying Saucer." *Life Magazine,* June 26, 1950.

FBI Records: The Vault. "Project Blue Book." Accessed August 28, 2020. https://vault.fbi.gov/Project%20Blue%20 Book%20%28UFO%29%20/Project%20Blue%20Book%20 %28UFO%29%20part%201%20of%201/view.

Federal Aviation Administration. "FAA Releases Documents on Reported UFO Sighting Last November." U.S. Department of Transportation press release. February 4, 1987. http://www .nicap.org/docs/861117_flight1628.pdf.

Fernandez, Peris. *30 Años de Literatura OVNI en Espana (1950–1980)*. Barcelona: Plaza y Janes,1984.

"Floating Mystery Ball Is New Nazi Air Weapon." *New York Times*, December 14, 1944. https://www.nytimes.com/1944/12/14 /archives/floating-mystery-ball-is-new-nazi-air-weapon.html.

Jafari, Parviz. Press conference at the National Press Club in Washington, DC. November 12, 2007.

Gilgoff, Dan. "Saucers full of Secrets." *Washington City Paper*, December 14, 2001. https://www.washingtoncitypaper.com /news/article/13023374/saucers-full-of-secrets.

Good, Timothy. *Above Top Secret: The Worldwide UFO Cover-up*. London: Sidgwick & Jackson, 1987.

———. *Beyond Top Secret: The Worldwide UFO Security Threat*. London: Pan, 1997.

Gross, Loren. *UFO's: A History 1952: July 21st - July 31st*. Fremont, CA: Privately published, 1986. https://sohp.us/collections /ufos-a-history/pdf/GROSS-1952-July-21-31.pdf.

Haines, Richard, K. Efishoff, D. Ledger, L. Lemke, S. Maranto, W. Puckett, T. Roe, M. Shough, and R. Uriarte. "Report of an Unidentified Aerial Phenomenon and its Safety Implications at O'Hare International Airport on November 7, 2006." National Aviation Reporting Center on Anomalous Phenomena. May 14, 2007. https://static1.squarespace.com /static/5cf80ff422b5a90001351e31/t/5d02ec731230e20001528 e2c/1560472703346/NARCAP_TR-10.pdf.

Haines, Richard and Paul Norman. "Valentich Disappearance: New Evidence and a New Conclusion." *Journal of Scientific Exploration* 14, no.1 (2000): 19–33.

Halt, Charles I. Memorandum to United Kingdom's Ministry of Defense. January 13, 1981. http://www.ianridpath.com/ufo/appendix.htm.

Hamilton, William. Phoenix Sightings Summary Report.

"Harassed Rancher Who Located 'Saucer' Sorry He Told about It," *Roswell Daily Record*. July 9, 1947.

Hastings, Robert. "Huge UFO Sighted Near Nuclear Missiles During October 2010 Launch System Disruption." The UFO Chronicles. June 21, 2011. https://www.theufochronicles.com/2011/06/huge-ufo-sighted-near-nuclear-missiles_19.html.

Haydon, S.E., "A Windmill Demolishes It." *The Dallas Morning News*, April 19, 1897.

Heath, Gord. "The Kinross Incident, Investigation Report by Gord Heath." Accessed July 17, 2019. ufobc.ca/Kinross.

Hilkevitch, Jon. "In the Sky! A Bird? Plane? A…UFO?" *Chicago Tribune*. January 1, 2007. https://www.chicagotribune.com/travel/ct-xpm-2007-01-01-chi-0701010141jan01-story.html.

House Committee on Science and Astronautics. "Symposium of Unidentified flying Objects." Nineteenth Congress. Volume 2. July 29, 1968.

Huang, Mary. "UFO in China's Skies Prompts Investigation," *ABC News,* July 14, 2010.

Hylton, Will. "The Gospel According to Jimmy." *GQ Magazine*, December 6, 2005. https://www.gq.com/story/jimmy-carter-ted-kennedy-ufo-republicans.

Hynek, J. Allen. *The UFO Experience: A Scientific Inquiry*. Chicago: Henry Regnery Company, 1972.

"Iranian Air Force Jets Scrambled," NICAP, November 1976, http://www.nicap.org/reports/760919tehran_NICAP.pdf.

Shincho, Shukan. "JAL Pilot's UFO Story Surfaces after 20 Years. JAL Pilot's UFO Story Surfaces after 20 Years." JapanToday. December 8, 2006.

Kean, Leslie. *UFOs: Generals, Pilots, and Government Officials Go On the Record*. New York: Random House, 2011.

Klass, Philip K. "New Research Suggests Kenneth Arnold's UFOs Were Meteor—Fireballs." *Skeptics UFO Newsletter* 46 (July 1997): 1–2. https://skepticalinquirer.org/the-skeptics-ufo-newsletter/.

Klemperer, W.B. Interview with Captain Willis T. Sperry. February 4,1955.

Kurczy, Stephen. "China UFO Spotted Again. Why Skepticism is Warranted." *The Christian Science Monitor.* July 16, 2010. https://www.csmonitor.com/World/Global-News/2010/0716/China-UFO-spotted-again.-Why-skepticism-is-warranted.

Lagrange, Pierre. "A Moment in History: An Interview with Bill Bequette." *International UFO Reporter* 23 (n.d.).

Levy, Nigel, dir. *Britain's Closest Encounters*, episode 4, "Aldernay Lights." Aired July 30, 2008, on Channel 5 in the UK.

Ley, Tim. "Tim Ley Family—Eyewitnesses of 3/13/97 Arizona UFO Flyover Event Called 'Phoenix Lights.'" *Tim Ley* (blog). 1998. http://www.artgomperz.com/a1999/aug/b7.htm.

Maccabee, Bruce. "Analysis and Discussion of the Images of a Cluster of Periodically Flashing Lights Filmed Off the Coast of New Zealand, 1987." *Journal of Scientific Exploration* 1, no. 2 (1987), 149–190. https://www.scientificexploration.org/journal/volume-1-number-2-1987.

———. High Flying Squid Boat, Dr. Bruce Maccabee Research Website. www.brumac.mysite.com.

———. "The Fantastic Flight of JAL 1628". International UFO Reporter.

Marrs, Jim. Alien Agenda: Investigating the Extraterrestrial Presence among Us. New York: HarperPaperbacks, 1998.

Marshall, General George. Memorandum to President Roosevelt, February 26,1942.

McDonald, James E., "Evaluation of the Fort Monmouth Incident." NICAP, http://www.nicap.org/reports/monmouthan .htm.

McDonald, James. House Committee on Science and Astronautics, July 29, 1968.

Memo to the Commanding General, 15th of September 1950.

Menzel, Donald H., and Lyle G. Boyd. The World of Flying Saucers: a Scientific Examination of a Major Myth of the Space Age. Garden City, NY: Doubleday, 1963.

MUFON Case File. Investigation led by Bill Case.1973.

"Mysterious 'Foo Fighters,' Balls of Fire, Trail U.S. Night Flyers." St. Louis Post Dispatch, January 2, 1945.

Nash, William B. and William H. Fortenberry. "We Flew Above Flying Saucers." TRUE Report on Flying Saucers, 1967. http:// www.seektress.com/above.htm.

National Aeronautics and Space Administration, "Cosmos 96," NASA Space Science Data Coordinated Archive, accessed September 14, 2020, https://nssdc.gsfc.nasa.gov/nmc/spacecraft /display.action?id=1965-094A.

National Investigations Committee on Aerial Phenomena. The UFO Evidence. Edited by Richard Hall. Washington, DC: Quarto, 1964.

National Press Club press conference. Aired September 27, 2010 on CNN. https://www.youtube.com/watch?v=zT0EP4mP1lI.

"New Mexico Rancher's 'Flying Disk' Proves to be Weather Balloon-Kite," *Fort Worth Star-Telegram*, July 9, 1947.

New Zealand Defense Force. "Investigations of Unidentified & Radar Sightings East Coast South Island." December 1978. http://files.afu.se/Downloads/Documents/New%20Zealand/AIR-1080-6-897-Volume-1-1978-1981.pdf.

NOAA National Climate Data Center. "March 12–14, 1997 Wind Direction in Phoenix, AZ."

Olmos, Vicente-Juan Ballester and Juan A. Fernandez Peris. *Enciclopedia de los Encuentros Cercanos con ONVIS*. Barcelona: Plaza y Janes, 1987.

Olmos, Vicente-Juan Ballester. "UFO Declassification—The Spanish Model." *European Journal of UFO and Abduction Studies* (1999). http://www.cisu.org/ejv0n0.htm.

Peebles, Curtis. *Watch the Skies!: a Chronicle of the Flying Saucer Myth*. Washington: Smithsonian Institution Press, 1994.

Philcox, N.W. FBI Memorandum, 1952.

Powell, Bill. "At Long Last—Authentic Photographs of Flying Saucer." *Telephone Register Newspaper*, June 8,1950.

Press Conference held by Major General Samford, July 29, 1952.

Press conference at the Ministry of Aeronautics, May 23, 1986.

Price, Richard. "Arizonians Say the Truth About UFOs Is Out There." *USA Today*, June 18, 1997.

Project Blue Book declassified documents. https://www.fold3.com/image/9552585.

Project Grudge. "Special Report No. 1." December 28, 1951.

Project Sign. "Estimate of Situation." 1948.

Project Twinkle Final Report, P.H. Wyckoff, File number K243.6012. November 27, 1951. http://www.nicap.org/twinkle/ProjectTwinkleFinalReport.pdf.

'RAAF Captures Flying Saucer on ranch in Roswell Region', *Roswell Daily Record*. July 8, 1947. Paraview Special Editions. 1992.

Randle, Kevin D. *The Government UFO Files: The Conspiracy of Cover-Up*. Detroit, MI: Visible Ink Press, 2014.

Randle, Kevin D. *Crash: When UFOs Fall from the Sky: a History of Famous Incidents, Conspiracies, and Cover-Ups*. Franklin Lakes, NJ: New Page Books, 2010.

Randles, Jenny. *UFO Crash Landing? Friend or Foe?: the Full Story of the Rendlesham Forest Close Encounter*. London: Blandford, 1998.

Report sent to the Commanding General by Lieutenant Wilbert Rogers, http://www.nicap.org/docs/MAXW-PBB8-1503-04.pdf.

Rojas, Alejandro. Interview with Luis Elizondo, June 8, 2019.

Rogerio, Chola. "Unidentified Spherical Flying Objects in the Skies of Brazil on May 19,1986." NICAP. March 2010. https://static1.squarespace.com/static/5cf80ff422b5a90001351e31/t/5d02eefd935aac0001695a10/1560473343396/narcap_ProjSph_3.1.1_Brazil.pdf.

Ruppelt, Edward J. *The Report on Unidentified Flying Objects: The Original 1956 Edition*. New York: Cosimo Classics, 2011.

Schuessler, John. "Metal from a crashed UFO?" MUFON. https://web.archive.org/web/20070204053124/http://www.mufon.com/famous_cases/Aurora%20Texas%20Crash%20Part%201%20MUFON%20Case%20File.pdf.

"Search for Pilot Who Saw UFO, Then Disappeared, Discontinued." *Lodi News-Sentinel*. October 16, 1978.

Sheaffer, Robert. "Hovering UFO Closes Chinese Airport" *Skeptical Inquirer* 34, no.6 (November/December 2010): 27–29.

———. "President Carter's 'UFO' Is Identified as the Planet Venus." *The Humanist*, July/August 1977.

———. *UFO Sightings: the Evidence*. Amherst, NY: Prometheus Books, 1998.

Shields, Henry. "Now You See It, Now You Don't!" Declassified December 4, 1981.

Siese, April. "The Pentagon has confirmed its $22M program to investigate UFOs," December 16, 2017.

Smith, Jack. "Army Says Alarm Real." *Los Angeles Times*, February 26, 1942.

SOBEPS, Vague d'Ovni sur la Belgique, 1991.

Southey, Robin. "UFO Mystery." *The Australian*, October 23, 1978.

"Supersonic Flying Saucers Sighted by Idaho Pilot." *The Chicago Sun*, June 26, 1947.

Swords, Michael D. *UFOs and Government: A Historical Inquiry*. San Antonio: Anomalist Books, 2012.

Symington, Fife. " I Saw a UFO In the Arizona Sky." *CNN*. November 9, 2007.

Terauchi, Kenju. "Meeting the Future," translated by Sakoyo Mimoto. FAA Alaskan Region Airway Facilities Division. January 2, 1987, https://documents.theblackvault.com /documents/ufos/jal1628/733667-001-007.pdf.

"This Strange Flying Object was Seen by Thousands and Chased by Jets." *The Sunday Express,* September 17, 1995.

To the Stars Academy of Arts & Sciences. Interview with Commander David Fravor. November 2017. https://thevault .tothestarsacademy.com/2004-uss-nimitz-pilot-interview/tag /David+Fravor.

———. "2015 Go Fast Footage." https://thevault .tothestarsacademy.com/2015-go-fast-footage.

——— "GIMBAL: Authenticated UAP video." https:// thevault.tothestarsacademy.com/gimbal/tag/UFO.

Transcript of Colonel Halt's Tape. Transcribed by Ian Ridpath. http://www.ianridpath.com/ufo/halttape.htm.

The Tribune-Review. "'Unidentified Flying Object' Falls Near Kecksburg." December 10, 1965.

UFO Casebook. "The Belgium UFO Wave." August 24, 2014. https://www.ufocasebook.com/Belgium.html.

"UFO Sighting in Shanghai and Beijing." China.org.cn. August 23, 2010, http://www.china.org.cn/china/2012-08/23/content_26311826_5.htm.

"The UFO Sighting in Pori Still Speaks," UUTISET, Last modified July 12, 2009, https://yle.fi/uutiset/3-5971507.

"UFOs Spotted Off Irish Coast Under Investigation." *BBC News*, November 13, 2018. https://www.bbc.com/news/world-europe-46181662.

United States Air Force. "USAF Fact Sheet 95-03." Accessed August 2020. http://www.gutenberg.org/files/25674/25674-h/25674-h.htm.

VASAviation. "[Real ATC] Several Aircraft Witness a UFO Right Over Ireland!" YouTube, November 13, 2018. 7:17. https://www.youtube.com/watch?v=pv7x4dRye3U.

"War Diary 415th Night Fighters Squadron Ochey Air Base, France, December 1944," CUFON, entry 23, http://www.cufon.org/cufon/foo.htm.

Warrick, Joby. "Head of Pentagon's secret UFO office sought to make evidence public" December 16, 2017.

Young, Robert. "'Old-Solved Mysteries': The Kecksburg Incident." *Skeptical Inquirer* 15, no. 3 (1991).

To Write to the Author

If you wish to contact the author or would like more information about this book, please write to the author in care of Llewellyn Worldwide Ltd. and we will forward your request. Both the author and publisher appreciate hearing from you and learning of your enjoyment of this book and how it has helped you. Llewellyn Worldwide Ltd. cannot guarantee that every letter written to the author can be answered, but all will be forwarded. Please write to:

Warren Agius
℅ Llewellyn Worldwide
2143 Wooddale Drive
Woodbury, MN 55125-2989
Please enclose a self-addressed stamped envelope for reply,
or $1.00 to cover costs. If outside the U.S.A., enclose
an international postal reply coupon.

Many of Llewellyn's authors have websites with additional information and resources. For more information, please visit our website at http://www.llewellyn.com